CROSSCURRENTS

ATLANTIC AND PACIFIC MIGRATION IN THE MAKING OF A GLOBAL AMERICA

REED UEDA

New York   Oxford
OXFORD UNIVERSITY PRESS

Oxford University Press is a department of the University of Oxford.
It furthers the University's objective of excellence in research,
scholarship, and education by publishing worldwide.

Oxford   New York
Auckland   Cape Town   Dar es Salaam   Hong Kong   Karachi
Kuala Lumpur   Madrid   Melbourne   Mexico City   Nairobi
New Delhi   Shanghai   Taipei   Toronto

With offices in
Argentina   Austria   Brazil   Chile   Czech Republic   France   Greece
Guatemala   Hungary   Italy   Japan   Poland   Portugal   Singapore
South Korea   Switzerland   Thailand   Turkey   Ukraine   Vietnam

For titles covered by Section 112 of the US Higher Education
Opportunity Act, please visit www.oup.com/us/he for the
latest information about pricing and alternate formats.

Published in the United States of America by
Oxford University Press
198 Madison Avenue, New York, NY 10016
http://www.oup.com

Library of Congress Cataloging-in-Publication Data

Ueda, Reed.
   Crosscurrents : Atlantic and Pacific migration in the making of a global
America / Reed Ueda (Tufts University).
      pages cm
   Includes index.
   ISBN 978-0-19-975744-2 (paperback : acid-free paper) 1. United
States--Emigration and immigration--History. 2. Islands of the Atlantic--
Emigration and immigration--History. 3. Islands of the Pacific--Emigration
and immigration--History. 4. Europe--Emigration and immigration--
History. 5. Asia--Emigration and immigration--History. 6. Interregionalism--
History. 7. Immigrants--United States--History. 8. Cultural pluralism--
United States--History. 9. Intercultural communication--United States--
History. 10. Globalization--Social aspects--United States--History. I. Title.
II. Title: Cross currents.
   JV6450.U33 2015
   304.8'73--dc23

                                                            2014042374

Printing number: 9 8 7 6 5 4 3 2 1

Printed in the United States of America
on acid-free paper

For Mildred, Nancy, Goro, Eddie, Irene, Yukiyo, Nan, and Pol

CONTENTS

Color map insert follows Introduction

LIST OF FIGURES
AND MAPS

Color Map Insert

LIST OF TABLES

ABOUT THE AUTHOR

Reed Ueda is Professor of History at Tufts University where he has taught since 1981. He has also held teaching positions at Brandeis University and Harvard University. In his research, Ueda explores the intersection of migration, globalization, and institutional history. His many studies include Avenues to Adulthood, Postwar Immigrant America, and The New Americans (with Mary C. Waters and Helen Marrow). He was a research editor of the Harvard Encyclopedia of American Ethnic Groups (Stephan Thernstrom, editor), awarded the Waldo Leland Prize of the American Historical Association. Ueda has received fellowships from the Woodrow Wilson International Center, the National Endowment for the Humanities, the American Council of Learned Societies, and the Charles Warren Center of Harvard University. He has been a Distinguished Lecturer of the Organization of American Historians, and is an elected fellow of the Massachusetts Historical Society. Professor Ueda has engaged in the expansion of interdisciplinary studies through his role as co-editor of the Journal of Interdisciplinary History and co-chair of the Inter-University Committee on International Migration at the MIT Center for International Studies.

INTRODUCTION

"It should be emphasized that ships were the living means by which the points within that Atlantic world were joined."

Paul Gilroy, *The Black Atlantic*

"To any meditative Magian rover, this serene Pacific once beheld must ever after be the sea of his adoption. It rolls the midmost waters of the world, the Indian ocean and Atlantic being but its arms."

Herman Melville, *Moby Dick, or the Whale*

The Norwegian Majesty, an Atlantic Ocean cruise ship traveling from Boston to Bermuda in 2004, arrived at the dock to be welcomed by a band playing the theme music from the legendary television series of the imagined Pacific, *Hawaii Five-O*. The boatload of tourists, with which my family had traveled, were encountering a cultural corridor that bridged the societies of the Atlantic and Pacific basins. This particular incident possessed a general significance, showing that beneath the surface of the contemporary world lies a historical pattern of deep connections between the Atlantic and Pacific regions. For the study of history, it indicates the importance of asking two fundamental questions: When and how did the trajectories of Atlantic history and Pacific history overlap and converge with each other through travel and migration? What historically rooted processes drove people originally separated by immense physical and cultural distances into mutual encounters, close exchanges, and collective creativity in building an interhemispheric social and cultural life based on group diversity?

A preliminary step to investigating these questions is to adopt a perspective that captures the shifting interaction of regional histories that led to the creation of global connections. This viewpoint yields a picture of the varieties of transoceanic and transcontinental migrations between the Atlantic and Pacific basins as connecting vectors in a far-flung zone of interregional development.[1] Migrations functioned as a set of interchanges—a collection of ramps, exits, and entrances between the highways or trajectories of Atlantic regional history and Pacific regional history. This view of migration serves to align this volume with recent historical research that is directed toward moving beyond regional compartments in order to uncover transnational interlinkages of migration, trade, and cross-cultural change.

As migrants built new lives across hemispheric divides, an interoceanic American world evolved, and a transnational and transcultural field emerged in the Pacific coast region of the United States. This complex world was more than a geographic borderland. It was also an area for the emergence and convergence of mass migrations, their demographic components of families and lineages, and their stores of cultural, social, and human capital brought from countries in Europe, Asia, the Americas, Africa, and Oceania. Its dynamic essence can be captured by the metaphor of "crosscurrents," turbulent stretches of water, caused by the interplay of multiple currents. The United States played the central role in the creation of this borderland world of migration and interaction in the nineteenth and twentieth centuries. The westward thrust of its dominant economic and political-military power, the magnitude of its westward internal migration and international migration, made the United States, in the words of a leading historian of expansion, "the single most powerful—and most powerfully single-minded—force on the North American frontier."[2]

The interplay of crisscrossing currents of migration at the Pacific edge of the United States propelled the rise of local and regional integration, on one hand, and the radiation outward of national and global connections, on the other. These different scales of development evolved interdependently and concurrently to produce innovative changes in social, economic, and cultural activity. This study holds these scales together so as to maintain a perspective on the concrete characteristics of each one of them and their mutual relationships. It utilizes social history to register the presence and dislocations of the lifeworlds of communities in specific places, the crucibles of action and agency of people which can elude the historian who regards only the immense sweep of transnational and global forces, or the social scientist fixed on modernization theories.[3] Historian Arif Dirlik has commented that the globalism of post-national diaspora studies "tends to erase differences based on place and the different histories that are articulated through place," noting further that "history informed by a sense of place not only resists erasure by globalist reification but serves also as a reminder of the very concrete experiences and activities through which people have constructed and defined their activities."[4]

The growing American presence in the far west connected this region with the hegemonic forces of change radiating from the Atlantic world and inspired the imperial visions of the great world's fairs held in the early twentieth century. The 1904 St. Louis World's Fair (The Louisiana Purchase International Exposition), the 1905 Portland World's Fair (The Lewis and Clark Centennial Exposition), the 1909 Seattle World's Fair (The Alaska-Yukon-Pacific Exposition), and the 1915

San Francisco World's Fair (The Panama-Pacific International Exposition) provided a stage for presenting the United States as the great occidental power bestriding the union of Pacific and Atlantic worlds.

In an immense arena of human and natural diversity, the imperial aspirations of American and European supremacists shaped a new emergent order out of international competition and conflict. Nevertheless, historian John Kuo Wei Tchen observed, "Alongside racism, the contact with non-Western peoples wrought mixed port cultures and frontier settlements in which were forged new hybrid human identities and cultures. Rough forms of social intermingling and acceptance seemed to prevail. Furthermore, rural trading outposts and urban commercial streetscapes . . . [were] important initial openings for more mixed cultural interactions to develop. These zones were not only and not always defined by hostility and exploitation, but also by friendships, interminglings, and the birth of new multicultural peoples."[5] As they settled in new communities in multiple regions of the United States, migrants originating from inside and outside the U.S. created intergroup boundaries and racial hierarchies concurrently with new opportunities for crossing these divides. Among these would be found migrants of European, Asian, African, Spanish, and indigenous origin who became part of an intercultural settler world.

The Pacific Ocean, as recent historical surveys have described, was marked by a variety of subregions within its geographical perimeter. The Pacific coast borderland of the Americas provided a pivotal connection between migration history and the repositioning of regional and subregional histories within the framework of global history. As its integration was facilitated by the growth of European empires, the Atlantic world existed and functioned as a region among regions. The growing integration of areas in the Atlantic basin fed upon the flow of forces—especially migrations—between neighboring oceanic worlds. The responses of the Atlantic world to global changes were filtered through a migration frontier between Atlantic societies and societies in the Pacific Ocean and Indian Ocean regions. The Pacific coast borderland of the western hemisphere was a crossroads of migrant settlements and the cultural corridors they created to maintain contact with their homelands. Viewed from the Atlantic side, this area acquired an enlarged outer framework of peripheral connections with the Pacific and Indian Oceans which were extended through the flows of international population movements.[6]

This fluid interhemispheric zone produced a transforming network of global linkages emanating from the Pacific coast of the United States. Around this network revolved American national development, Asian and American cultural and economic interchange, and a new global diversity productive of innovation.

This study examines the historical underpinnings for these transformative developments. It utilizes a variety of primary sources, including public records and personal writings, quantitative data sets, and visual material, to highlight, rather than to be fully comprehensive of, its vast subjects. In framing historical questions and themes, the author has been guided by the scholars who have presented and criticized papers at the meetings of the International Seminar on

Atlantic History at Harvard directed by Bernard Bailyn, the Center for South Asian and Indian Ocean Studies at Tufts directed by Ayesha Jalal, the South Asia Initiative at Harvard directed by Sugata Bose, and the South Asia Institute at Harvard directed by Tarun Khanna. Their work has pioneered the study of the relationships among oceans, regions, empires, and nations. I wish to express my gratitude to Jorge Canizares-Esguerra and Erik R. Seeman, who read previously drafted portions of the manuscript, and Sugata Bose, who read it in its entirety. I also am grateful for the reviews commissioned by Oxford University Press, including the reports sent in by Madeline Hsu, University of Texas at Austin; Gordon Chang, Stanford University; Peter Coclanis; University of North Carolina, Chapel Hill; John Rosa, University of Hawai'i, Manoa; Hasia Diner, New York University; Tomas Jiminez, Stanford University; J. Wu, Oregon State University; Kevin Hatfield, University of Oregon; and other anonymous reviewers. Building on the insights of the scholars cited here, I have endeavored to explore mass migrations as part of a modern panorama of transoceanic emergence, innovation, and convergence involving multiple peoples from very distant lands.

I am indebted to the members of Oxford University Press who worked on the production of this volume: Lynn Luecken, Beverly Kraus, Christian Holdener, Debbie Ruel, Francelle Carapetyan, and Debbie Needleman. I am especially grateful to my editor, Charles Cavaliere, who saw this volume through from inspiration and research to publication.

Finally, my deepest appreciation is owed to my wife, Peggy Ueda, for helping me chart the course of my field research that yielded the key insights of this study.

Notes

1. Jorge Canizares-Esguerra and Erik Seeman, eds., *The Atlantic in Global History, 1500–2000* (Upper Saddle River, N.J.: Pearson Prentice Hall, 2007), Introduction; Peter Coclanis, "Drang Nach Osten: Bernard Bailyn, the World-Island, and the Idea of Atlantic History," *Journal of World History* 13, no. 1 (Spring 2002): 169–182.
2. Gregory H. Nobles, *American Frontiers: Cultural Encounters and Continental Conquest* (New York: Hill and Wang, 1997), pp. 241–242.
3. Vicente L. Rafael, "Regionalism, Area Studies, and the Accidents of Agency," *American Historical Review* 104, no. 4 (October 1999): 1210.
4. Arif Dirlik, ed., *Chinese on the American Frontier* (Lanham, Md.: Rowman & Littlefield, 2001), p. xvii. Also, see David Igler, *The Great Ocean: Pacific Worlds from Captain Cook to the Gold Rush* (New York: Oxford University Press, 2013), pp. 11–12.
5. John Kuo Wei Tchen, *New York before Chinatown* (Baltimore, Md.: Johns Hopkins University Press, 1999), p. xix.
6. David Armitage and Alison Bashford, *Pacific Histories: Ocean, Land, People* (New York: Palgrave Macmillan, 2014), p. 1-1; Kornel S. Chang, *Pacific Connections: The Making of the U. S.-Canadian Borderlands* (Berkeley: University of California Press, 2012), Introduction; Kenneth Pomeranz, *The Great Divergence: Europe, China, and the Making of the Modern World Economy* (Princeton, N.J.: Princeton University Press, 2000), pp. 296–297.

Earlier versions of portions of the Introduction, Chapters 1, 2, and 3 appeared in Reed Ueda, "Pushing the Atlantic Envelope: Interoceanic Perspectives on Atlantic History," in Jorge Canizares-Esguerra and Erik R. Seeman, *The Atlantic in Global History, 1500–2000* (Upper Saddle River, N. J.: Pearson Prentice Hall, 2007), pp. 163–175; earlier versions of portions of Chapter 3 also appeared in Reed Ueda, "American National Identity and Race in Immigrant Generations," *Journal of Interdisciplinary History*, Vol. 22, No. 3 (Winter 1992), pp. 483–491; Ueda, "Second-Generation Civic America: Education, Citizenship, and the Children of Immigrants," *Journal of Interdisciplinary History*, Vol. 29, No. 4 (Spring 1999), pp. 661–681.

MAPS

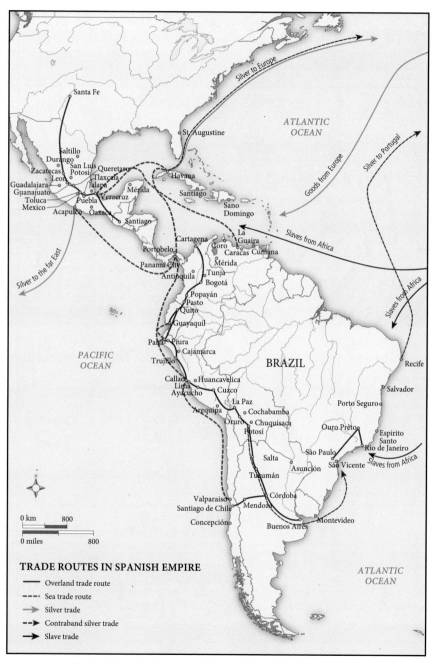

Map 1. Trade Routes in Spanish Empire in Hemispheric Context.

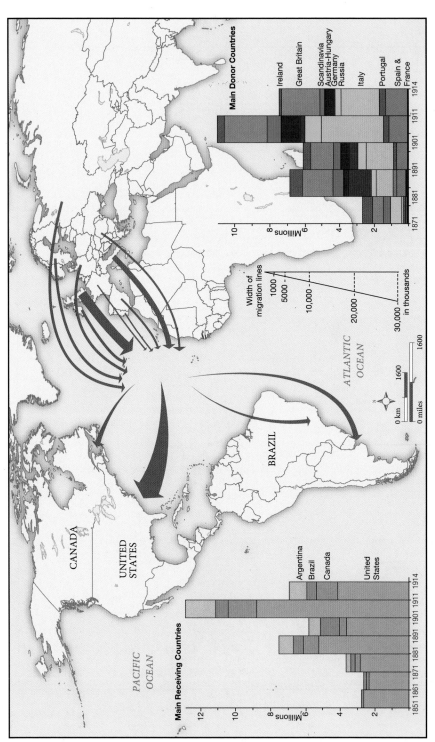

Map 2. Atlantic Migrations (1870–1914).

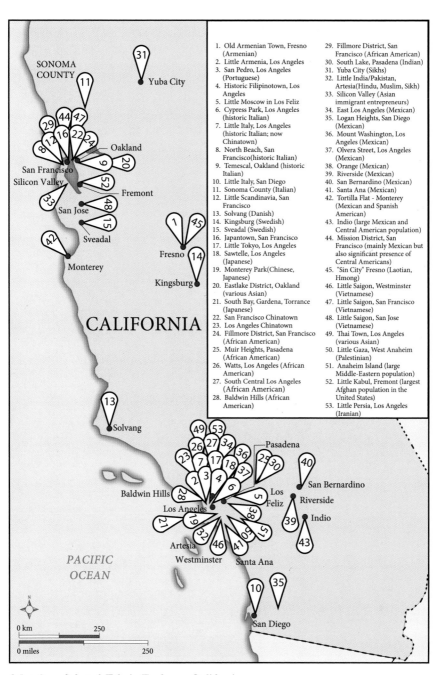

1. Old Armenian Town, Fresno (Armenian)
2. Little Armenia, Los Angeles
3. San Pedro, Los Angeles (Portuguese)
4. Historic Filipinotown, Los Angeles
5. Little Moscow in Los Feliz
6. Cypress Park, Los Angeles (historic Italian)
7. Little Italy, Los Angeles (historic Italian; now Chinatown)
8. North Beach, San Francisco (historic Italian)
9. Temescal, Oakland (historic Italian)
10. Little Italy, San Diego
11. Sonoma County (Italian)
12. Little Scandinavia, San Francisco
13. Solvang (Danish)
14. Kingsburg (Swedish)
15. Sveadal (Swedish)
16. Japantown, San Francisco
17. Little Tokyo, Los Angeles
18. Sawtelle, Los Angeles (Japanese)
19. Monterey Park (Chinese, Japanese)
20. Eastlake District, Oakland (various Asian)
21. South Bay, Gardena, Torrance (Japanese)
22. San Francisco Chinatown
23. Los Angeles Chinatown
24. Fillmore District, San Francisco (African American)
25. Muir Heights, Pasadena (African American)
26. Watts, Los Angeles (African American)
27. South Central Los Angeles (African American)
28. Baldwin Hills (African American)

29. Fillmore District, San Francisco (African American)
30. South Lake, Pasadena (Indian)
31. Yuba City (Sikhs)
32. Little India/Pakistan, Artesia (Hindu, Muslim, Sikh)
33. Silicon Valley (Asian immigrant entrepreneurs)
34. East Los Angeles (Mexican)
35. Logan Heights, San Diego (Mexican)
36. Mount Washington, Los Angeles (Mexican)
37. Olvera Street, Los Angeles (Mexican)
38. Orange (Mexican)
39. Riverside (Mexican)
40. San Bernardino (Mexican)
41. Santa Ana (Mexican)
42. Tortilla Flat - Monterey (Mexican and Spanish American)
43. Indio (large Mexican and Central American population)
44. Mission District, San Francisco (mainly Mexican but also significant presence of Central Americans)
45. "Sin City" Fresno (Laotian, Hmong)
46. Little Saigon, Westminster (Vietnamese)
47. Little Saigon, San Francisco (Vietnamese)
48. Little Saigon, San Jose (Vietnamese)
49. Thai Town, Los Angeles (various Asian)
50. Little Gaza, West Anaheim (Palestinian)
51. Anaheim Island (large Middle-Eastern population)
52. Little Kabul, Fremont (largest Afghan population in the United States)
53. Little Persia, Los Angeles (Iranian)

Map 3.   Selected Ethnic Enclaves, California.

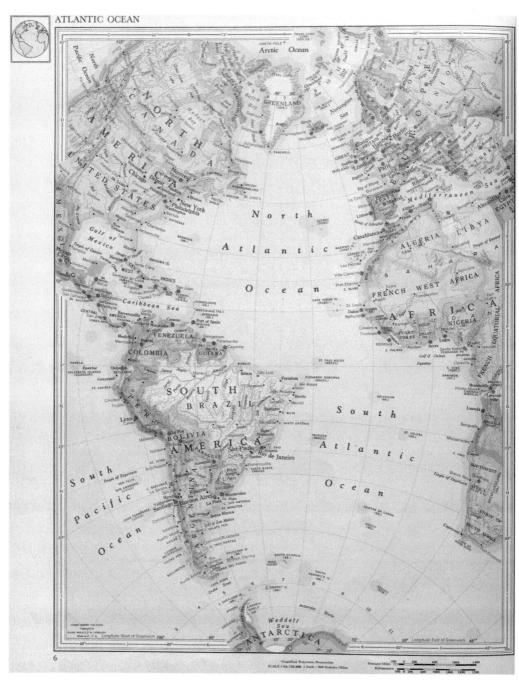

Map 4.   Rand McNally's Postwar Map of the Atlantic Basin, a Region that Previously had not Received its own Map.

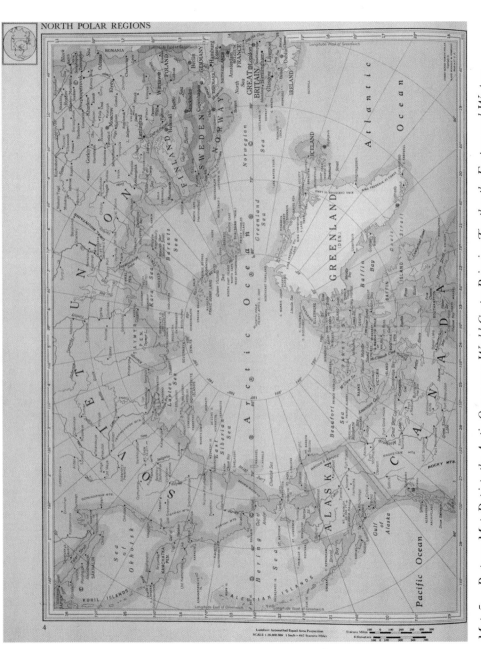

Lambert Azimuthal Equal Area Projection
SCALE 1:39,000,000 1 Inch = 442 Statute Miles

Map 5.   Postwar Map Depicts the Arctic Ocean as a World Center Bringing Together the Eastern and Western Hemispheres.

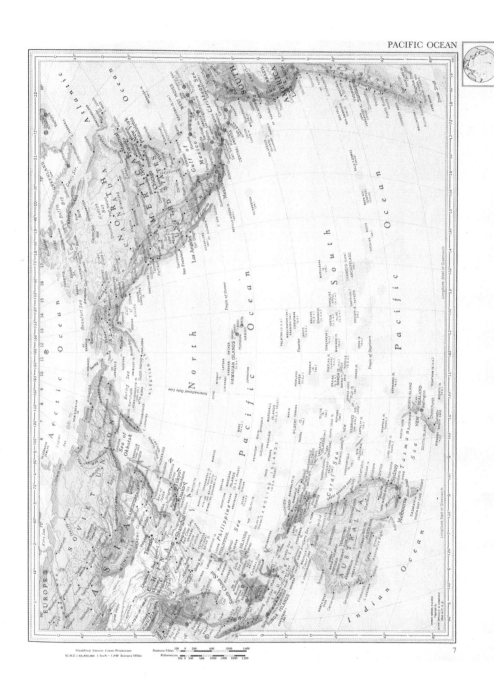

Map 6.   Postwar Map of the Pacific as a Basin or Rim.

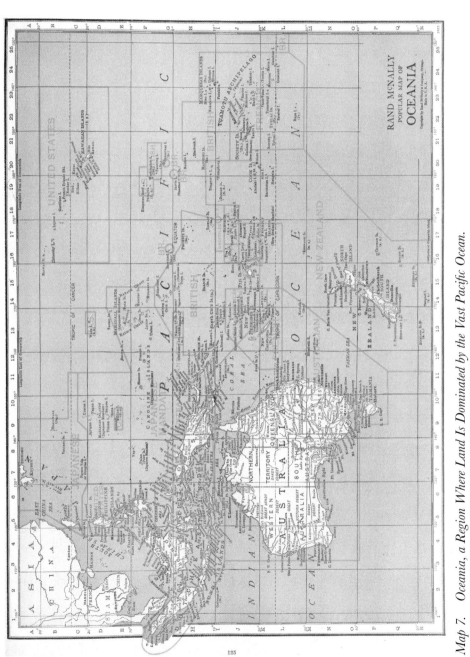

Map 7. *Oceania, a Region Where Land Is Dominated by the Vast Pacific Ocean.*

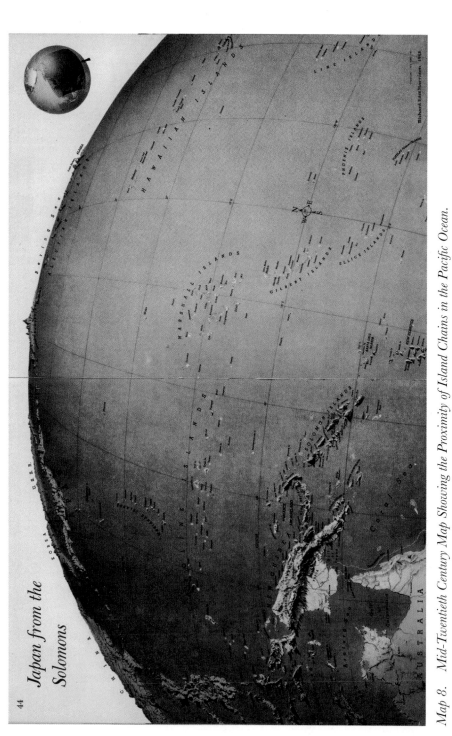

Japan from the Solomons

Map 8.   Mid-Twentieth Century Map Showing the Proximity of Island Chains in the Pacific Ocean.

ONE

Precursors

PACIFIC BORDERLANDS

The Pacific Ocean is a supra-region, "an enormous water world covering one-third of the Earth's surface, framed by continents, joined by islands," in the words of a historian looking across time and space from the vantage of the twenty-first century.[1] The Pacific Ocean is connected to smaller, subsidiary seas, as is the Atlantic Ocean. The Pacific is joined with the South China Sea, the Sea of Japan, the Coral Sea, and the Bering Sea, while the Atlantic forms a waterway network with the Mediterranean, Caribbean, the Baltic, Norwegian, and North Seas. By connecting smaller, adjoining seas, the Pacific and Atlantic Oceans facilitate interaction and integration of their internal subregional worlds. On an outward planetary scale, the Pacific and Atlantic Oceans operate together as two interoceanic highways that link the world's continents and island chains in long, sweeping arcs across the globe.[2]

At the end of the Middle Ages, Europeans attained a new level of nautical skill and geographic knowledge and launched transoceanic movements of people and trade to create a world of imperial nations and their colonies (Map 1-1). In the age of global empire, people from the trans-Atlantic colonies of Spain, Portugal, Britain, Netherlands, and France, and their independent successor states, encountered each other in the coastal regions and islands of the Pacific. Voyagers from the Atlantic world contacted through maritime exploration, travel, and trade the ancient Asian civilizations of China, Japan, and India and the archipelago societies of Indonesia, Malaysia, Micronesia, Melanesia, and Polynesia. The worldwide expansion of European power turned the Pacific Ocean into a contested realm for claims of imperial authority and possession declared by mariners such as Vitus Bering from Russia and James Cook from Britain.[3]

Imperial Spain was the earliest of the European empires to establish, from the Atlantic direction, a primary Pacific settler presence and orientation toward far Asian shores.[4] A Spanish explorer, Vasco Nunez de Balboa, traversed the Isthmus of Panama and reached the shores of the Pacific Ocean in 1513, the first European

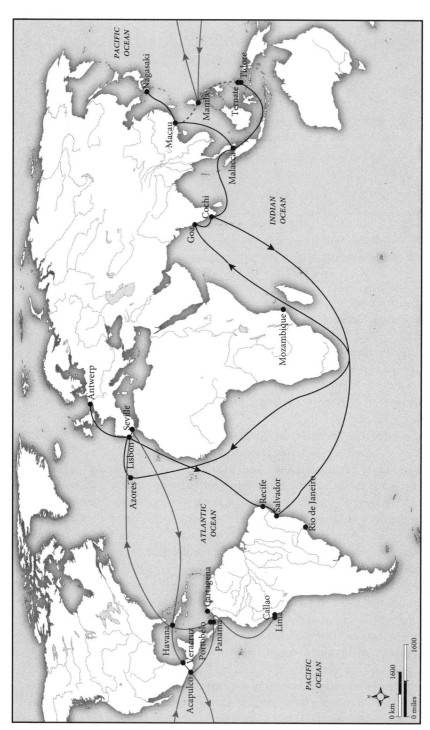

Map 1-1. *Sixteenth-century Spanish and Portuguese trade routes.*

2

to make this crossing by land. The Portuguese voyager Ferdinand Magellan sailed into the Pacific for Spain in 1520 and claimed the Philippine Islands.

Manila became the gateway for European trade with China, Japan, Korea, and India. The treasure-laden Manila galleon sailed once a year from the Philippines to Acapulco, Mexico, and then back. Through its voyages silver from the Andean mines of Potosi was traded for silks, porcelain, cotton textile, tea, and other high-priced goods which circulated in the Spanish colonies and as far as the market-places of Europe (Map 1).

To enlarge the empire of souls, the Spanish Catholic Church established an archbishopric in the Philippines in 1579. The indomitable Franciscan missionary Father Junipero Serra blazed a trail along the coast of California to build a series of missions from San Diego to San Francisco. The Spanish domains on the Pacific—Alta California, Mexico, Ecuador, Columbia, Peru, and Chile—became rapidly growing communities of converts for a transoceanic spiritual empire.

When white American settlers, Chinese immigrants, European immigrants, and African Americans began moving into California after its incorporation in the United States, they were moving into a land where Hispanic people possessed a well-developed consciousness of its role as a bridge between the Pacific and the Atlantic. Indeed, the forging of "Transcontinental Empire," in the words of historian David J. Weber, was the initial achievement of the Spanish who spanned the continent and linked the Atlantic and Pacific Oceans, through their twin outposts of New California (from San Francisco to San Diego) and the Floridas East and West in the late eighteenth century.[5]

Russian explorers and colonists gazed at the Aleutian Islands and the Pacific coast of North America as a natural extension of Siberia. The Tsar hired the Danish navigator Vitus Bering to explore and gather geographic information from Kamchatka to Alaska and its islands, where he discovered the strait between the Pacific and Arctic Oceans that was named after him. By the start of the nineteenth century, Russia had forged a chain of hunting and trading posts from the Aleutian Islands, to the Hawaiian Islands, and to northern California (Figure 1-1).

Shortly after the American Revolution, mercantile entrepreneurs in the United States launched new organized ventures into the Indo-Pacific region. New England merchants established commercial relations with a far-flung network of trading centers in southeastern India where American goods were exchanged for spices, fabrics, and tea.[6] They managed a profitable business of exporting ice to India in exchange for commercial tea. Throughout the early nineteenth century, American merchants continued to search for new opportunities to trade and to engage in whaling across the Pacific (Table 1-1). A group formed ties with Chinese merchants in the Canton region of southern China to import tea, silk, and other commodities. In 1853, Commodore Matthew Perry forced his way into the harbor of Tokyo and obtained an agreement for commercial exchanges between the United States and Japan.

President Thomas Jefferson arranged the Louisiana Purchase in 1803 and sponsored the Lewis and Clark exploratory and surveying expedition into the great hinterland that established a new geographic horizon for the United States on the

Figure 1-1.   Fort Elizabeth of the Russian American Company, Kaua'i, Hawaiian Islands, 1817.

northwest Pacific coast.[7] The coastal area to the north of California became a regional arena for imperial rivalry between Russia, Great Britain, and the United States. The United States negotiated a treaty in 1846 with Britain to secure the northwestern boundary line between the United States and British Columbia. Officials of the United States warily eyed Alaska from which Russia had extended settlements as far south as the Pacific coast of northern California. A Russian naval expedition built and occupied a fort on the Hawaiian island of Kaua'i. The United States acquired California and other far western regions through its victory in the Mexican War, and directly purchased Alaska from Russia two years after the end of the Civil War. Overland travel through regularized "trail" routes and transcontinental railroads boosted internal migration to the Pacific coast.

Table 1-1.   Ship Arrivals in Hawaiian Ports, 1824–1861.

	Whaling Ships	**Merchant Ships**
Honolulu	4,708	2,959
Lahaina	4,424	
Other Ports	1,169	484

Source: Patrick V. Kirsch and Marshall Sahlins, Anahulu: The Anthropology of History in the Kingdom of Hawaii, Volumes One and Two (Chicago: University of Chicago Press, 1992); Volume One, Marshall Sahlins with Dorothy B. Barrere, Historical Ethnography, Table 5-1, p. 103.

Along interoceanic routes, Hawai'i became a destination for missionaries and hundreds of trading and whaling ships departing from New England seaports. Shipping to the Hawaiian Islands from New England linked the Atlantic and Pacific worlds. Pre-eminent maritime historian Samuel Eliot Morison once described Honolulu as an interoceanic crossroads with the role of the "commercial Gibraltar of the Pacific." Anthropologists Patrick V. Kirsch and Marshall Sahlins summarized Sir George Simpson's view of the Hawaiian Islands as the centerpiece of the Hudson's Bay Company imperial vision, describing how they were "at once accessible to the shores of North and South America and on the most convenient route between the American coast and the Celestial Empire."[8]

The whaling industry launched thousands of seamen into the ports of Hawai'i. Lahaina, Maui, the capital of the Hawaiian monarchy, became a gathering place for New England whalers, creating an enclave that was an interoceanic equivalent of a New England seaport. Kirsch and Sahlins described "crews of whale ships let loose for weeks . . . drawn from the flotsam of New England ports . . . [and] crew losses (as by desertion) were made up through recruitment of Pacific islanders, including many hundreds of Hawaiians." Indeed, crew lists of many New England–based sailing ships recorded the names of sailors that appeared to suggest that their origins were in the Pacific islands.[9] Native Hawaiians "signed on as crew members, making two- and three-year voyages before returning to their homes—just as New England seamen made similar trips," according to historian Jo Anne Roe who has described the journeys of these Polynesians as follows:

> [The monarch of the Hawaiian Islands] King Kamehameha encouraged his subjects to make voyages in the ships that touched Hawaiian shores. Since they were, by nature, seafaring men, they adapted to western ways and became excellent sailors. . . . Inevitably Hawaiian sailors left their ships in British Columbia and other ports to explore new lands. In the Pacific Northwest it was not uncommon for Hawaiians to work at diverse shoreside jobs, some marrying the daughters of Indians or settlers. During the early settlement of the American Northwest, there were large numbers of Hawaiians working as sheepherders on San Juan Island. . . . Hawaiian crewmen also appeared on the decks of the earliest ships to enter the Columbia River and trade at Astoria or Fort Vancouver. In Oregon, Owyhee County, Owyhee River, and Owyhee Mountains ["Owyhee" was an early American linguistic distortion of Hawai'i] commemorate those Hawaiians. . . .[10]

Many Hawaiian migrants established settlements in the Washington and Oregon area that became multigenerational communities. The seaman Henry Haumea, who landed from a trans-Pacific sailing ship in the San Juan Channel near Bellingham, Washington, became the progenitor of several generations of part-Hawaiian descendants who remained in that area for well over a century.[11]

The industrialization and agricultural development of Atlantic economies, the global expansion of slave, indentured, and wage labor markets, and increases of population caused by demographic transition in Europe and Asia shaped a new matrix of push and pull forces that propelled migration. The worldwide "plantation complex" described by historian Philip Curtin spreading from the Mediterranean to the Atlantic and to the Pacific, followed by the international-ization of the industrial labor system, created a global economic force field that spurred mass migrations across the Atlantic and Pacific.

Countries such as the United States, Canada, Peru, Cuba, Trinidad, Mexico, and Brazil became magnets for European and Asian immigration. From the middle of the nineteenth century, the United States became the leading destina-tion country in the western hemisphere for immigrants from Europe and from countries in the Pacific region.[12] The United States was also at the forefront of the transcontinental expansion of Atlantic societies to the Pacific region, rapidly es-tablishing new settlements and spheres of influence in its far western reaches.[13]

The Pacific far west exhibited the role of population history in the develop-ment of an interoceanic world from the nineteenth century to the twentieth century. Transoceanic population movements drove the transformation of Hawai'i of the Polynesian monarchy into the U.S. territory and state of Hawai'i. The transcontinental movement of people to California changed its core population as a Spanish colony, a state of Mexico, and then as a state of the United States. In Hawai'i and California, the fabric of local communities was sewn together from multiple cultural threads carried by migrations across the lands and seas of the Atlantic and Pacific regions over a long series of historical eras.[14]

In the first decade after the founding of the United States, the new nation's leaders—particularly Alexander Hamilton, James Madison, and Thomas Jefferson—placed their imprimatur on the drive to enlarge national boundaries. They were immediately concerned about the new republic's expanding geopolitical frontiers abutting the empires of Great Britain, France, Russia, and Spain whose domin-ions ringed the fledgling country and encroached from the Pacific Rim.[15] The statesmen of the new republic had defied the standard view of political theory that republics had to be small in scale. Instead, they were confident that, because of its strong representative and federal institutions, the United States could expand into a large state and still maintain itself as an effectively functioning republic. Some even held that the political logic of a republic required enlarging the size of the population and its territory. Expansion would limit the potential for political factions to become dominant because there would be more regional communities checking and balancing each other.

In the immense tract of land west of the Mississippi River acquired from the Louisiana Purchase—the "trans-Mississippi west"—the United States struggled for control of long and amorphous new international borders and internal settle-ment zones with the Spanish and British Empires, as well as their "off-shoot" countries of Mexico and Canada. Regional control often meant migration con-trol. California and the northern region of Mexico around the Rio Grande River attracted migrants and traders from the United States, a potential de-stabilizing force in disputed land. These settlers intermixed with the Hispanic elites of California (Californios) and New Mexico (Hispanos) and helped to create a transnational Anglo-Hispanic culture. Eventually, however, the growing number of American newcomers sought to take over this borderland. Supporting American settlers in Texas who espoused the cause of breaking away from Mexico, the United States defeated Mexico in 1848 in an international war, and gained Texas and the large area from New Mexico to California.[16]

American slaveholders also turned their eyes southward toward Spanish colonies in the Caribbean as possible sites for plantation-based production of commercial crops such as sugar and fruits. Southern slaveholders and their supporters joined with slaveholders in Cuba to lobby for the annexation of Cuba. They came together to coordinate military expeditions to Cuba from 1849 to1851, but they were unable to achieve a successful takeover.

By the 1850s, the United States had established de facto and official control of the lands west of the Mississippi to the Pacific, and between Canada and Mexico. Settlers from the east who organized themselves into local interest groups and federal government leaders surveyed the former borderlands of the British and Spanish empires with an ambitious long-range vision for developing the west. Their vantage would lead them into efforts to establish trans-Pacific international relations that would secure the fringes of the far west. The U.S. government began official contacts with Japan when Commodore Perry sailed into Yokohama Bay near Tokyo to initiate trading and diplomatic relations. Tokyo sent a diplomatic party to Washington, D.C., the first Japanese embassy, in 1860.

The destiny of the trans-Mississippi west became part of a plan for resolving the relationship between the expanding white communities and Indian tribes east of the Mississippi. The federal government decided that these two populations could never co-exist as integrated parts of a future American society. The eastern tribes were forced to migrate to what became known as "Indian country," the lands to the west of the Mississippi River such as the territory of Oklahoma, carved out as a zone of resettlement for Indian tribes like the Creek, Cherokees, Choctaws, and Chicasaws who were forcibly relocated by the federal government from their homelands in the southeast. The lands of the original Indian inhabitants of the trans-Mississippi west were rapidly penetrated by settlers, hunters, farmers, and traders moving in from the states and territories to the east. Whites moving from the Mississippi River to the Pacific coast brought changes in land usage that for Indians produced an all-encompassing new environment incompatible with their tribal modes of existence.[17]

The growing presence of Americans in the Pacific led to efforts to establish their cultural institutions among indigenous Pacific Islanders. The first group of missionaries from New England arrived in the Polynesian kingdom of Hawai'i in 1820, one year after the monarch King Kamehameha I, who had unified the chain of islands, passed away. His heirs were willing to accommodate the New England missionaries as they converted thousands of native Hawaiians to Christianity in the form of New England Congregationalism (Figure 1-2). This religious transformation was the first in a wave of cultural exchanges between Hawai'i and New England.[18]

Figure 1-2. Mokuʻaikaua church, first Christian church in Hawaiian Islands (founded 1820, built 1835–1837).

A native Hawaiian youth, Opukahaiʻa, who sought to escape from family and tribal feuding, boarded in 1808 the ship of a New England sea captain anchored in Hilo Bay in the "big island" of Hawaiʻi, the largest of the Hawaiian Islands (Figure 1-3a, b, c). After a voyage back to the home port of New Bedford, Massachusetts, he was adopted into the captain's family so he could attend school and study for the ministry. He Anglicized his name to Henry Obookiah and lived with Yale president Timothy Dwight, who tutored him in Christianity and literature. Obookiah also stayed at Williams College and at the Andover Theological Seminary. He resettled in Connecticut to ready himself for a return to Hawaiʻi as a missionary, but he died at the age of twenty-six in Cornwall, where he was buried in the parish graveyard.[19]

Whaling expeditions from New England brought about unexpected personal contacts between Japan and the United States. American whalers rescued dozens of Japanese sailors who survived shipwrecks in the Pacific. Nakahama Manjiro, a shipwrecked fisherman from Japan, was rescued by an American whaling ship. He returned with the ship's crew to New Bedford and became the ward of a local Yankee family in the nearby town of Fairhaven. Manjiro adopted "John" as his American name and attended a local Unitarian church. He learned English,

Figure 1-3.   Encounters with Pacific Islanders and Asians: (a) Opukahaiʻa [Henry Obookiah] (circa 1792–1818). First indigenous Hawaiian immigrant in the United States; (b) Nakahama "John" Manjiro (1827–1898); (c) Joseph Pierce in his Union Army uniform (1842–1916).

studied literature and scientific subjects as a student in an American school. Manjiro returned to Japan after his American sojourn. He was appointed a government official and ennobled as a samurai in service to the Japanese national government, largely because of his ability to supply the regime with knowledge about America and its culture.[20] Also through experiences in the U.S. whaling industry, a traveler and adventurer, Ranald MacDonald, became a kind of Manjiro in reverse. Born in Astoria in the Columbia River valley of Oregon, this son of an officer of the Hudson's Bay Company and a Chinook Indian mother obtained passage with a New England whaling ship and arranged with its captain to be cast off in a row boat off the northern coast of Japan in 1848 where he made landfall. He was held by Japanese officials who ordered MacDonald to teach English to Japanese translators who later became interpreters with Commodore Perry when he arrived in Japan. This first teacher of English in Japan traveled further to Australia and the Pacific coast of Canada. Both Manjiro and MacDonald were representative of an increasing number of globalist social types, individuals who circulated in long-distance journeys and sojourns, and provided a life-thread of cultural contacts that formed connections which integrated and bridged regions.[21]

   The life of Joseph Pierce, a Chinese immigrant and Civil War veteran, revealed that migration from across the Pacific could intertwine at a personal level with the major events of U.S. history. The journey that took him from southern China, beset by famine and disorder, to the Fourteenth Connecticut Infantry in the U.S. Civil War began when he was ten years old. Joseph Pierce was "sold" by his impoverished father to Amos Peck, the captain of an American ship that had stopped for trade in Canton in 1852. The boy was given the name "Joe" by the crew on the two-month return voyage to New England. Joe accompanied Captain Peck to his home in Berlin, Connecticut, and received the surname "Pierce" after

Franklin Pierce who was president of the United States in 1853. Captain Peck was a bachelor, so his mother took charge of Joe's upbringing, and taught him English, reading, and arithmetic. Joe eventually attended a country school in Berlin along with Captain Peck's younger brothers and sisters.

When the Civil War began, Pierce was working on the Peck homestead as a farmer. In July, 1862, at the age of twenty-one, he volunteered for military service and joined the Fourteenth Regiment Connecticut Volunteers Infantry, a regiment in the Army of the Potomac. Pierce fought at the Battle of Chancellorsville and Gettysburg where he helped to repel "Pickett's Charge." Promoted to corporal in 1864, he fought in the Virginia campaigns until Lee's surrender at Appomattox in April 1865. By the end of the war, Pierce's regiment had lost more men than any other unit from Connecticut. Pierce returned to Connecticut and started a successful and long career as an engraver in the silver industry located in Meriden. He met and married Martha Morgan in 1876, and raised three children with her in Meriden. When he died, the local newspaper's obituary did not mention his background or origin and stated with simple respect that Joseph Pierce was "well known and liked."[22]

BRIDGES ACROSS THE WATERS

The cultural and material forces of the Atlantic world flowed into the Pacific basin and from there into the eastern periphery of the Indian Ocean through a set of archipelagic links. The Philippines, the Aleutians, the Fiji Islands, the Hawaiian Islands, the Samoas, and French Polynesia were turned into interoceanic connecting points by the seaborne expansion of European imperial power. These archipelagos, positioned at geographically strategic locations in the Pacific basin, played a key role in the development of interconnections between Atlantic and Indo-Pacific regions.

Island worlds of the North Atlantic near the European and African land masses had once played a similar role in connecting the early modern economy and population of the Mediterranean region with an emerging set of colonies in the Atlantic basin. The Canaries, Azores, Madeiras, and eastern West Indies were corridors through which institutions, economic patterns, and people of the Mediterranean region began to pass into the Atlantic Ocean. Historian Felipe Fernandez-Armesto pointed out that the "completion of the conquest of the Canary Islands is very close in time to the first conquests in the New World," and therefore can be seen as an episode in the long sequence of Spanish expansion into the Atlantic. Philip Curtin noted that this geopolitical projection was an evolutionary process as well: "The Atlantic islands in the fifteenth century thus came to be an intermediate step between the colonial institutions of the medieval Mediterranean and those of the Americas." As a location for the interaction of population, commerce, ecological factors, and cultural diffusion, archipelagos were natural bridges between oceanic worlds. Historian J. G. A. Pocock has commented, "Islands are in oceans, not in narrow seas; and from the English south-west, the Gaelic west, and the Norse far north of the Stuart monarchies, the seas of Europe open out into the Atlantic and the global or world-girdling ocean."[23]

In an age when maritime travel reigned as the most efficient form of transport, archipelagos were highly accessible geographical sites for long-distance movers. Positioned on sea lanes, they were small enough to be quickly settled and subjected to externally imposed changes. Removed by the barrier of distance from other societies, they became containers for the reciprocal exchange of inserted cultural modes and products, and evolved quickly into local communities defined by creole cultures and languages. Island worlds nurtured syncretic cultural complexes with the capacity to participate in interregional communication and to influence distant societies.[24]

In the nineteenth century, the Hawaiian Islands became part of the economic periphery of the Atlantic world. The sugar plantation and its labor system, a characteristic feature of the early modern Atlantic economy initially brought from the Mediterranean region, were established in Hawai'i by the 1830s. Philip D. Curtin has charted the Atlantic-to-Pacific migration of this "plantation complex:"

> [The] particular sugar revolution of the seventeenth century [in the eastern Caribbean islands] was only one among many. Each time the complex moved to a new place, it had brought on a new sugar revolution. The onward movement from Madeira to Brazil was a sugar revolution; the forward movement from the eastern Caribbean to Saint Domingue and Jamaica after 1700 was another; and still others lay in the future for Cuba, Mauritius, Natal, Peru, Hawai'i, and Fiji—among others.[25]

Cattle ranching and whaling, which had developed in the Atlantic basin, also found a receptive site in Hawai'i. Cattle ranches were established on the "big island" of Hawai'i and Maui, which also served as the Pacific home base of the New England whaling fleet. The products of commercial plantation agriculture, ranching, and whaling were crucial for integrating the Hawaiian economy with the Atlantic economy. Ninety percent of Hawai'i's export total in 1878, 99 percent in 1899, and 98 percent in 1930 went to the United States. Sixty-seven percent of Hawai'i's import total in 1878, 78 percent in 1899, and 90 percent in 1930 came from the United States. Trade and development pivoted on the interlinkage of structures of economic organization from the Atlantic region to Hawai'i. The productive and commercial base of Hawai'i, formed as offshoots of the Atlantic regional economy, turned these islands into an emergent central Pacific hub of transoceanic migration, ecological exchange, and cultural diffusion.[26]

The plantation, ranching, and whaling tripod of Hawai'i brought settlers from New England who played a key role in the development of economic institutions. Hundreds of Protestant families, descended from or related to missionaries who began to arrive in 1820, formed an elite group of "malihini" (newcomers from the outside) implanted among the "kamaaina" ("people of the land," homegrown or native), and founded a commercial empire of sugar, pineapple, and coffee plantations. The development of nineteenth-century Hawai'i rested on an agricultural economy of scale controlled by a creole oligarchy that paralleled the political economy of planter societies in the Atlantic basin. James Dole came to Hawai'i soon after graduating from Harvard and created a pineapple growing and processing business that evolved into the mammoth Dole Pineapple Company. The Parker Ranch, pioneered by John Palmer Parker of Newton, Massachusetts, who arrived on the "big island" of Hawai'i in 1809 on a New England whaler, grew into one of the largest cattle ranches on U.S. territory.

European immigration and Atlantic Islander migration had a profound impact on the new society emerging in nineteenth-century Hawai'i. Under the government of the Hawaiian monarchy and the successor U.S. territorial government that took over in 1898, immigrants from Portugal, Germany, Scotland, Norway, Russia, Spain, and Puerto Rico were recruited to work in the plantations and ranches established by the first New England settlers and their descendants. From 1878 to 1887, 12,000 Portuguese immigrants arrived from the Azores and Madeira Islands. From 1906 to 1913, a second burst of immigration from these islands brought 13,000 more Portuguese newcomers. Six hundred Norwegians arrived in 1881; 1,400 immigrants from northwest Germany came in the 1880s and 1890s; these were followed a little later by more than 2,000 Russians. The early years of the twentieth century brought 5,200 Puerto Ricans, 7,600 Spaniards, and smaller numbers of immigrants from Greece and Sweden. Large numbers of Scots migrated to Hawai'i continuously from the nineteenth century; as a result, the 1980 U.S. Census enumerated 24,300 persons of Scottish ancestry in Hawai'i. As a cumulative product of these flows, migrants from Atlantic settler societies and Europe constituted by 1910 a subpopulation of 44,000 persons, or approximately one-fifth of the entire Hawaiian Islands population, who lived among a non-white majority consisting of indigenous Hawaiians, and Chinese, Japanese, Korean, and Filipino immigrants who came to work on the plantations.[27]

Viewed from a worldwide perspective, Hawai'i's peopling process was suggestive of how island societies, in the context of economic and technological change, played important roles in interlinking oceanic regions. Hawai'i—the central Pacific island world—was settled to a striking extent by peoples from other island worlds: first from the Atlantic—the Azores, the Madeiras, Britain, and Puerto Rico—then from the Pacific: Japan and the Philippines (concurrently with the influx from Puerto Rico). Island peoples proved to be widely available for participation in the mass migratory movements spurred by the revolution in seagoing transportation and commerce.

INTELLECTUAL PATHFINDERS

The provincial settlements from the days of the British Empire had developed into the United States and created a national identity based on new movements of religious revival, humanitarianism, romanticism, and individualism. These constituted one facet of a trans-Atlantic cultural movement against Calvinism, Catholicism, feudalism and other formal systems that also inspired writers, artists, and philosophers in England, France, Italy, and Germany. In the United States, the philosophical movement known as transcendentalism resonated with the idealism of British writers such as Thomas Carlyle, William Wordsworth, Samuel Taylor Coleridge, and Percy Shelley and the German philosophers Immanuel Kant, Georg Wilhelm Friedrich Hegel, and Arthur Schopenhauer.

As they participated in a trans-Atlantic philosophical and literary culture, the transcendentalists were also influenced by the European discovery of Asian thought. Ralph Waldo Emerson and Henry David Thoreau were American students of the Orient who studied ancient religious and philosophical texts from India, Persia, and China through translations in English and other European languages. They were particularly influenced by Hindu and Buddhist teachings that provided moral and spiritual guidance in times of change and complexity. Emerson paid homage to the *Bhagavad Gita*, a key scripture of Hinduism as "the first of books." "[I]t was as if an empire spoke to us," Emerson recalled, "nothing small or unworthy, but large, serene, consistent, the voice of an old intelligence which in another age and climate had pondered and thus disposed of the same questions which exercise us." Thoreau exulted, "I bathe my intellect in the stupendous and cosmogonical philosophy of the *Bhagavad Gita*, in comparison with which our modern world and its literature seem puny and trivial." Fortified with knowledge of the East's wisdom, Emerson and Thoreau rejected formal, superficial systems and urged their followers to look inward to their inner spiritual power and to become spiritually self-regenerating. Their trailblazing explorations encouraged fellow Americans to open their minds to the achievements of Asian civilizations as gifts to all humankind. In the late nineteenth century, Edward Morse, Ernest Fenolossa, William Sturgis Bigelow, and Okakura Tenshin assembled the Asian collection of the Boston Museum of Fine Arts, the finest in the United States and an unparalleled window onto Asian culture and civilizations.[28]

The far west became a vivid tableau on the imaginative horizon of easterners through the writings of two Massachusetts authors who, unlike Thoreau and Emerson, traveled far and wide in pursuit of their subjects. Francis Parkman of Boston wrote *The Oregon Trail,* which was a historical saga of the pioneers who journeyed to new lands in the Pacific northwest. Its epic qualities inspired Theodore Roosevelt to write a four-volume history, *The Winning of the West*. Helen Hunt Jackson of Amherst, a friend of poet Emily Dickinson, toured the west and documented the unjust treatment of Indian tribes by the federal government in *A Century of Dishonor*. She traveled to southern California to explore the plight of the Indian communities of the old Spanish missions. Jackson wrote *Ramona*, a novel about the sufferings and struggles of a part-white Indian woman on a California farm, which was second only to Harriet Beecher Stowe's *Uncle Tom's Cabin* as a best-selling American novel in nineteenth-century America. It was reprinted three hundred times, sold hundreds of thousands of copies, and was turned into a movie in 1910 which was directed by D. W. Griffith and starred Mary Pickford as Ramona. *Ramona* was also turned into a play that became the centerpiece of the yearly Ramona Pageant held outdoors in the town of Hemet, a festival that helped jump-start mass tourism in southern California.[29]

Scientists from U.S. institutions contemplated the far west as a tremendous opportunity for the development of American science. They were following up on the wave of curiosity, speculation, and theorization by Europeans inspired by the Enlightenment to classify and organize knowledge of the natural world, particularly in relation to the newly discovered biota, geology, and geography of the western hemisphere. The French philosopher Charles Marie de La Condamine was among those who went beyond mental journeys and imaginings from the armchair and went to the Andes to engage in first-hand reconnaissance.[30] Surgeons on ships from U.S. Atlantic states and from seaports in England, Russia, France, and Germany often had doubled as naturalists on voyages to the Pacific coast of the Americas. By following the trail blazed by a "mountain man" pioneer explorer, Jedidiah Smith, two academic experts in botany and ornithology from Philadelphia, Thomas Nuttall and John Townsend, came to California in 1834 and stayed for two years collecting specimens. In the 1840s, a growing number of naturalists and geographers followed and produced discoveries that excited national interest in the Pacific coast. The Yale geologist James Dwight Dana and the Philadelphia naturalist Titian Peale were in the civilian Scientific Corps of the expedition led by Navy Lieutenant Charles Wilkes that explored the area from the Columbia River to San Francisco Bay in 1841. The German cartographer Charles Preuss accompanied the inland expedition of Army Captain John C. Fremont, whose reconnaissance complemented the Wilkes coastal survey, and produced detailed maps of the interior far west. Fremont himself had gained experience with exploratory science as an officer in the Army Corps of Topographic Engineers and as a field collaborator with the famed cartographer Joseph Nicolet.[31]

TRANSATLANTIC MOVEMENTS

The United States was unlike any country in Europe, since it possessed a long, open borderland known as the western frontier. Functioning as a demographic "expansion tank," it received the growing numbers of Americans who left more crowded eastern communities in search of new opportunities as well as immigrants from Europe willing to make the long journey to the west. Wave after wave of westward, repeated migrations produced a widening bridgehead of settlement edging its way toward the Pacific.

The growth of the United States can be re-framed as a chapter in the global history of transoceanic mass migrations. The creation of European overseas empires laid the foundations for this phase of international development. Enslaved Africans and colonists from northern and western European nations moved across the Atlantic from the sixteenth to the eighteenth century in the first large-scale transoceanic organized recruitment of settler populations. They swiftly populated the eastern seaboard and its hinterlands.

The conception of emigration to the United States as providing a "safety valve" to the opportunistic masses played upon the thoughts of influential European commentators and officials. In their view, emigration from their countries re-adjusted the balance between population and inherent economic resources. In Germany, the European country which sent the greatest number of immigrants to the United States, a debate occurred throughout the nineteenth century that focused on the possibilities of trans-Atlantic emigration as an overflow that relieved social pressure. The "Iron Chancellor" who unified Germany, Otto von Bismarck, claimed that the peopling of North America by Europeans was "the decisive fact in the modern world."[32] For many emigrants, as a historian has pointed out, migration was "conceived of as a means of escape from oppressive spiritual conditions, constriction of social life, generalized exploitation, and the reality of larger economic cycles." Their departure represented a type of nonviolent social protest and a "part of a process of bargaining over the allocation of resources and resistance to unacceptable conditions either by demographic and economic developments or by political and social systems."[33]

Patterns of European immigration in the nineteenth century departed radically from the influx of the eighteenth century. The ethnic, cultural, and religious diversity of new arrivals multiplied exponentially (Map 2). The first dramatic change in the foreign population occurred through the arrival of a large group of Roman Catholics, coming chiefly from Ireland and southern German states such as Bavaria, Wurtemberg, and Baden. Another difference in the pattern of the nineteenth century was that it contributed a greater share to American population growth than did migration during the colonial era. Finally, the number of immigrants settling in urban areas increased sharply. Irish and German immigrants flocked to Boston, New York City, Philadelphia, Cincinnati, and St. Louis.

The rise in immigration sprang from a new set of conditions promoting population growth. Reorganization of the agricultural economy in Europe provided an improvement in the quantity and quality of the food supply. European farmers introduced new marketing arrangements and technical changes. The innovation of crop diversification prevented to a greater degree a catastrophic break in the food supply chain when areas dependent on one staple crop failed to meet normal levels of production for subsistence. Plants from the New World such as potato, maize, and green vegetables supplemented the diet of the peasantry. The agricultural revolution raised nutritional norms, thus sustaining high birth rates while lowering death rates in the nineteenth century. Concurrently, parental and communal controls on marriage began to loosen, allowing more and earlier independence to individuals in their decisions to marry. Patterns of economic change often influenced marriage. For example, the spread of cottage industries in some rural areas provided a means for securing a livelihood and the capital to start a family.

These economic and demographic changes produced an overall rise in population in regions of northern and western Europe. Farms were becoming miniaturized or "morselized" as they were subdivided among an expanding pool of people who lived off of farming. In the Rhine Valley, half of all farms were less than five acres in size, and a quarter were less than one acre. At the same time as population increased and farmland was intensively subdivided, landlords started consolidating and integrating their agricultural domains to create conditions for more efficient farming. The rural peasantry faced new limits on the available supply of farmland. A large displaced surplus population began to accumulate, and they prepared to migrate in search of new livings. The gradual abolition of feudal tenure removed the legal restraints that had kept the rural masses tied to the lords' landed estates. Rural migration flowed toward local or nearby urban centers. People farther away from provincial urban centers moved to more distant state capitals such as London, Paris, and Vienna, and also became available to migrate across international land boundaries or overseas.[34]

Across northern European countries, industrialization began to create new difficulties for earning a livelihood. Artisans working in small shops and peasants who practiced crafts in their cottages faced overwhelming competition from the spread of markets supplying new mass-manufactured goods. Scottish and German cottage weavers lost out in the expanding marketplace for low-priced factory-made textiles. The regions experiencing commercial change became increasingly vulnerable to the alternation of economic "boom" and "bust." Economic instability put new pressures on the households of common laborers who had little extra margin to survive regular recurrences of lean times. As this process of economic change moved from countries in northern and western Europe to those in southern and eastern Europe, a pool of surplus labor expanded.[35]

The cycles of economic growth were unevenly phased among the industrializing societies of the northern Atlantic world in such a way as to promote migration. During the 1840s, when the British economy slackened, the expanding American economy attracted farmers, artisans, and laborers from England, Scotland, Wales, and Ireland to the United States. The geographic distribution of industrial employment opportunities across the northern Atlantic world propelled labor migration from European countries to the United States. In the early to middle decades of the nineteenth century, the shortage of skilled labor in the United States drew artisans from Britain and Germany, because they were able to obtain higher wages as American immigrants than by remaining in their homelands. Displaced by "push" forces of economic and political reorganization in homeland societies, immigrants were attracted by the "pull" forces of material opportunities and political liberties in the new American lands. The yearly totals of European immigrants entering the United States rose and fell according to the expansion and contraction of the economy.[36]

A revolution in long-distance mass transportation in Europe greatly improved travel connections for immigrants. Railroads, canals, and vehicular roads linked provincial areas to urban centers, creating an internal revolution in transportation. Another part of the transportation revolution occurred in transoceanic mass travel. Ever faster and larger ships, first under sail and then, by midcentury, under steam lowered the cost of travel and reduced its inconvenience and insecurity. Travel time was shortened, carrying capacity was increased, travel conditions became safer, and departure and arrival schedules were regularized. Common laborers were able to secure a ticket from a European to an Atlantic coast port in the United States for a month's wages.[37]

Supplementing the transportation revolution was a communications and information revolution that heightened popular knowledge of migration opportunities. The printing and marketing of travel guidebooks about the United States expanded throughout Britain and western Europe as popular literacy rose. The result was a more informed public consciousness of the opportunities that awaited in America. The market for immigration guidebooks was manipulated by agents and entrepreneurs on both sides of the Atlantic. State and territorial governments in the west, land-selling companies, and railroads supported the production of immigrant guidebooks written in several European languages.[38]

Immigration from Catholic Ireland as well as from Britain, Germany, and Scandinavia in the middle decades of the nineteenth century formed the first great wave of new trans-Atlantic migrants. It was succeeded by a second and even larger wave of immigration originating from southern and eastern Europe and also, to a lesser degree, from Asia, Mexico, and the Caribbean. The European newcomers of the second wave were labeled the "new immigrants" to contrast them with the "old immigrants" of the first wave. The second wave declined sharply in the late 1920s and the Great Depression era.

European immigrants formed an industrial working class that powered population growth in urban centers. In the workplace, immigrants constituted a driving force behind the organization of labor unions. In the urban neighborhoods, European immigrants became the constituencies of mass political parties rooted in ethnic voting blocs. They spurred urban institutional and communal development in the United States to a greater extent than immigrants did in Canada, Brazil, and Australia.

In other immigration-receiving countries, European immigrants were recruited primarily to build the middle class or to provide manpower for agriculture. In Canada, British immigrants found their central economic roles in white-collar and commercial fields. In Australia, the Irish filled the demand for farm labor. On the Argentine Pampa, Irish immigrants started farms and ranches. In Buenos Aires, immigrants from Italy, Spain, and Russia constituted the urban middle-class core that would Europeanize the civilization of a nation emerging from raw colonial roots. In Brazil, German immigrants served a similar civilizing developmental function in its southern states and large urban centers.[39]

European immigrants in the United States, by and large, did not come from the most under-developed countries, and they did not originate from the most deprived classes of their homelands. They were rural and urban laborers who had already initiated adaptations to population pressure and limited resources. The experiences of this process made them "available" to the attractive forces of opportunities they perceived to lie outside their local worlds. Poor men and women from the countryside moving in search of better opportunities to nearby provinces, towns, cities, and neighboring countries became part of regional worlds in motion. These unrooted people frequently moved back and forth between distant workplaces and home. They formed a growing pool of transient migrant labor that spilled into streams of immigrants seeking permanent new homes in the United States and other developing overseas areas.[40]

Many saw their move to the United States as an extension of the circular or transient currents of local migration and thus returned home after sojourns. As a result, the United States experienced a large bi-directional flow after the advent of modern ocean and land transportation systems. Transient immigration reached its historic zenith in the early twentieth century. Immigrants from southern and eastern Europe formed the bulk of those involved in this pattern. From 1908 to 1910, for every 100 northern Italians arriving, sixty-three departed; for every 100 southern Italians arriving, fifty-six departed. For Russians, the rate was forty-one departures for every 100 arrivals; for Hungarians, it was sixty-five departures; for Slovaks, it was fifty-nine departures; for Croatians and Slovenians, it was fifty-seven departures; for Poles, it was thirty-one departures. In the first quarter of the twentieth century, approximately three immigrants departed from every ten who arrived in the United States.[41]

The regularity and magnitude of two-way migration produced a continual flow of popular traditions between the United States and Europe. International migration was a conduit that brought the institutions and cultures of European North Atlantic countries into constant and close contact with the new communities being built in the United States. International mass migrations from Europe, in other words, established cultural corridors between receiving communities in the United States and European homelands that linked together the two Atlantic regions.

Immigrants were not passively like particles in a historical force field. Their decision to migrate turned always on their possession of two attitudes that set them apart from countrymen who stayed behind. These individuals were open to risk-taking and possessed the willingness to search for the widest fields of opportunity for their offspring—to invest in future generations. As they moved to new countries, immigrants from Europe relied upon a process of mutually assisted migration based on specific local attachments called chain migration. According to an influential theoretical study, chain migration was a movement "in which prospective migrants learn of opportunities, are provided with transportation, and have initial accommodations and employment arranged by means of primary social relationship with previous migrants." Relatives and friends who had already immigrated provided information and help in obtaining jobs, housing, loans, and connections to newcomers in transit in the United States.[42]

By the middle of the nineteenth century, immigrants from Ireland settled in the major urban enclaves, and immigrants from northern and central Europe followed the flow of American settlers to the territories around the Great Lakes, which were quickly being turned into new states. Prompted to migrate to the United States by the poverty and the limited opportunities of their homeland villages and towns, Norwegians and Swedes carved out farms in Wisconsin, Michigan, and Minnesota. German immigrants fanned out even more widely to start farms in Missouri, Kansas, Iowa, Nebraska, and Texas, as well as the Great Lakes region. Other German newcomers flocked to midwestern urban centers. St. Louis, Milwaukee, and Cincinnati, which became hosts to large German enclaves, came to be known as the "German triangle."

Geographic and economic expansion ensured constant change in the American population. Before the nineteenth century, the process of peopling the colonies by voluntary migration involved settlers from Britain and the countries of western Europe. In the mid-nineteenth century, the Anglo-American population rooted in the colonial era made room for a new foreign-born population that became known popularly as "immigrant America." The coastal towns and cities and the farmlands of the midwest were dotted by enclaves of newcomers who came from the Celtic fringes of Britain and the countries of northern and central Europe, bringing with them the Roman Catholic faith and new varieties of Protestantism.

Native-born Americans of the mid-nineteenth century, who were the great-grandchildren of the generation that had founded the United States, were astonished by the rapid pace of social change in their new republic. The United States began the nineteenth century as a nation with a miniature population in comparison to the countries of the eastern hemisphere. In 1800, the United States had only 5.3 million inhabitants, while France had 27.4 million, the German states had 23.0 million, and Britain had 20.8 million. The Asian countries of China, India, and the Ottoman Empire dwarfed the United States in population.

The United States at the start of the nineteenth century was a sparsely populated land, but it started to expand at a growth rate surpassing those of European countries. From 1800 to 1850, the United States' population quadrupled to over 23 million inhabitants, while France's and Germany's populations grew by about a quarter. Two forces propelled the unusually rapid rise of the American population. The first was a high rate of fertility, which from 1800 exceeded that of European countries. In 1800, an average of seven children were born to a woman in the United States, compared to slightly over five in England and slightly over four in France. Although the U.S. fertility rate gradually declined, it continued to lead over the fertility rate of France and England. The second factor that raised the pace of population growth in the United States was an accelerating rate of mass immigration. The number of foreign-born people annually entering the United States grew steadily from several thousand in the 1820s to over 300,000 in the 1850s. These arrivals represented a substantial loss of population in the poor rural areas of Europe from which they had escaped.

The immigrants arrived at a unique moment, when urbanization grew faster than at any other time in the country's history. In 1790, nine out of ten Americans derived their living from farming; in 1860, nearly half of all employed persons worked in non-agricultural occupations. Village-size communities based on family and personal relations gave way to larger and denser settlements that attracted masses of people from a variety of distant places. Immigrants who settled in these urban centers worked together to rebuild communal institutions in an unfamiliar and impersonal environment. The immigrants toiled in factory-like shops where they were treated as "hands," and they lived in poor and segregated neighborhoods without paternalistic care or supervision.

The nation's population grew at the rate of doubling every twenty-five years. With a population of 31 million people in 1860, the United States was nearly as large as France, the most populous country in Europe. As a result, the "geographic center of population," the point from which the national population was equally distributed in every direction, kept moving progressively westward. In 1790, it was located in Maryland; by 1860 it was in Ohio. As population surged to the west, new territories multiplied and a new state gained admission to the union on an average of every three years. The sixteen states that composed the United States in 1800 multiplied to thirty-three states in 1860.

LABOR FOR THE FAR WEST

In the mid-nineteenth century, the abolition of African slavery by imperial Britain and France, coupled with a rising demand for labor in the colonies of European empires and their successor states, produced a global shift in immigration patterns. The search for sources of labor moved away from Africa toward India and China, and from northern and western Europe toward southern and eastern Europe. It is estimated that between thirty and forty million Indian laborers and ten to fifteen million Chinese laborers moved to the peripheral areas of economic development, chiefly to the Indian Ocean and Pacific basin outbacks of the empires of Britain, France, Germany, Spain, Portugal, and the Netherlands. Over fifty million immigrants from all regions of Europe moved across the globe from the nineteenth to the early twentieth century. The trio of immigration flows from India, China, and Europe accumulated to approximately 100 million international migrants during the mature phase of European imperialism and industrial transformation.[43]

The social changes brought by industrial and urban growth were accompanied by new and intensifying inequalities. As the productivity of the American economy reached new heights in the first stages of the industrial revolution, the distribution of wealth grew more hierarchical. Industrial workers faced the proletarianizing conditions of wage labor, and gender inequality grew in urban employment. Abolitionists gathered more support to their crusade, but as a whole the northern populace remained deeply opposed to racial equality between whites and blacks. Furthermore, the power of slavery to expand into new territories seemed irresistible. In cities where immigrants from Catholic areas of Ireland and Germany and from China arrived, an unprecedented nativist backlash occurred. The policy of forced Indian removal to designated Indian territory west of the Mississippi expressed the view of the nation's political leaders that whites and Indians could not occupy the same society and share membership in the American nation.

The transformation of the American population by the middle of the nineteenth century through migration, industrialization, and urban growth presented public institutions with a new version of an old and fundamental problem of American life: How diverse communities of multiple origins would act together under conditions of openness and change, seeking a destiny that they were collectively a new people dedicated to republican institutions in a unique way, while facing new social divisions caused by economic and geopolitical expansion.

From the nineteenth century, the Pacific basin was a zone of primary economic development. The seemingly limitless resources of the region possessed the potential to provide a bonanza of raw materials for industry. The far west region of the United States, as part of the Pacific basin, functioned as a complementary, peripheral area of the urban-industrial core regions of Europe and the eastern United States. The far west served as a site for the development of a secondary capitalism that relied on eastern and foreign investments, external markets for raw materials, long-range transportation systems, and an elastic labor supply characterized by mobility and low skill level. Laborers had to flock quickly to different sites (with low upkeep) across the vast western distances, be quickly pooled into a workforce and then let go when the job was finished to leave the region or country. Transient labor migration was facilitated by technological modernization of the international transportation and communications systems, which reduced the transfer costs involved in changing residency. This occurred directly through the lowering of passenger fares, increasing the speed and regularity of travel by rail and steamship, and the diffusion of information about jobs, housing, and general conditions for the migrant propelled by the telegraph and print media.

OUT FROM ASIAN ENCLOSURES

Asian immigrants to the United States were part of a much larger pattern of labor migration from the countries of Asia that flowed to the new international zones of development created by the advent of Western capitalism and imperial power. The migration of Asian laborers to the United States was largely self-organized through internal networks of assistance and support for transportation, rather than systems of mass indenture, that were employed in the Indian Ocean and Latin America.

In contrast to provincial regions of Asia, the United States was a far more advanced and dynamic sector of economic growth. Both agricultural and industrial labor were more valuable in the United States. Even semiskilled and unskilled workers improved their chances for employment. Workers made more than their counterparts in the homelands. Chinese laborers in the United States were able to earn $200 to $300 a year, ten times their annual income in China. Furthermore, these immigrants sent money to their families and communities in China. The California State Senate estimated in 1878 that the average annual remittance of a Chinese emigrant was $30, enough to feed a wife and two children for a year.[44] Japanese plantation workers in Hawai'i earned wages several times higher than in Meiji-era Japan. With the advantage of superior earnings in the United States and Hawai'i, immigrants sent remittances back to their relatives and communities in their homelands. They sent small amounts, ten to twenty dollars a year, which added up to large flows of foreign exchange in aggregate over the years. It was estimated that from Hawai'i, Japanese immigrants sent $2.6 million in remittances to their home villages from 1885 to 1894.[45]

The homelands of immigrant laborers were located in the areas of Asia acutely exposed to the currents of rapid change. Rural laborers were responsive to the new opportunities to work in far-off regions because their local prospects suffered from economic underdevelopment, high population-to-land ratios, vulnerability to political upheavals and civil disorders, and external commercial pressures. The Pearl River delta of China, southern Japan, coastal Korea, the Punjab of India, and the northern Philippines were penetrated by new political and imperial controls (in some cases imposed by military power) that overturned traditional patterns of work and existence. These areas were also gripped by deep-seated and destabilizing changes in the infrastructure that supported living standards. Population growth, political disturbances, and economic distress were interconnected vectors that reduced the margin of existence sufficiently to make the option of migration attractive.[46] In Japan, the modernization of agriculture and landholding after the Meiji Revolution of 1868 resulted in new taxes and burdens on farmers in southern Japan. In the Canton area of southern China, dockhands as well as laborers who transported merchandise inland had employment prospects reduced by the advent of European carriers. Peasants lost supplementary income from household manufactures when imported foreign goods flooded the local market. Cotton textile manufacturing in the Punjab area of northwest India was set back by British imports.

War and civil insurrections—concurrent with political disorder and economic dislocation attendant with the arrival of foreign imperialism—further encouraged immigration from China, Korea, the Philippines, and India. The first Opium War (1839–1842), won by Great Britain, set into motion new forces of mass uprooting. The postwar treaty removed the imperial ban on emigration present since the fifteenth century, thus opening China to a popular exodus. The levy of indemnities on China to pay for war reparations increased the taxation of peasants and thus reduced their margin of survival. The Taiping Rebellion (1851–1864) erupted in a tremendous backlash against the Qing dynasty imperial government that had proven too weak to resist foreign imperialistic aggression. This mass uprising, roughly contemporaneous with the Sepoy revolt in India against British rule, dwarfed the Civil War in the United States, causing a huge loss of life estimated at twenty million deaths. The Taiping Rebellion began in southern coastal provinces already experiencing emigration, and then overspread a wide interior region, bringing warfare, military conscription, and economic deterioration.[47]

The expansion of the Japanese Empire triggered emigration from Korea. In 1876, the Japanese government imposed on Korea, which had existed for several centuries as an isolationist nation much like Japan, an unequal treaty arrangement for special trading rights like the unequal treaties imposed by Western powers on China. By establishing an interest in Korea, Japan became a rival of China for influence over Korea. Korea was one of the stakes in the Sino-Japanese War of 1895. Japan made Korea a protectorate in 1905 and finally annexed it in 1910, conducting its takeover with a military invasion and a large-scale restructuring of Korean institutions.

Filipino workers who migrated to the United States came at a moment when the transition from Spanish colonial rule to United States takeover in the Philippines produced a period of economic and physical displacement. Crop prices fell as internal agricultural markets were crippled by fighting and chaos. The island of Luzon, from which most Filipino immigrants came, was especially hard-hit during the guerilla war between American forces and Filipino nationalist insurgents from 1899 to 1902.

The liberalization of travel and movement in nineteenth-century states and territorial dominions contributed to mass emigration. The arrival of British power in China prompted the legalization of emigration in 1842. In Japan, a new imperial government lifted the ban on emigration in 1885. Prior to the eighteenth century, Hindu prohibitions on sea travel limited emigration. The British Indian Raj abolished the system tying agricultural laborers to land which allowed them unprecedented mobility. Legal mass emigration began from 1842, when officials permitted recruitment of laborers in Calcutta, Madras, and Bombay.

Southeastern China turned into a centrifuge of migration at the same moment as did Ireland, Britain, and the countries of northwestern Europe. Long-settled farmers and laborers in southern China began to emigrate to the United States and Hawai'i to find better personal and economic security. Many came from rural areas close to the commercial urban centers of Hong Kong and Canton. The first immigrants from China represented a prototype of transient labor migration to the United States, namely young male workers sent overseas by their family households to obtain new sources of income. They played key roles in two economic systems: the household of rural China from which they were displaced and the industrializing economy of the United States. As workers who were instrumental supports to their family households, they sent back to China a steady stream of remittances derived from their earnings in America to provide the margin of survival to their families. Many planned to return eventually to their home villages with what they had saved while working in the United States.[48]

Chinese laborers who emigrated as a result of a family strategy for income earning by sending them to work abroad were not a unique phenomenon. Many immigrants from various places in southern and eastern Europe also came for temporary work in the United States and as such were termed "birds of passage." They traveled overseas to obtain earnings which they sent back home in a steady stream of remittances to provide assistance to their families in the villages of Italy, Greece, and Poland.[49] Most of the first Chinese immigrants had been rural laborers whose economic prospects in their home villages had suffered. They were a spillover of currents of rural migration set into motion by the sudden impact of imperialism and attendant disturbances in southern China. Only a small minority were urban craftsmen or merchants, and many were single laborers or married men who had become temporary "bachelors" to work in the United States until they returned to their homes with their savings. The Chinese were eager to take any paying job because of the pressure to earn income to help improve their family household's economic prospects. However, many immigrants who had left China fully with the intention to return changed their minds and decided to make new homes in the United States.

Immigration from Asia to the United States sprang from very localized geographic origins. Chinese, Japanese, Korean, Filipino, and Indian immigrants had homelands of very limited size with an intensively local social network—a ready-made framework for mutually assisted chain migration. The Chinese came from the Pearl River Delta around Hong Kong and Canton and nearby provincial areas. Japanese immigrants came principally from the four southwestern provinces of Hiroshima, Yamaguchi, Fukuoka, and Kumamoto. Koreans migrated from urban centers that had been disrupted by Japanese invasion and efforts to control them. Filipinos came from the Ilocos rural district of the northernmost main island in the Philippine archipelago, Luzon. Indian emigrants to the United States came from five contiguous subdistricts within the rural Punjab: Jullunder, Hosiarpur, Gurdaspur, Amritsar, and Ludhiana.

The first Korean immigrants departed while the Japanese were consolidating their control over Korea. Their exodus took place in a shorter span of years than migration from Japan or China, from 1903 to 1905. In that interval, about 7,000 immigrants, most of whom were young male laborers, arrived in Hawai'i to work in plantation agriculture. Unlike the Chinese and Japanese immigrants who left from rural provinces, these Korean immigrants came from cities, mostly in their country's most urbanized area around Seoul, Inchon, and Suwon.[50] In 1905 the Japanese government imposed political rule and also suspended emigration from Korea to improve social control and stability. In 1907, the U.S.-Japan Gentlemen's Agreement reinforced the Japanese imposed ban on emigration from Korea because under its terms Korea was considered part of the Japanese Empire. After 1907 until 1924, most of the migration from Korea consisted of roughly one thousand "picture brides," who were exempt from the terms of the Gentlemen's Agreement.

Indian laborers who migrated to the United States came from the Sikh community of the state of Punjab. In bands of several individuals, they journeyed by a two-stage migration first to Hong Kong and then to North America. Nearly all Sikh emigrants were young male laborers from the small land-owning class (like Japanese immigrants) who planned to return to their home villages. Many were married and had left their wives. They sent back regular remittances to their families which were used to buy land, pay off debts, build housing, and for money lending, and they looked forward to returning home with savings accumulated during their sojourn abroad.

The Punjabi Sikh emigration was the result of familial and communal decisions. Shareholders in property groups decided who would leave as emigrants.

Male household heads decided frequently to send the second or youngest son as an overseas migrant. Veterans of the British Indian Army or Police in Hong Kong, Singapore, and Shanghai provided unusual leadership as organizers of chain migration among kinship groups. These veterans were literate and had overseas connections or were actually living in way station points such as Hong Kong. They were familiar with the transportation routes and overseas opportunities, and they were positioned to respond to the solicitations of labor recruiters and steamship companies.

The emigration of Punjabi Sikhs to the United States was a spillover of migration to western Canada. Sikh emigration to Canada had been orchestrated by Canadian labor recruiters who collaborated with middlemen sponsors and advertised in the Punjab. Steamship companies served as the transoceanic transportation link that brought the Sikhs to do heavy labor in lumbering and railroad building.

RESTRICTIONIST ADMISSIONS POLICY

The influx of immigrants from Asian regions constituted a small fraction of total U.S. immigration in the late nineteenth and early twentieth centuries—somewhat less than 2 percent. The small size of the Asian population in the U.S. owed to the deployment of immigration restrictions against Asian countries at a time earlier than the imposition of restrictions against European nations. These restrictions were imposed consecutively against individual Asian countries rather than simultaneously against all. Repeated cycles of intense labor demand and popular opposition to the assimilation of Asians produced this serial pattern of restriction. By the 1920s, Asians and southern and eastern Europeans were the two categories of immigrants most restricted from admission by federal laws.

Asian immigrants faced a host of legal and administrative barriers to immigrating to the United States not faced by immigrants from other parts of the world. Chinese immigration was curbed in 1882 with the passage of the Chinese Exclusion Act that barred Chinese laborers. Japanese and Korean immigration, which grew larger after Chinese exclusion, was unrestricted until 1908 when the Gentlemen's Agreement excluded Japanese and Korean laborers. Asian Indians began arriving shortly after the Koreans, but they were totally excluded by the creation of the Asiatic Barred Zone in 1917. The entry of all Asian aliens was universally proscribed in 1924. Finally, Filipinos, who had migrated freely as American nationals after the United States acquired the Philippines in the Spanish-American War, were restricted by the imposition of an annual quota for the Philippines. Opponents of the immigration of "pinoys" succeeded in passing the Tydings–McDuffie Act of 1934 that limited the number of immigrants admissible from the Philippines to fifty persons yearly.[51]

As a consequence of consecutive group restrictions, immigration from Asian countries to the United States occurred in bursts followed by continuing though sharply reduced influxes after the enactment of restricted admissions (Figure 1-4).

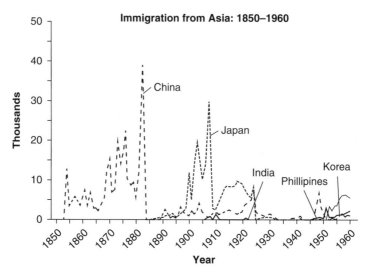

Figure 1-4.   Immigration from Asia: 1850–1960.

The Chinese, Japanese, and Filipinos comprised the bulk of Asian immigration to America, while Koreans and Asian Indians constituted miniature migratory waves.

The major periods of immigration from each Asian country occurred in a series of waves spread over intervals. Between 1850 and 1924, 455,000 Chinese immigrants entered the United States. From 1890 to 1924, 290,000 immigrants from Japan came. From 1899 to 1924, 9,200 Koreans and 8,200 Asian Indians immigrated. Between 1910 and 1934, over 50,000 Filipinos arrived.

After the enactment of restrictions on Asian admissions, a shrunken flow from China, Japan, and Korea continued through loopholes that permitted businessmen, professionals, students, and relatives of citizens to immigrate. Thus Chinese, Japanese, and Korean communities received very limited demographic reinforcement. After the Chinese Exclusion Act of 1882 until 1940, 150,000 Chinese entered the United States. After the Gentlemen's Agreement excluded Japanese laborers in 1908, 166,000 Japanese immigrants arrived through 1940.

The Chinese Exclusion Act and the Gentlemen's Agreement established principles for control of immigration from Asia. The former set a precedent for utilizing country of origin and race as criteria for restriction of admissions and exclusion from citizenship. It also established occupational status as an admissions standard, barring immigrants who were classified as laborers while admitting merchants, professionals, and other commercial employees, along with their spouses and children. Under the Gentlemen's Agreement, Japanese adult male immigrants were permitted to bring spouses and prospective spouses. The *jus soli* nativity clause of the Fourteenth Amendment, confirmed by the U.S. Supreme Court in the case of *United States. v. Wong Kim Ark* in 1898, allowed U.S.-born Chinese to be American citizens and thus to travel to China and be re-admitted to the United States upon their return. Even after the onset of exclusionary policies, these admissible categories and claims by applicants for admission based on their alleged descent from U.S. citizens enabled immigration from China to continue. The transoceanic cultural corridors Chinese and Japanese immigrants had initiated in the nineteenth century were refreshed by these categories of migrants who journeyed between the United States and Asian countries well into the twentieth century.[52]

A pattern of two-way repeat migration (trips back to the home country and returns to the United States) between enclaves in the United States and Hawai'i, on one hand, and communities in their homelands, on the other, also strengthened trans-Pacific social and cultural connections. A study of the Japanese community of San Pedro, California, found that 32 percent of the population had returned to Japan for a visit once, 38 percent had returned twice, and 18 percent three or more times.[53] Immigration and return migration between Asian countries and the United States formed a smaller-scaled parallel to the massive two-way flow of European immigration and return migration that shaped trans-Atlantic cultural corridors connected to European homelands.[54]

CLOSING PACIFIC AND ATLANTIC GATES

"Asiatic" immigrants—as the Chinese, Japanese, Koreans, Indians, and Filipinos were labeled in U.S. immigration reports—constituted less than 2 percent of total immigration from 1850 to 1920, but their racial and cultural differences were judged to be so great and their economic threat as "cheap labor" so powerful that they were eventually excluded from the country. Moreover, the anti-Chinese agitation in the United States was part of a global anti-Chinese movement in other areas of Anglophone settlement. Equivalent exclusionist policies were directed toward the Chinese in Australia in 1888 and in South Africa in 1904. Restrictions on Chinese immigration constituted merely one phase in a worldwide movement to divide employment opportunities along racial lines. White labor organizers in Anglophone colonies and offshoot countries opposed the coming of the Japanese, Asian Indians, and Koreans largely on the same grounds used to exclude the Chinese laborers.[55]

As Italians, Jews, Poles, Hungarians, Russians, Rumanians, Greeks, Armenians, and Lebanese began to outnumber the arrivals from northern and western Europe, they too were seen as a culturally and racially alien element posing unprecedented problems of assimilation. According to nativists, the coming of these "new" immigrants from Europe and nearby areas, like the arrival of Asians, appeared to start dangerous changes in the role of ethnic groups in American life. Because they were unlike the core population of British and northern and western European stock, the new waves of immigrants threatened to create a divided society. Thus, whether to exclude these newcomers from entering the country became a paramount policy issue, nothing less than an issue of national security.

The penetration of Chinese workers into industrial employment eventually raised fears that they would take jobs away from the white worker. They soon became the focus of nativist reactions that grew with distorted ideas about sub-human living and working standards of the Chinese to which whites would be reduced. A powerful anti-Chinese movement was spawned by nativist working-men in the stronger labor unions. These labor leaders received support from small farmers and demagogic politicians in search of an exploitable issue.

The railroads, large agriculturalists, and industrialists endeavored to keep American ports open to the Chinese against this populist movement which used racist appeals. Their support for Chinese immigration hinged to a degree on their anticipation that racial differences would inhibit intergroup alliances in the ranks of labor. Indeed, the anti-Chinese movement was proof of the accuracy of their analysis. But the most important motivation for corporate interests was the cost-efficiency of Chinese labor. By adding new scale and elasticity to the labor supply the Chinese pushed down the cost of industrial wages. Wages in the west were previously inflated due to the scarcity of labor, but with the addition of Chinese immigrants to the labor supply, wages moved downward to levels found more typically on the east coast. The Chinese impact on the wage structure was a part of the shifting equilibrium of supply and demand in the labor market.

Missionaries in the far west also tended to favor the continuance of free im-migration for the Chinese. Citing the scriptural belief in the common origin of all men in a single act of creation by God, they asserted that it was their mission to Christianize the "heathen Chinamen."

Nevertheless, popular agitation and fears gained the upper hand and the door closed against the Chinese. The anti-Chinese movement grew into a well-organized political party based in San Francisco, which became the leading anti-Asian city in America. Anti-Chinese conventions were held which passed resolves to drive the Chinese from the country. Denis Kearney, an Irish immigrant sailor, became the leader of the California Workingmen's Party that strategically exploited the Chinese issue to promote union organization. Armed with the rallying cry "The Chinese Must Go!" the unions and the Workingmen's Party were crucial in lobbying successfully for the termination of free immigration from China, and their ideological attacks set a precedent for the reception of future Asian immigrants, especially the Japanese.[56]

Xenophobic nativists perceived Chinese immigrants as a form of dehuman-ized, servile labor, resembling enslaved black labor, that could displace whites and disorganize social structures and institutions. The Chinese were seen as a menace to the nineteenth-century industrial paradigm of the individualist work ethic, economic deregulation, the nuclear family, free wage labor, democratizing institutions, urbanization, and social mobility coupled with social stability. Be-cause this social synthesis of emerging industrial order was so newly achieved and exposed to forces of change, Americans were apprehensive of its stability and durability. The Chinese had just arrived as historical processes began to crystal-lize this synthesis: on the eve of Chinese mass migration the United States expe-rienced, according to historian David Hackett Fischer, "the beginning of rapid intensive economic growth, . . . the start of sustained urbanization; demographic

transition toward modern fertility patterns; marked change toward social strati-
fication by wealth and growing inequality in the distribution of wealth; rapid
pragmatic adaptation in the law; shifts from unitary to pluralistic networks in
personal association; unprecedented expansion in primary education; democra-
tization in the political process; invention of a new language of political and
social thought; and—not least—with respect to family life, the appearance of
'domesticity.'"[57]

Increasingly the Chinese became victims of legal persecution and violent attacks. San Francisco city ordinances of 1870 outlawed the Chinese porter's practice of carrying loads on a pole and excluded Chinese from employment in public
works. In 1873, a special tax was levied on Chinese laundries; in 1880, an anti-
ironing ordinance shut down night-time laundry operation.[58] An epidemic of riots
broke out against the Chinese in mining and railroad towns, such as the mob
attack in Rock Springs, Wyoming, in 1885, which killed twenty-eight Chinese.

The Qing imperial government, crippled by corruption and the incursions of
foreign powers, struggled to protect countrymen far away in a strange land. In
the 1880s, the Qing Dynasty took new custodial interest in emigration to the
United States. Officials of the imperial government visiting the United States
would stop to consult with leaders of the Six Companies organizations in San
Francisco Chinatown on the status of Chinese immigrants in America. The
Qing government wanted political and economic support from immigrants for
modernization, famine relief, and national defense, and it saw the Chinese im-
migrant communities as a safety valve for socioeconomic pressures. Chinese
immigration to the Pacific coast was seen in trans-Pacific perspective by the
Chinese state. Popular concern about the fate of Chinese immigration to the
United States grew into a powerful movement in China. In 1905, a boycott of
American goods in China protested Chinese exclusion laws in the United States
as well as American trade policies. At the same time, Qing rulers worried about
American Chinese communities becoming sanctuaries for reformers and revo-
lutionaries, and were concerned over maintaining a hold on younger Chinese
generations who tended to support reform in China and assimilation in the
United States.[59]

In the United States, the opposition to Chinese labor was transferred to subsequent immigrants arriving from Asia. White workers opposed the coming of the
Japanese, Asian Indians, and Koreans largely on the same grounds used to exclude the Chinese laborers. As Japanese immigrants began to arrive in numbers
comparable to the earlier waves of Chinese labor migrants, congressmen proposed
to extend the ban on Chinese immigrants to the Japanese as well. They also sought
to exclude Korean immigrants whose homeland had been annexed by Japan in
1905. Restrictionists received an unexpected breakthrough in 1907 and 1908,
when the so-called Gentlemen's Agreement was arranged between Washington
and Tokyo. The Japanese government pledged to stop emigration of Japanese laborers to the United States in exchange for the admission of Japanese American
pupils to public schools in San Francisco. The cumulative experience gained in

excluding Asian nationalities encouraged federal lawmakers to think that immigration policy could be used to preserve the ethnic character of the nation.

The Immigration Act of 1917 was a major step toward discrimination and restriction based on national origins. This law introduced the long-sought literacy test that had been proposed in various legislative bills since the 1890s. Its supporters believed the test would have the practical effect of denying admission to immigrants from southern and eastern Europe. Massachusetts Congressman Henry Cabot Lodge expressed this intention in an article published in the *North American Review* in 1891 and entered into the Congressional Record. Arguing that "We have the right to exclude illiterate persons from our immigration," Lodge pushed for a test that promised "in all probability" to "shut out a large part of the undesirable portion of the present immigration." The 1917 law also established an Asiatic Barred Zone from which no laborers could be received. The Zone was a gigantic imaginary triangle that covered Afghanistan, Arabia, India, the rest of South Asia, East Asia (except for areas already affected by the Chinese Exclusion Act and the Gentlemen's Agreement), and the Pacific. What the 1917 Immigration Act accomplished was to expand greatly the principle of exclusion based on national origins that was first established by Congress in the Chinese Exclusion Act of 1882.

By the 1920s, federal lawmakers also began to explore the need for a finely graded scale of admissions in which particular nationalities were preferred over others. In this new form of discriminatory immigration policy enacted by the Quota Acts of 1921 and 1924, large visa quotas would be given to countries believed to be sending assimilable immigrants, while small visa quotas would be granted to countries from which the immigrants designated as less assimilable came.

Nativists who defined the American national core as Anglo-Saxonist and immigrant cultures as enduringly foreign rejected the possibility of assimilation and became advocates of immigration restriction. They gave mass immigration the appearance of a destructive force that gravely endangered the United States. For the sake of reducing the influx of newcomers, restrictionists concentrated their energies on demarcating the line between "old" immigrants and "new" immigrants. This simplistic bifurcation provided the clinching justification for enacting a policy of restriction to replace the traditional policy of openness to immigration that originated with the founders of the republic. By the 1920s, Asians and southern and eastern Europeans were the two categories of immigrants most severely restricted by federal legislation. The United States became a nation defined by a ring of administrative barriers to immigration that interrupted international population movements as a force for integrating the Atlantic and Pacific worlds. In this context, the federal immigration receiving facility at Angel Island in San Francisco Bay, which processed immigrants of Asian, European, Latin American, and Pacific Islander ancestry, became a more representative symbol of global immigration control than was Ellis Island, which primarily dealt with European immigration control.[60]

Notes

1. Matt K. Matsuda, "The Pacific, AHR Forum: Oceans of History," *American Historical Review* 111, no. 3 (June 2006): pp. 758–780.

2. Donna R. Gabaccia and Dirk Hoerder, eds., *Connecting Seas and Connected Ocean Rims: Indian, Atlantic, and Pacific Oceans and China Seas Migrations from the 1830s to the 1930s* (Leiden: Brill, 2011) pp. 9–10.

3. Walter A. McDougall, *Let the Sea Make a Noise: A History of the North Pacific from Magellan to MacArthur* (New York: Basic Books, 1993), p. 19; Patricia Seed, *Ceremonies of Possession in Europe's Conquest of the New World* (Cambridge, Eng.: Cambridge University Press, 1995), pp. 35–36.

4. David Igler, *The Great Ocean: Pacific Worlds from Captain Cook to the Gold Rush* (New York: Oxford University Press, 2013), p. 9.

5. David J. Weber, *The Spanish Frontier in North America* (New Haven, Conn.: Yale University Press, 1992), p. 270.

6. Susan Bean, ed., *Yankee India: American Commercial and Cultural Encounters with India in the Age of Sail, 1784-1860* (Salem, Mass.: Peabody Essex Museum, 2001). This is a source for the history of commerce with Indian Ocean and Pacific Ocean regions.

7. Anne F. Hyde, *Empires, Nations and Families: A History of the North American West, 1800–1860* (Lincoln: University of Nebraska Press), ch. 2.

8. Patrick V. Kirsch and Marshall Sahlins, *Anahulu: The Anthropology of the History in the Kingdom of Hawaii,* vol. 1 (Chicago: University of Chicago Press, 1992), Table 5.1, pp. 102–103.

9. Crew list of Brig Albatross (Records of the Collector of Customs, District of New London, Connecticut, July 24, 1826), National Archives and Record Administration (Boston): a record indicating the diverse origins of sailors serving on a New England-based ship.

10. Jo Ann Roe, *Ranald MacDonald: Pacific Rim Adventurer* (Pullman: Washington State University Press, 1997), 38–39.

11. Tom Koppel, *Kanaka: The Untold Story of Hawaiian Pioneers in British Columbia and the Pacific Northwest* (Vancouver: Whitecap Books, 1995), p. 137.

12. U.S. Congress. Senate. Committee on the Judiciary. *The Immigration and Naturalization Systems of the United States* (Washington, D.C.: U.S. Government Printing Office, 1950) supplies a statistical picture of global migration.

13. Leonard Pitt, *The Decline of the Californios: A Social History of Spanish-Speaking Californians, 1846–1890* (Berkeley: University of California Press, 1966; 1998), chs. 5, 6.

14. Douglas Monroy, *Rebirth: Mexican Los Angeles from the Great Migration to the Great Depression* (Berkeley: University of California Press, 1999), pp. 7–45; Albert Camarillo, *Chicanos in a Changing Society: From Mexican Pueblos to American Barrios in Santa Barbara and Southern California* (Cambridge, Mass.: Harvard University Press, 1979), ch. 3, 9.

15. Paul W. Mapp, *The Elusive West and the Contest for Empire, 1713–1763* (Chapel Hill: University of North Carolina Press, 2011), Introduction, ch. 3–6.

16. Patricia Nelson Limerick, *The Legacy of Conquest: The Unbroken Past of the American West* (New York: W. W. Norton, 1987), ch. 7.

17. Gregory H. Nobles, *American Frontiers: Cultural Encounters and Continental Conquest* (New York: Hill and Wang, 1997), pp. 205–206, 212–241.

18. "To the Friends of Civilization and Christianity." Sandwich Islands, October 3, 1826 (Massachusetts Historical Society Library) expresses the aspirations of the New Englanders who arrived in Hawai'i as missionaries.

19. LaRue W. Percy, *Hawaii's Missionary Saga: Sacrifice and Godliness in Paradise* (Honolulu: Mutual Publishing, 1992), pp. 1–6.

20. The personal account by John Manjiro of his travels and sojourn in the United States can be found in *Drifting toward the Southeast: The Story of Five Japanese Castaways* (New Bedford, Mass.: Spinner Publications, 2003).

21. Roe, *Ranald MacDonald*, pp. 1–4, 96–100. For an exemplary treatment of a life-thread that integrated a regional world in the Indian Ocean, see Sugata Bose, *A Hundred Horizons: The Indian Ocean in the Age of Global Empire* (Cambridge, Mass.: Harvard University Press, 2006), ch. 7, on the poet, Rabindranath Tagore.

22. Association to Commemorate the Chinese Serving in the American Civil War, "Moy's Research on Joseph Pierce," Parts 1–5, by Irving Moy. https://sites.google .com/site/accsacw/Home/moy (July 31, 2014).

23. Felipe Fernandez-Armesto, *Before Columbus: Exploration and Colonization from the Mediterranean to the Atlantic, 1229–1492* (Philadelphia: University of Pennsylvania Press, 1987), p. 212; Philip D. Curtin, *The Rise and Fall of the Plantation Complex, Essays in Atlantic History*, 2nd ed. (Cambridge, Eng.: Cambridge University Press, 1998), p. 22; J. G. A. Pocock, *The Discovery of Islands: Essays in British History* (Cambridge, Eng.: Cambridge University Press, 2005), p. 55.

24. Patricia Nelson Limerick, "The Multicultural Islands," *American Historical Review* 97, no. 1 (February 1992): pp. 121–135; Gary Y. Okihiro, *Island World: A History of Hawai'i and the United States* (Berkeley: University of California Press, 2008), ch. 7.

25. Curtin, *The Rise and Fall of the Plantation Complex*, 2nd ed., p. 73.

26. Reed Ueda, "Pushing the Atlantic Envelope: Interoceanic Perspectives on Atlantic History," in Jorge Canizares-Esguerra and Erik R. Seeman, eds., *The Atlantic in Global History, 1500–2000* (Upper Saddle River, N. J., 2007), pp. 163–175.

27. Eleanor C. Nordyke, *The Peopling of Hawai'i*, 2nd ed. (Honolulu: University of Hawaii Press, 1989), pp. 42–52.

28. Arthur Versluis, *American Transcendentalism and Asian Religions* (New York: Oxford University Press, 1993); Thomas A. Tweed, *The American Encounter with Buddhism, 1844–1912: Victorian Culture and the Limits of Dissent* (Bloomington: Indiana University Press, 1992); Charles Capper, "'A Little Beyond': The Problem of the Transcendentalist Movement in American History," in Charles Capper and Conrad Edick Wright, eds., *Transient and Permanent: The Transcendental Movement and Its Contexts* (Boston: Massachusetts Historical Society, 1999), p. 29; Palmer Rampell, "Laws That Refuse to Be Stated: The Post-Sectarian Spiritualities of Emerson, Thoreau, and D. T. Suzuki," *The New England Quarterly* 84, no. 4 (December 2011): pp. 621–654; Sebastian Smee, "Looking East," *Boston Globe*, January 20, 2013.

29. Francis Parkman, *The Oregon Trail: Sketches of Prairie and Rocky Mountain Life* (Boston: Little, Brown, 1904); Theodore Roosevelt, *The Winning of the West*, 4 vols. (New York: G. P. Putnam, 1895); Helen Hunt Jackson, *A Century of Dishonor: A Sketch of the United States Government's Dealings with Some of the Indian Tribes* (New York: Harper and Brothers, 1881); Helen Hunt Jackson, *Ramona: A Story*, 2 vols. (Boston: Little, Brown, 1900).

30. Jorge Canizares-Esguerra, *How to Write the History of the New World: Histories, Epistemologies, and Identities in the Eighteenth-Century Atlantic World* (Stanford, Calif.: Stanford University Press, 2001), pp. 13–22.

31. Michael L. Smith, *Pacific Visions: California Scientists and the Environment, 1850–1915* (New Haven, Conn.: Yale University Press, 1987), pp. 14–17; William H. Goetzmann,

Exploration and Empire: The Explorer and the Scientist in the Winning of the American West (New York: Alfred A. Knopf, 1966), Parts 1 and 2.

32. Bernard Bailyn, *The Peopling of British North America: An Introduction* (New York: Alfred A. Knopf, 1986), p. 5.

33. Klaus Bade, Dirk Hoerder, and Jorg Nagler, eds., *People in Transit: German Migrations in Comparative Perspective, 1820–1930* (Cambridge, Eng.: Cambridge University Press, 1995), pp. 4–5.

34. Thomas J. Archdeacon, *Becoming American: An Ethnic History* (New York: The Free Press, 1983), ch. 2, 5.

35. Philip Taylor, *The Distant Magnet: European Emigration to the U.S.A.* (New York: Harper, 1971), pp. 20–57.

36. For general patterns, see Harry Jerome, *Migration and Business Cycles* (New York: National Bureau of Economic Research, 1926); Richard A. Easterlin, *Population, Labor Force, and Long Swings in Economic Growth: The American Economy* (New York: National Bureau of Economic Research, 1963). The case for economic cycles is made by Brinley Thomas, *Migration and Economic Growth: A Study of Great Britain and the Atlantic Economy*, 2nd ed. (Cambridge, Eng.: Cambridge University Press, 1973), ch. 7, 14. For conditions in European countries, see H. J. Habakkuk and M. Postan, *The Cambridge Economic History of Europe, The Industrial Revolutions and After: Incomes, Population, and Technological Change*, vol. 6 (Cambridge, Eng.: Cambridge University Press, 1965), ch. 2.

37. Taylor, *The Distant Magnet*, pp. 150–164.

38. Marcus Lee Hansen, *The Atlantic Migration, 1607–1860* (Cambridge, Mass.: Harvard University Press, 1940), ch. 1, 2.

39. John Higham, *Send These to Me: Immigrants in Urban America* (Boston: Atheneum, 1975), ch. 1; Frederick C. Luebke, *Germans in Brazil: A Comparative History of Cultural Conflict During World War I* (Baton Rouge: Louisiana State University Press, 1987), ch. 1, 2.

40. John Bodnar, *The Transplanted: A History of Immigrants in Urban America* (Bloomington: Indiana University Press, 1985), ch. 1.

41. Michael Piore, *Birds of Passage: Migrant Labor and Industrial Societies* (Cambridge, Eng.: Cambridge University Press, 1980), Table 6-1, p. 151.

42. John S. MacDonald and Leatrice D. MacDonald, "Chain Migration, Ethnic Neighborhood Formation, and Social Networks," in Charles Tilly, ed., *An Urban World* (Boston: Little Brown, 1974), pp. 226–236.

43. J. R. McNeill and William H. McNeill, *The Human Web: A Bird's Eye View of World History* (New York: W. W. Norton, 2003), p. 261.

44. June Mei, "Socioeconomic Origins of Emigration: Guangdong to California, 1850–1882" in Lucie Cheng and Edna Bonacich, eds., *Labor Immigration under Capitalism: Asian Workers in the United States before World War II* (Berkeley: University of California Press, 1984), p. 240.

45. Alan Moriyama, "The Causes of Emigration: The Background of Japanese Emigration to Hawaii, 1885–1894" in Cheng and Bonacich, eds., *Labor Immigration under Capitalism*, pp. 268–270.

46. Changing conditions for emigration from homeland districts are described in historical articles on immigrants from China, Japan, Korea, and the Philippines by H. Mark Lai, Harry H. L. Kitano, Hyung-chan Kim, and H. Brett Melendy in Stephan Thernstrom, ed., *The Harvard Encyclopedia of American Ethnic Groups* (Cambridge, Mass.: Harvard University Press, 1980).

47. Frederic Wakeman, Jr., *Strangers at the Gate: Social Disorder in South China, 1839–1861* (Berkeley: University of California Press, 1966), Introduction.

48. Mei, "Socioeconomic Developments among the Chinese in San Francisco, 1848–1906," in Cheng and Bonacich, eds., *Labor Immigration under Capitalism*, p. 240.

49. Piore, *Birds of Passage*; Tamara Hareven, *Family Time and Industrial Time: The Relationship between the Family and Work in a New England Industrial Community* (Cambridge, Eng.: Cambridge University Press, 1982); Mark J. Stern, *Society and Family Strategy: Erie County, New York, 1850–1920* (Albany: State University of New York Press, 1987), pp. 41–43, 74–77.

50. Wayne Patterson, *The Korean Frontier in America: Immigration to Hawaii, 1896–1910* (Honolulu: University of Hawaii Press, 1988), p. 103.

51. Bill Ong Hing, *Making and Remaking Asian America through Immigration Policy* (Stanford, Calif.: Stanford University Press, 1993); Lucy E. Salyer, *Laws as Harsh as Tigers: Chinese Immigrants and the Shaping of Modern Immigration Law* (Chapel Hill: University of North Carolina Press, 1995), Part 5.

52. Erika Lee, *At America's Gates: Chinese Immigration during the Exclusion Era, 1882–1943* (Chapel Hill: University of North Carolina Press, 2003), pp. 141–145; Roger Daniels, *The Politics of Prejudice: The Anti-Japanese Movement in California and the Struggle for Japanese Exclusion* (Berkeley: University of California Press, 1962), pp. 41–45.

53. Kanichi Kawasaki, "The Japanese Community of East San Pedro, Terminal Island, California" (master's thesis, University of Southern California, 1931), p. 165.

54. Thomas Archdeacon, *Becoming American: An Ethnic History* (New York: The Free Press, 1983), Table V-3, pp. 118–119; Piore, *Birds of Passage*, Table 6-1, p. 151.

55. Kornel Chang, "Circulating Race and Empire: Transnational Labor Activism and the Politics of Anti-Asian Agitation in the Anglo-American Pacific World, 1880–1910," *Journal of American History* 96, no. 3 (December 2009): pp. 678–701.

56. Alexander Saxton, *The Indispensable Enemy: Labor and the Anti-Chinese Movement in California* (Berkeley: University of California Press, 1971), ch. 12.

57. Nancy F. Cott, *The Bonds of Womanhood; "Woman's Sphere" in New England, 1780–1835* (New Haven, Conn.: Yale University Press, 1977), p. 3.

58. Stanford Lyman, *Chinese Americans* (New York: Random House, 1974), pp. 81–83; Jack Chen, *The Chinese of America* (San Francisco: Harper and Row, 1980), pp. 137–139.

59. Salyer, *Laws as Harsh as Tigers*, pp. 162–163; Shih-Shan Henry Tsai, *The Chinese Experience in America* (Bloomington: Indiana University Press, 1986), pp. 50, 77, 80, 81.

60. Erika Lee and Judy Yung, *Angel Island: Immigrant Gateway to America* (New York: Oxford University Press, 2010), Appendix, Table 2.

TWO

EMERGENCE BETWEEN
THE HEMISPHERES

"Arnold Toynbee has suggested that the most important figures of history are those who bridge two or more civilizations."[1]

Hilary Conroy, *The Japanese Frontier in Hawaii, 1868–1898*

Despite periods of restrictionist immigration control, the United States combined global leadership in the intake of immigrants from Europe with the role of the leading destination country in the Americas for immigrants from Asia. The United States led all western-hemisphere nations in the admission of trans-Atlantic immigrants, receiving from 1871 to 1914 nearly 25 million immigrants, while Canada received 4.6 million, Argentina 4.5 million, and Brazil 3.2 million.[2] From the nineteenth to the twentieth century, the United States received a much larger flow of immigrants from Asia than did any other country in the western hemisphere. According to the 2010 census, the United States had over 17 million Asians who came from every country in East Asia and South Asia. By contrast, the total numbers and multinational diversity of Asians in every other country in the Americas were much more limited in the early twenty-first century. Peru had an East Asian population of only 2.5 million, mostly produced by Chinese and Japanese immigration a century earlier. Brazil had 2.5 to 3 million people of Japanese ancestry. About 1.3 million Asians lived in Canada coming from many countries of East Asia and South Asia. In Mexico, 200,000 people were partly descended from Filipino immigrants and 10,000 or so from other parts of Asia. Chile had 100,000 people derived mainly from China, Korea, and Japan.[3]

The historical outcome was a unique pattern of diversity in the United States in which migrants from the Asia Pacific became a core element in a diasporic pluralism. The United States functioned in an unparalleled way in the global migration system. More than any other country, it became a destination country bridging the Atlantic and Pacific by sea, land, and later by air, an interoceanic zone of emergence for a new composite pattern of global diversity derived from the Americas, Europe, Africa, and Asia, a space where groups coalesced that were in the process of superseding the limitations of their original environments.[4]

From a global vantage point, the Atlantic world can be seen as an intensively developed core region with an extensive periphery that merged increasingly into a surrounding Pacific and Indian Ocean context in the course of the nineteenth century. The building of transcontinental societies and economies appears from the perspective of the Atlantic core to take the form of centrifugal forces causing the disintegration of the Atlantic world. But these same processes can be seen, from the periphery, as extending the Atlantic world into interregional border spaces that facilitated the knitting together of societies of different oceanic regions in such a way as to precondition the globalization process of the late twentieth century. The building of transcontinental societies and economies— through railroads, domestic markets, and geographic mobility—may have ended the Atlantic world as it had existed from the sixteenth century to the nineteenth century, as suggested by J. R. McNeill's pithy remark, "The Portuguese caravel opened the Atlantic world, and the railroad closed it."[5]

But, in this interval, there was much occurring to suggest another dimension of change in which the periphery of the Atlantic world began to push outward into new zones of interaction with other regional peripheries. The process of westward expansion in the United States and Canada brought not only natives of European ancestry from the eastern seaboard but also settlers directly from Europe to the Pacific region. Diverse groups of European origin swiftly began the arduous process of rebuilding core institutions in a wide range of settings unlike the homeland. For example, immigrants from Portugal on the "big island" of Hawai'i built Roman Catholic churches in the open fields of sugar plantations (Figure 2-1).

Societies that had been integrated into north Atlantic and south Atlantic regional patterns began to link with the societies of the Pacific world through the westward movement of population, which accelerated in the nineteenth century. Westward expansion turned the United States into a continental corridor, or a "country of transit," through which people who originated in the Atlantic world flowed into and connected with the Pacific Rim, enabling the former's western coastal extremity to become an integral part of the Pacific region. By the twentieth century, the United States became a transcontinental and transoceanic society, an Atlantic and a Pacific power.

The Pacific coast was the primary destination point for an advancing wave of settlers from multiple homelands in Europe, the Americas, and Asia. It had long been a frontier settled by Spanish colonists in Mexico, Ecuador, Peru, and Chile. During the nineteenth century, it also became a borderland developing from the infusion of Asian immigrants.[6] Their primary advancing line pushed out of East Asia and South Asia into Hawai'i and the Pacific coast of the Americas, where they shaped social and economic development and diffused eastward to Atlantic-centered communities. A secondary advancing line of immigrants emanating from British India and southern China traversed the Indian Ocean as a bridge to the Atlantic Ocean where they continued their long interoceanic voyage to

Figure 2-1. Portuguese immigrants at Catholic church on Island of Hawai'i.

arrive finally in the islands and Latin American shores of the Caribbean.[7] From the mid—to late nineteenth century, more than a half-million Chinese immigrated to the western Hemisphere—over 320,000 to the United States, 125,000 to Cuba, 100,000 to Peru, and 16,000 to British Guiana. Concurrently with the flow from China, laborers from India arrived in the Caribbean basin: 200,000 Indians migrated to British Guiana, 100,000 to Trinidad, over 30,000 to Suriname and Guadaloupe each, and 20,000 to Jamaica. Shortly after the first waves of emigrants from China and India arrived in the western hemisphere, 300,000 Japanese immigrated to the United States from the turn of the twentieth century to World War I. And, in the early decades of the twentieth century, 200,000 Japanese immigrated to Brazil, while Japanese immigrants settled in Canada and Peru in the tens of thousands. Creating an arc of migration from eastern Siberia to the Pacific Rim of North America, over 50,000 Russians in the nineteenth century streamed across Alaska, to British Columbia, and finally to Washington, Oregon, and California. After the turn of the century, 7,000 Indians and a few thousand Koreans immigrated to the United States.[8] From World War I to the Great Depression, about 50,000 laborers from the Philippines immigrated to the Pacific coast of the United States.

Asian immigrants affected the development of many countries in the western hemisphere. Chinese communities grew in Cuba, and Indians formed sizable enclaves in Trinidad and British Guiana. In the twentieth century, the Japanese population of Sao Paolo, Brazil, far surpassed the population of any Japanese local community in the far western United States or Canada, and rose to over half a million. In these areas and others across the Americas where immigrants from China, Japan, and India settled, businesses run by these newcomers had a vital economic impact. Out of 12,700 Chinese in Cuba in 1899, almost 2,000 were merchants. In Peru, Chinese immigrants owned half the grocery stores in the city of Lima. Japanese immigrants became a primary factor in the commercial produce business of Los Angeles. In the state of Sao Paolo, Japanese immigrants in the decade before World War II ran enterprises that produced 30 percent of its agricultural output—which included 46 percent of cotton, 57 percent of silk, and 75 percent of tea produced—and concomitantly owned over a million acres of land. Indian immigrants became successful in British Guiana as commercial farmers and worked in various other business fields. The large Indian community of Trinidad produced one-third of the doctors and two-fifths of the lawyers in this island nation, influencing much of its professional business life.[9]

Immigrants from China, Japan, India, Korea, and the Philippines constituted an invaluable source of manpower in the labor-short regions of the far western United States, where they helped to build farms, factories, mines, and railroads. American corporate magnates owned and ran these enterprises from remote points of control, accentuating the growth of a pyramid-like social structure from whose pinnacle they lorded over a vast hinterland of clashing immigrant groups such as Chinese, Cornish, Irish, and German miners; Scandinavian, Japanese, Italian, Sikh, Basque, and Armenian farmers; and a native American middle class transplanted from the east.[10] After the Civil War, hundreds of mobile and adventurous Chinese spilled out of the far west into rural districts, towns, and cities of the South and the Atlantic coast.[11] New York City had attracted Chinese immigrants before the Civil War. They built a downtown neighborhood that grew into the second largest Chinatown in the United States, only exceeded by San Francisco's.[12] Finally, migrating peoples from Asia contributed to the international circulation of capital and commercial goods that connected the Pacific Rim and the countries of the Atlantic world. In the late nineteenth century, Chinese fishermen of California's Monterey Bay region harvested abalone, which they shipped to international markets in France, Germany, and China; they caught and processed squid, which they sold to consumers in Hong Kong. Chinese merchants in San Francisco and Japanese merchants in Los Angeles brought to American markets enormous varieties of goods from China and Japan, including processed food products, clothing, hardware, utensils, decorative objects, and other household items. An immense capital flow of remittances ran through Asian immigrant diasporic networks in western-hemisphere countries to homelands in the Punjab of western India, the Pearl River Delta of southern China, the prefectures of southern Japan, and the Ilocos district of the Philippines. In 1876 alone, Chinese immigrants in the United States sent 11 million U.S. dollars in remittances to their families and villages in Guangdong province, and this flow of foreign exchange from the overseas Chinese would continue unabated well into the twentieth century.[13]

An interoceanic perspective on Atlantic history from the nineteenth century reveals the deepening involvement of societies in the Atlantic world in growing transregional patterns that reached beyond it to other regional worlds. Charting their development requires a visualization of how oceanic worlds flowed into each other through migration, interacted with transcontinental societies, and created overlapping connective structures that prefigured twentieth-century patterns of globalization. The modern history of the American Pacific coast suggests that the "end of the Atlantic world" in the nineteenth century can also be viewed as the beginning of a new, connected world in which the Atlantic focus of the western hemisphere shifted westward to form a broader geographic framework of collective activity with Oceania, East Asia, and South Asia.

MIGRATIONS AND REGIONAL DEVELOPMENT

The American far west beckoned as the external frontier to opportunistic migrant workers from East Asia and South Asia who had traveled for generations to destinations in their home regions to find better prospects. The American Pacific coast and the Hawaiian Islands appeared as new realms of an eastern frontier across the Pacific for Asian migrants. "Working on the other edge of the Pacific," in the words of historian Madeline Y. Hsu, became "an employment option regularly chosen, and even highly preferred" by Chinese migrants sponsored by their families and supported by communal associations transplanted abroad.[14] Asian immigrants saw the American Pacific coast as a region that offered rewards for their initiative and enterprise, where American industrialists tended to see the immigrants as a convenient form of intensive and mobile labor in mining, agriculture, manufacturing, and transportation. Hawai'i has been described as an "American frontier," but as a historian remarked "it was also a Japanese frontier, and the Hawai'i of the late nineteenth century provides a fascinating tale of frontier competition. . . ."[15]

In the early twentieth century, a majority of Japanese, Korean, and Asian Indian male immigrants who returned home usually had sojourned in the United States from a few years to a decade (Table 2-1). An even greater percentage of returning Chinese had lived and worked in the United States for more than a decade. The official statistics on this pattern of transient migration captured only the surface of a large movement of Asian migrants who came to the United States on a temporary and sometimes undocumented basis. Asians served on the crews of British and other foreign vessels, and some "jumped ship" in American ports and eventually were able to reside and be absorbed into Asian American and other minority enclaves.[16]

Many more Asians came to the United States classified as "non-immigrants" by the federal immigration bureaucracy, a category which from 1925 to 1948 included over 4,300,000 arrivals (primarily visitors, relatives, students, and

Table 2-1.   Asians Departing from the United States.
Sex and Age of Emigrant Departures, 1908–1917 (Percent)

	Chinese	Japanese	Korean	Indian
Male	97.5	81.7	88.7	96.7
Female	2.5	18.3	11.3	3.3
Under 14	0.7	4.1	2.2	1.1
14–44	35.0	79.5	81.6	84.4
44 & Over	64.3	16.4	16.3	14.5
Total N	25,158	22,300	743	1,229

Asian Emigrant Departures by Length of Residence in the United States, 1908–1917 (Percent)
Number of Years Continuously Resident in United States

	Chinese	Japanese	Korean	Indian
5 and under	13.4	41.0	51.0	59.2
5–10 years	15.1	32.6	34.6	37.1
10–15 years	14.3	15.7	13.6	1.6
15–20 years	13.7	7.4	0.8	0.2
Over 20 years	43.4	3.1	0	0.6
Unknown	0.1	0.3	0	1.4
Total N	25,158	22,300	743	1,229

Number of Asian Emigrants Departing from the United States, 1899–1924

Chinese	51,343
Japanese	44,392
Korean	9,214
Asian Indian	8,234

European Migrants Admitted to and Departing from United States, 1908–1910

Immigrants Admitted	Emigrant Aliens Departed	N Departed per 100 Admitted
2,297,338	736,835	32

Source: U.S. Commissioner-General of Immigration, Annual Reports.

businessmen) who became temporary residents in American neighborhoods, and of which 4,000,000 departed.[17] In other words, besides immigrants from Asian countries who came to make homes in the United States, there were Asians who circulated in and out of the United States whose lifeworlds consisted of a transnational pool of co-migrants and their networks.

Asian international labor migration can be compared to westward internal migration in the United States and European labor migration in terms of transiency and cost factors. As a labor supply, Asian immigrants were like American miners, farmers, and workers who moved temporarily across the country to the Pacific basin to find new opportunities and who later returned to their home communities back east. Asian immigrants also resembled European immigrants who returned frequently to their home countries: thirty-two immigrants from Europe departed from the United States for every one hundred who entered from 1908 to 1910. Labor migration from Asia and Europe was facilitated by technological modernization of the international transportation and communications systems which reduced the transfer costs involved in long-distance residential changes to levels competitive with transfer costs of internal migrations.

Chinese immigrants provided the earliest responsive solution to the labor conditions of the far western economy. Their transiency and their exclusion from citizenship insured that they could not develop the political power to raise their labor cost in the form of higher wages or improved working conditions. The Chinese were also desirable because, as a nearly all-male adult population, they could move far and live inexpensively. Their geographic mobility was not encumbered by the on-site and on-the-move support of families.

Chinese and other Asian labor migrations were also a response to the limits of international labor migration from Europe and Mexico and the internal labor migration of blacks from the American south. Recruitment of Asians from across the Pacific seemed most practical, even necessary. Western entrepreneurs lacked strategic geographic access to European labor. Mexican workers could not be counted on yet, because the numbers willing to immigrate remained small until the first decade of the twentieth century. Black labor gravitated toward the industrial cities of the northeast and upper midwest and was less available in the west.

The American territory of Hawai'i was a unique receiving area of Asian immigration and served as a jumping-off point for departures to the mainland. Hawai'i had been an independent monarchy ruled by a Polynesian royal family until it was annexed by the United States in 1898. U.S. restrictionist laws thereafter applied in the islands to produce a mirror image of the truncated Asian migration of the mainland. In the nineteenth century 56,000 Chinese journeyed to Hawai'i, but after U.S. annexation imposed the Chinese Exclusion Act, only 4,800 arrived through 1924.

The history of the far west, the growth of its economy and infrastructure, could not have occurred without wider, interregional connections and leveraging of the capital and labor markets. East coast and European capital investments financially powered the construction of railroads, mines, and oil facilities and the development of supplies of water and usable land. Industrial, agricultural, and transportation development in western regions and the contributions of societies in the Asia Pacific to these changes would not have been possible without the decisive influx of immigrant labor from Asia. Chinese, Japanese, Korean, Asian Indian, and Filipino immigrant workers made the Pacific into a region where globalized labor circulated rapidly and over long distances at the key moment of industrial and agricultural start-up in the mid-nineteenth century. In mining, oil, agriculture, construction, transportation, and trade, a zone began to form of economically dynamic Asian and American interaction, fraught with exclusionary rivalry and competition, but with new human networks, economic connections, and cultural capital that had the enormous potential to create a more global society in the United States.

The Pacific coast of the United States formed an interregional supra-borderland consisting of multiple sub-borderlands of migration frontiers populated by various races.[18] Once described as "a new racial frontier" by *Nation* magazine editor Carey McWilliams, the coast's core state of California sprouted enclaves of Asian immigrants, immigrants crossing overland from Mexico and Canada, immigrants arriving from across the Atlantic, African American ex-slaves escaping from the "Jim Crow" south, and native white Americans migrating from the east, midwest, and south.[19] In the wider geographic perspective, the U.S. Pacific coast was a hemispheric gateway for international migration that was augmented by a transcontinental migration corridor. The latter brought migrants from the older communities rooted in the history of the Atlantic region seeking new outlets for opportunity, enterprise, and social life. The federal government carried out by military force the removal of Indian tribal populations and their relocation to reservation communities that made available vast tracts of land for settlement.

Waves of immigrants arrived in the far west from Europe and nearby regions on the European periphery. Foreign-born whites constituted a large proportion of the west's population. In the late nineteenth century, they formed from one-fourth to one-third of the populations of Montana, Wyoming, Idaho, Utah, Nevada, Arizona, Washington, and California. In 1900, the percentages of European immigrants in the populations of many far western states equaled or surpassed the percentage of European immigrants in the entire U.S. population. In California, Washington, and Oregon, the proportion of European immigrants in each state were respectively 24.7 percent, 21.5 percent, and 15.9 percent; in the total U.S. population, the percentage of immigrants was 13.6 percent. When foreign-born white persons and native-born white persons of foreign parentage were totaled together, they constituted 46.9 percent of California's population, 40.8 percent of Washington's, and 30.7 percent of Oregon's (Tables 2-2a, b, c). The Germans, English, Canadians, Italians, Swedes, Norwegians, Russians, and Irish were among the largest foreign-born groups in the western states, as they were in the country as a whole. Jews from central Europe could be found in the major cities of Washington, Oregon, California, and Nevada. In 1940, the national groups of European immigrants represented in the west approximated their representation in the country as a whole.[20]

The north Atlantic world projected its international influences to the far west through corridors extending from multiple European countries and from eastern communities of the United States. A highly articulated social geography of enclaves emerged in the Pacific coast region and reflected the cohesive patterns of settlement among migrants from eastern-hemisphere and western-hemisphere

Table 2-2a.   Number and Percentage of Total Population of Foreign-Born White Persons and Native-Born White Persons of Foreign Parentage in Pacific Coast States, by Country of Origin (1900).

	Washington (Total = 518,103)		Oregon (Total = 413,536)		California (Total = 1,485,053)	
	N	%	N	%	N	%
Austria	3,845	0.7	1,586	0.4	8,355	0.6
Bohemia	824	1.2	478	0.1	922	0.1
English Canada	27,545	5.3	11,675	2.8	44,841	3.0
French Canada	3,862	0.8	2,169	0.5	5,392	0.4
Denmark	6,564	1.3	3,319	0.8	16,416	1.1
England	25,519	4.9	16,394	4.0	84,690	5.7
France	2,354	0.5	1,905	0.5	22,983	1.6
Germany	43,555	8.4	36,547	8.8	154,809	10.4
Hungary	342	0.1	260	0.1	1,087	0.1
Ireland	23,548	4.6	14,058	3.4	152,006	10.2
Italy	2,997	0.6	1,536	0.4	41,632	2.8
Norway	18,814	3.6	5,566	1.4	8,522	0.6
Poland	931	0.2	583	0.1	2,450	0.2
Russia	3,830	0.7	3,136	0.8	5,376	0.4
Scotland	10,013	1.9	6,542	1.6	25,225	1.7
Sweden	21,361	4.1	8,270	2.0	23,728	1.6
Switzerland	3,527	0.7	5,472	1.3	19,742	1.3
Wales	3,600	0.7	1,098	0.3	5,020	0.3
Other	8,077	1.6	6,324	1.5	73,893	5.0
TOTAL	211,108	40.8	126,918	30.7	697,089	46.9

Source: Frederick Luebke, ed., European Immigrants in the American West: Community Histories (Albuquerque: University of New Mexico Press, 1998), Table 2, p. xiii.

"sides" of the north Atlantic: from Europe and the eastern Mediterranean, on one hand, and the Atlantic coastal regions and its hinterlands in the United States and Canada, on, the other. German-born Johann Augustus Sutter immigrated from Switzerland to the Sacramento area of California in the 1830's, when it was still a state of the Republic of Mexico, and established an outpost called "Sutter's Fort" which served as a base of operations as he developed into a local land baron. Pioneer ethnic communities that were established after California state-hood included Scandinavian settlements such as Solvang, Kingsburg, Hilmar, and Sveadal, Italian wine-making colonies in Sonoma and Napa Counties, San Francisco enclaves of Italian businessmen around Ghirardelli Square and Italian fishermen in North Beach, Irish Catholic Telegraph Hill and the Mission in San Francisco, and Armenian and Basque communities near the Sierra foothills. As farmers moved to urban centers, "Little Portugals" sprouted in San Jose and

Table 2-2b. Place of Birth, Jewish Adult Males, Selected Western Towns, 1880.

Place of Birth	Portland	Albany OR	Seattle	Los Angeles	Virginia City	Carson City	Reno	Total No.	% of Total
France/Alsace	4	5	1	11	2	1	2	26	5.7
Bavaria	26	4	6	13	4	0	1	54	12.4
Prussia	54	8	9	37	17	16	12	153	35.2
Baden, etc.	9	0	2	4	1	2	2	20	4.6
"Germany"	17	0	3	14	0	0	0	34	7.8
Aust-Hung	2	6	1	1	3	0	0	13	3.0
Other	12	3	1	17	10	1	2	46	10.6
USA									
East Coast	16	1	3	10	1	1	2	34	7.8
Midwest	1	0	0	3	1	0	0	5	1.1
Oregon	9	1	0	0	0	0	0	10	2.3
California	14	0	1	15	2	1	2	35	8.0
Other West	0	0	1	0	2	0	0	3	0.7
Canada	0	0	1	0	0	0	1	2	0.5
Total	164	28	29	125	43	22	24	435	100.0

Source: Ava F. Klein, Jewish Life in the American West: Perspectives on Migration, Settlement, and Community (Los Angeles: Autry Museum of Western Heritage, 2002), p. 94.

Table 2-2c. Foreign-born Populations (White and Non-white) in the U.S. and the U.S. West, by Rank Order, 1940.

Population: United States		Population: The West	
Total Foreign Born	**11,659,621**	**Total Foreign Born**	**1,790,869**
1. Italians	1,623,580	1. Mexicans	338,545
2. Germans	1,237,772	2. Canadians	183,730
3. Canadians	1,065,480	3. Germans	137,612
4. Russians (U.S.S.R.)	1,040,884	4. Italians	137,015
5. Poles	993,479	5. English	125,559
6. Irish	678,447	6. Swedes	92,946
7. English	621,975	7. Russians	90,926
8. Austrians	479,906	8. Japanese	82,844
9. Swedes	445,070	9. Filipinos	68,000
10. Mexicans	377,433	10. Norwegians	63,320
11. Czechoslovaks	319,971	11. Irish	54,237
12. Scots	279,321	12. Scots	42,624
13. Norwegians	262,088	13. Danes	39,557
14. Greeks	163,252	14. Austrians	33,889
15. Yugoslavs	161,093	15. Swiss	28,304
16. Danes	140,279	16. Poles	26,968
17. Finns	117,210	17. Finns	26,434
18. Dutch	111,067	18. Chinese	25,576
19. French	102,920	19. Yugoslavs	24,651
20. Filipinos	98,132	20. French	24,373
21. Swiss	88,293	21. Greeks	23,844
22. Japanese	84,667	22. Portuguese	21,690
23. Portuguese	52,347	23. Czechoslovaks	19,927
24. Syrians	50,859	24. Dutch	18,692
25. Spanish	47,707	25. Spanish	15,633

Source: Elliott Robert Barkan, From All Points: America's Immigrant West, 1970s–1952 (Bloomington: Indiana University Press, 2007), Table 3.14, p. 475.

San Pedro, "Little Armenia" took shape in Los Angeles, and "Old Armenia Town" formed in Fresno.[21]

Jews from central Europe and from the U.S. east coast and midwest settled in Portland, Seattle, Los Angeles, San Francisco, and towns in Nevada. By the 1870s, San Francisco became second only to New York City in the size of its Jewish population. Anglo-westerners were generally more welcoming and accommodating to German Jews seeking new opportunities than were white natives in eastern states. Levi Strauss, August Helbing, and Isaias Hellman were the most prominent of German Jewish immigrants in manufacturing, mercantile, and banking businesses of San Francisco. Achieving election to high political office

Figure 2-2.   Temple Emmanu-El, San Francisco, 1867.

were Adolph Sutro, who built a silver mining empire in the Comstock Load and
became Mayor of San Francisco, and Julius Kahn, a leading attorney who won a
seat in the U.S. House Representatives. San Francisco's Jewish community
strongly supported Reform Judaism and was drawn to assimilation as ethnic
Jewish Americans. The magnificent Temple Emmanu-El embodied in architectural form the aspirations, prominence, and successful adaptation of Jewish immigrants to American life in San Francisco (Figure 2-2).[22]

California's developing economy attracted settlers from every part of the
world. It is arguable that the emergence of truly global diversity in the United
States occurred in the coasts and valleys of California (Map 3, I-3), even more
than in urban centers like Manhattan's Lower East Side or the South Side of
Chicago. Fresno County (Table 2-3), for example, was described by U.S. government agents as having a population of "very cosmopolitan character" where
races from "many parts of the world may be found."[23] The multi-racial, multiethnic, multi-religious quilt in communities surrounding the San Joaquin
River in the Central Valley formed in the face of, as well as out of, the fierce xenophobia of native old-stock whites. Historian Kathleen Weiler observed that
hostilities toward minority newcomers "were an integral part of the rural culture
that defined the dominant institutions of the area," and along with "particular

Table 2-3. Employees in Fresno County Vineyards, by Race (1900–1910).

Japanese	574
Miscellaneous White	168
Chinese	119
Italian	72
Asian Indian	55
Mexican	50
American Indian	42
Armenian	31
German Russian	11

Source: Reports of the Immigration Commission, Vol. 24, Immigrants in Industries, Part 25 (Washington, D.C.: U.S. Government Printing Office), Table 2, p. 579.

cultural identities" worked to pressure "groups such as the Armenians and Japanese to settle together and to establish their own churches and social organizations."[24]

The San Joaquin River Valley, the Sacramento River Valley, and the Santa Ynez River Valley formed an interconnected network of globally diverse enclaves. In Merced County, immigrants, African Americans, and Indians constituted nearly a third of the population. Among the Merced immigrants, Portuguese, Swedes, Italians, Mexicans, and Japanese were the most numerous, with the rest consisting of smaller enclaves of Armenian, Basque, German, Greek, Jewish, Filipino, and Slavic immigrants. In adjacent Stanislaus County, the town of Turlock became the Assyrian (Christian Iraqi) "capital" of the United States, admixed with Greeks, Punjabi Sikhs, Japanese, Filipinos, Chinese, and Mexicans. A large group of Italian wage laborers and farm workers arrived there around the turn of the century and established control of the farming and processing of tomatoes. A decade later, families of Portuguese immigrants arrived to start small, independently operated family farms that produced sweet potatoes and dairy products. In the area of Livingston, Swedish migrants who had traversed overland from the midwest established the Hilmar colony, the largest Swedish American farming enclave in the country boasting eight Swedish Lutheran churches before World War I. Danish immigrants also migrated from midwestern states to the Santa Ynez Valley to establish the farming village of Solvang. Assyrian immigrants and Armenians took up melon farming. Mexican workers made up a labor force of farm workers that seasonally circulated through the area. By 1920, according to federal population census returns, in Livingston (Township #5–1) the total of immigrants, African Americans, and American Indians was greater than the number of native whites.[25] Neighborhood grammar schools in Fresno enrolled substantial numbers of children from European and Asian countries, as well as the United States, making schoolrooms a reflection of the multiple ethnic enclaves coexisting in Fresno (Table 2-4).[26] Allensworth was an egalitarian African American

Table 2-4. Number of Children in the Thirteen Public Grammar Schools of Fresno, 1908, by Nativity and Race of Father.

	PS1	PS2	PS3	PS4	PS5	PS6	PS7	PS8	PS9	PS10	PS11	PS12	PS13	Total
Native-Born of Native Father														
White	377	66	270	82	459	56	230	9	31	278	278	337	7	2,480
Black	2	53	1	1	3	—	—	—	3	—	3	6	4	76
Foreign-Born														
Armenian	21	1	141	10	20	3	3	17	83	—	3	28	2	332
Chinese	3	22	—	—	1	—	—	—	22	—	—	2	4	54
English	24	7	8	3	17	2	11	—	—	—	—	—	—	53
French	2	4	7	1	6	—	1	—	7	3	2	15	5	53
German	24	6	24	1	39	1	9	2	32	12	14	27	1	192
German-Russian	12	—	16	—	—	—	—	122	312	—	6	4	472	—
Irish	15	8	4	6	—	1	1	—	2	1	1	9	—	48
Italian	—	112	2	—	9	—	2	—	11	7	—	4	59	206
Japanese	2	2	—	3	3	—	1	14	—	1	1	2	29	—
Mexican	—	17	—	—	3	2	1	1	3	2	—	1	4	34
Portuguese	—	12	6	—	5	—	9	8	4	1	13	5	—	63
Scandinavian	10	8	13	6	25	1	5	—	1	11	11	23	2	116
Scotch	18	—	1	2	5	—	3	—	—	2	—	6	—	37
Spanish	12	3	—	—	—	—	—	—	3	—	1	4	—	23
Miscellaneous	9	9	3	—	7	—	—	—	18	2	—	5	—	53
Total Foreign-Born	140	220	228	26	146	10	46	150	513	51	51	146	87	1,814
Grand Total	519	339	499	109	608	66	276	159	547	329	332	489	98	4,370

Note: PS = Public School
Source: Reports of the Immigration Commission, Vol. 24, Immigrants in Industries, Part 25 (Washington, D.C.: U.S. Government Printing Office), Table 2, p. 579.

farming community founded by an organized group of blacks escaping from the "Jim Crow" south, led by Allen Allensworth, a former slave who joined the Union Army and rose to the rank of colonel. Waves of immigrants came into the Sacramento Valley from South Asia and East Asia. Chinese laborers who began to come in the Gold Rush also built and worked agricultural land. Sikh laborers from the Indian province of Punjab took passage from British India to British Canada at the turn of the twentieth century, filtered into the Pacific northwest, and finally moved into California where they established the oldest continuous Asian Indian community in the United States in Yuba City, just north of Sacramento.

Japanese immigrants formed a major pattern in the kaleidoscope of global diversity in Merced County and Stanislaus County.[27] The Yamato Colony (a Japanese immigrant community with a large Christian core) was led by Reverend Kyutaro Abiko, who arrived in California as a twenty-year-old and preached to Japanese immigrants that they would achieve success and acceptance if they organized themselves into an ethnically defined corporate community of farmers who embraced Christianity. To that end, he purchased three thousand acres of land suitable for agriculture in Livingston, a town in the Central Valley, and recruited hundreds of immigrants from Japan, who settled and farmed the land.[28] Nisaburo Aibara was another Japanese immigrant leader who oversaw settlement in the Turlock area of Stanislaus County, where Japanese agricultural cooperatives, Christian and Buddhist religious institutions, and the Turlock Social Club of Japanese Americans formed the pillars of community.[29]

ASIAN FRONTIERS

At the turn of the twentieth century, Asian American communities consisted chiefly of transient male immigrants from China and Japan along with small representations of Koreans. The first generation developed their group culture and personal lives by following inherited traditions. Eventually, ethnic identity and culture changed with the creation of families and the emergence of the first American-born children. The social characteristics of Asian American communities underwent transformation as the process of intergenerational succession unfolded. The Asian population in the United States grew into a multigenerational community with more stability and permanence.

The evolution of Asian American communities involved shifts in how Asian populations were distributed geographically and organized in the social structure, the social "morphology" that changed over time.[30] As a historian explained, these types of patterns in social history require much more inspection: "Many important problems remain unexplored. We know little about movement into, out of, and within the city. We do scarcely more than guess whether some groups shifted about more swiftly than others. We only speculate about the forces that made some enclaves resist change, held their residents against the temptation of the suburbs, and fended off intrusions by outsiders. We are equally in the dark about the substantial numbers in the nineteenth century who drifted from place to place without ever settling down."[31]

The spatial patterns of the Asian population constitute a subject particularly in need of research and investigation. Asian enclaves started in seaports, mining towns, railroad towns, and farms and plantations of the far west; large Chinatowns and Little Tokyos developed in big cities like San Francisco, Seattle, Honolulu, Los Angeles and New York City. The dispersion inland of Asians to the midwestern, southern, and eastern United States produced dozens of minuscule new communities. Although the dynamic factors causing population distribution require more analysis, a description of basic patterns of concentration and dispersion can be derived from the published reports of the U.S. census. A useful source is the U.S. Census of 1910 when the federal census bureau issued for the first time a special report on Chinese and Japanese in the United States. It showed that these two major groups of the early Asian American population were primarily located in two distinctive geographic regions: the far western United States, especially the Pacific coast, and the Hawaiian Islands (Tables 2-5a, b). The Chinese were more widely dispersed over the mainland. Only a fifth of all Japanese lived outside the Pacific coast, while over a third of the Chinese did so. California had the largest Chinese population, and Hawai'i had the largest Japanese population.

Table 2-5a. U.S. States, Territories, and Cities with Largest Chinese and Japanese Populations, 1910. (In Rounded Numbers)

Chinese Population in States and Territories, 1910	
1. California	36,000
2. Hawai'i	22,000
3. Oregon	7,400
4. New York	5,200
5. Washington	2,700

Japanese Population in States and Territories, 1910	
1. Hawai'i	80,000
2. California	41,000
3. Washington	13,000
4. Oregon	3,400
5. Colorado	2,300

Source: Compiled from U.S. Bureau of the Census, Chinese and Japanese in the United States, 1910 (Washington, D.C.: U.S. Government Printing Office, 1914), Table 49, p. 20.

Table 2-5b. U.S. States, Territories, and Cities with Largest Chinese and Japanese Populations, 1910. (In Rounded Numbers)

Chinese Population in Cities

1. San Francisco	10,600
2. Honolulu	9,600
3. Portland	5,700
4. New York	4,600
5. Oakland	3,600

Japanese Population in Cities

1. Honolulu	12,000
2. Seattle	6,100
3. San Francisco	4,500
4. Los Angeles	4,200
5. Oakland	1,500

Source: Compiled from U.S. Bureau of the Census, Chinese and Japanese in the United States, 1910 (Washington, D.C.: U.S. Government Printing Office, 1914), Tables 49, 50, p. 20.

Tightening the demographic focus from regions to cities reveals that San Francisco and Honolulu were the chief urban centers of Asian American population in 1910. With 10,600 Chinese, San Francisco had the largest Chinese population of any American city, and with 4,500 Japanese the third-largest Japanese urban population in the United States. Honolulu had the largest Japanese population of any American city (12,000) and the second-largest Chinese population (9,600).

With respect to the white population, the demographic positions of Asians in Hawai'i and the United States were completely different. On the mainland they constituted an extremely small minority of the population relative to whites. The Chinese and Japanese each composed less than one-tenth of 1 percent of the total population. In Hawai'i, by contrast, Asians composed a majority population. This difference was the key to the development of two very divergent social experiences. In Hawai'i, the Chinese and the Japanese together numbered over 100,000 by 1900, making up 56 percent of the total population. In California, the Chinese made up 1.5 percent of the state's population, and the Japanese 1.7 percent.[32]

In Hawai'i, immigrants from Asia initially located almost wholly in the rural areas to work on the pineapple and sugar plantations. The plantation society was built upon ethnic villages called plantation camps, enumerated in the hand-written manuscript schedules of federal census takers (Figure 2-3), and vividly sketched in the recollections of those who grew up in them (Figure 2-4).

Life was rough and crude, as in the world of novelist William Faulkner's poor white southerners. The plantation was a cross-cultural community in which a melting pot proletarian culture evolved. Foreign mother tongues declined in

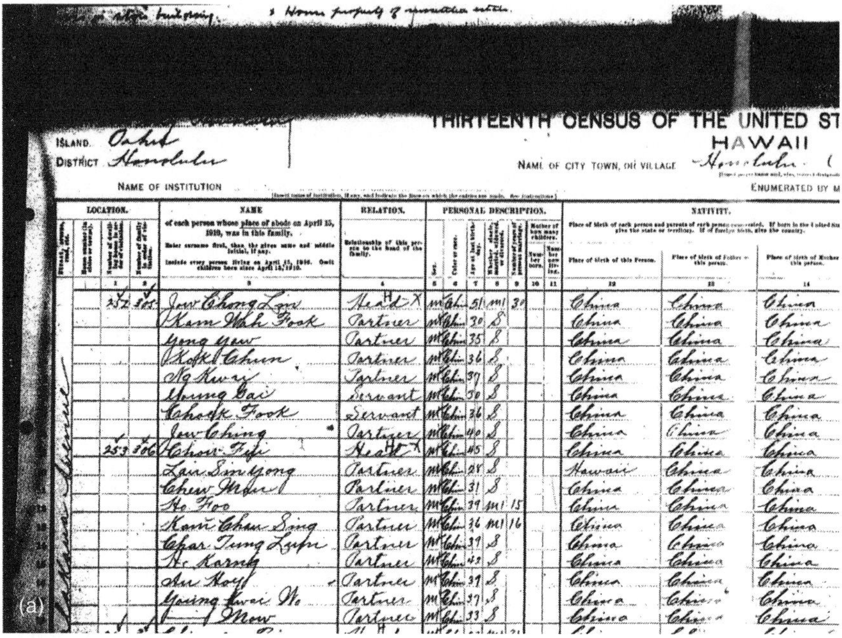

Figure 2-3. Asian immigrants in the Hawaiian Islands: (a) and (b) 1910 U.S. Census manuscript schedules, households of partner laborers and families.

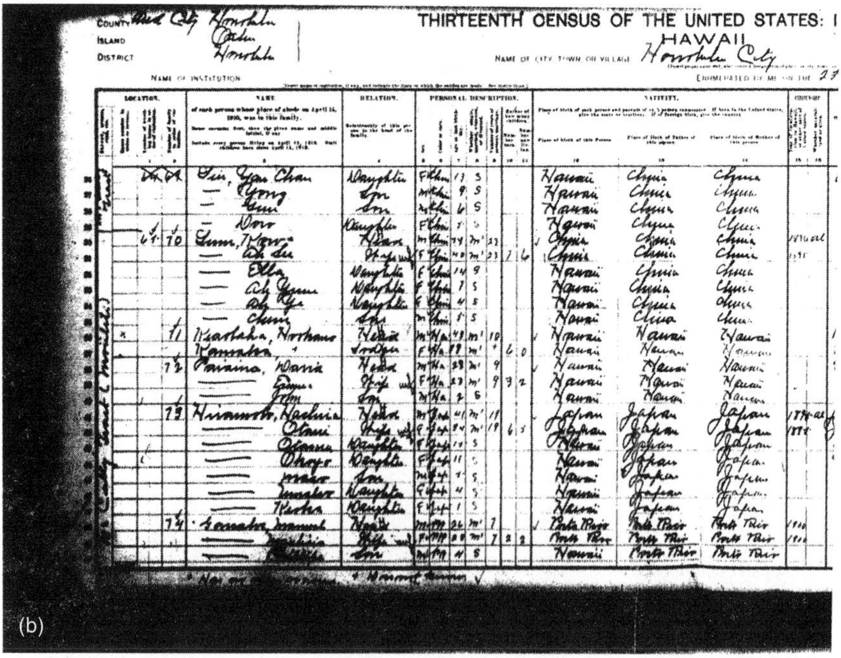

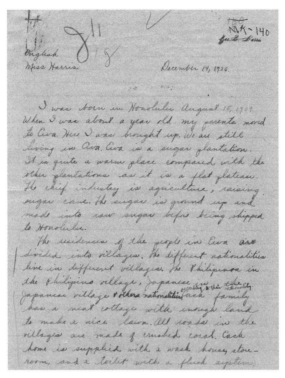

Figure 2-4. Autobiographical essay of a student.

usage, and a common pidgin language gradually formed to unite a working class consisting of different immigrant groups. Immigrant workers from China, Japan, Korea, and the Philippines negotiated and asserted their rights with plantation owners in a dialectic of accommodation and resistance to hegemonic control.[33]

The great majority of Asian immigrants in Hawai'i passed through an initial phase of building households on the plantations (Table 2-6). As the largest ethnic populations on the islands they were launched on a social trajectory of community change and development that differed significantly from the evolution of small, scattered Asian populations of the mainland United States. According to sociologist Sylvia Junko Yanagisako, Japanese Americans in Seattle, San Francisco, and Los Angeles were positioned far from the "radically different structural position of Japanese Americans in Hawai'i." Yanagisako, a Japanese American from Hawai'i, conducted a study of the Seattle Japanese and described her personal encounter with localized identities as follows:

> That I am not a member of the Seattle Japanese American community was as apparent to the "natives" as it was to me. My paternal and maternal grandparents had, like the Issei [the first generation or immigrant generation of Japanese Americans] I interviewed [in Seattle], emigrated from southwestern Japan at the turn of the

Table 2-6.   Pioneer Households of Asian Immigrants.

Households in Plantation Areas, Hawaiian Islands (Part A)

Korean	Percent
Honokaa, Island of Hawaiʻi	
Household Heads (N = 117)	
Married, Spouse in United States	3.4
Single	36.8
Married, Spouse in Korea	37.6
Widowed	22.2
Male	98.3
Female	1.7
Skilled	2.6
Semi-skilled	6.0
Unskilled	88.9
Housewife	1.7
Unemployed	0.9
Lodgers in All-Male Households (N = 64)	
Single	37.5
Married	35.9
Widowed	26.6
Kukuihaele Island of Hawaiʻi	
Household Heads (N = 64)	
Married, Spouse in United States	12.5
Single	42.2
Married, Spouse in Korea	29.7
Widowed	15.6
Male	93.7
Female	6.3
Professional	1.6
Skilled	0
Semi-skilled	4.7
Unskilled	87.5
Housewife	6.3
Lodgers in All-Male Households (N = 43)	
Single	46.5
Married	34.9
Widowed	18.6

Paauilo, Island of Hawai'i

Household Heads (N = 25)	
Married, Spouse in United States	0
Single	29.4
Married, Spouse in Korea	52.9
Widowed	17.6
Male	100.0
Female	0
Semiskilled	5.9
Unskilled	94.1

Pahala, Island of Hawai'i

Household Heads (N = 99)	
Married, Spouse in United States	6.1
Single	15.2
Married, Spouse in Korea	50.5
Widowed	28.3
Male	97.0
Female	3.0
Professional	1.0
White Collar	1.0
Semiskilled	4.0
Unskilled	92.0
Housewife	2.0

Philippine Immigrants	Percent

Kukaiau, Island of Hawai'i

Household Heads (N = 48)	
Married, Spouse in United States	0
Single	79.2
Married, Spouse in Philippines	16.7
Widowed	
Male	100.0
Female	0
White Collar	2.1
Unskilled	97.9
Lodgers in All-Male Households (N = 45)	
Single	77.8
Married, Spouse in Philippines	17.8
Widowed	4.4

(continued)

Table 2-6. Pioneer Households of Asian Immigrants. (*continued*)

Philippine Immigrants	Percent
Honokaa, Island of Hawai'i	
Household Heads (N = 43)	
Married, Spouse in United States	14.0
Single	86.0
Married, Spouse in Philippines	0
Widowed	0
Male	93.0
Female	7.0
Semiskilled	2.3
Unskilled	90.7
Housewife	7.0
Naalehu, Island of Hawai'i	
Household Heads (N = 68)	
Married, Spouse in United States	8.8
Single	79.4
Married, Spouse in Philippines	7.4
Widowed	4.4
Male	95.5
Female	4.5
Unskilled	95.6
Housewife	4.4
Paauhau, Island of Hawai'i	
Household Heads (N = 51)	
Married, Spouse in United States	23.5
Single	66.7
Married, Spouse in Philippines	7.8
Widowed	2.0
Male	88.2
Female	11.8
Unskilled	88.2
Housewife	11.8

PART A. *Source: U.S. Census, Manuscript Schedules, 1910.*

century. But the circumstances that brought them to work in the sugar and pineapple plantations of Hawai'i rather than in the lumber camps and farms of the Northwest led their children and grandchildren to grow up in a social world quite different from that of the Seattle Nisei and Sansei [the second and third generations of Japanese Americans who were U.S.-born]. Such grandparents gave me not only a Japanese American identity but a generational status, as a Sansei, in relation to those I interviewed. However, my lack of kinship connections with Seattle Japanese Americans and, until I began my research, any friendships with them, placed me outside the community. Whether my ambiguous status as, in the words of one Nisei, "one of us," or, in the words of another, "you Hawaiians," or, in the words of yet another, "you social scientists" endowed me with what I then thought was the best of all possible social identities is something of which I am now less certain. Nevertheless, the people I interviewed frequently voiced their assumption that as "Japanese Americans" we shared experiences, knowledge, attitudes, and vocabularies. At times we did.[34]

The Japanese American population on the mainland consisted of small, scattered, and isolated communities of minorities who sought opportunities for assimilation, while the Japanese Americans of Hawai'i were the largest ethnic group of an Asian demographic majority bloc and had the numbers to seek not only integration but regional socioeconomic and political dominance. The former and the latter shared a common homeland but diverged with the succession of generations to such a degree that they saw each other as different social types, as Yanagisako explained.

The creation of family life in the early stages of community building turned the Japanese population in Hawai'i and on the mainland into a generation-based and genealogical community. The genealogical consciousness of the Japanese immigrants created a diasporic conception of intergenerational succession as emanating from the origin point of the home country.[35] The Japanese-born called themselves the Issei (the first generation) and became parents of the Nisei (the American-born second generation), the first large generation of citizens in the Japanese American community, who in turn became parents of the Sansei (the third generation), and so on. The creation of a community that could sustain itself through natural increase and intergenerational succession put the survival of the Japanese American community out of the reach of exclusionary immigration laws. The key outcome of demographic change was the establishment of a permanent family system. It was facilitated by a mechanism of chain migration, the "picture bride system" for recruiting female spouses. After the negotiation of the Gentlemen's Agreement of 1907–1908, an unprecedented flow of single Japanese women traveled to the United States. From 1909 to 1923, over 33,000 Issei wives arrived. They came to marry husbands with whom marriage had been pre-arranged by the respective families of the couple in the homeland. Often the arrangement involved an exchange of photographs, hence the selected female spouses were called "picture brides."

The workings of the Japanese "picture bride" system is described by sociologist Helen Nakano Glenn as follows:

> Most of the Issei women who arrived in the United States between 1907 and 1924 were from the same southern rural backgrounds as the male immigrants. They had levels of education comparable to the men. . . . The typical Issei woman was in her early twenties and was married to a man ten years her senior who had lived for some years in the United States, working as a wage laborer or small entrepreneur.

Arranged "picture" marriage was a mechanism for family elders to marry off daughters without overt concern for their personal happiness. However, it also could serve as a means for young women to experiment with a new life away from the limitations of the homeland, perhaps to escape poverty or the onerous domination of elders and relatives. Many "picture brides" left Japan with a hopeful attitude that they would find new opportunities. Just as the Japanese male immigrants had left with the expectation of improving their prospects, the Issei women came with the hopes of helping their family of origin through a good marriage alliance and a more prosperous family life.

Despite variations in motivation to migrate, the Issei women shared a common situation. In leaving their family of origin, they were all following the Japanese patrilineal custom of leaving their household to take up residence in their husband's. Arranged marriage for a female immigrant functioned economically like the instrumental labor of the male sojourner that supported his family of origin. The migration of young women who married spouses in the U.S. and Hawai'i relieved their parents of pressure to support them in their households and allowed them to use the savings for other purposes. The income from the labor of Issei wives provided the extra margin of income needed by her new family to invest in property and in education. Most Issei wives in Hawai'i worked alongside their husbands in the sugar and pineapple plantations. They had been hands who worked the family farmlands in Hiroshima or Yamaguchi, so they were prepared for the backbreaking labor of the plantation. On the mainland farms, Issei wives who were used to labor on family farms back in Japan worked with husbands, hired hands, and older children.

Many Japanese women came as married immigrants or single adults, and so did not come in the "picture bride" system. For example, a woman married a widower with children in Japan and then decided to migrate with her husband to Hawai'i to escape from two sets of in-laws. Another woman from a declining samurai family migrated to Hawai'i to join her uncle's family when her arranged marriage partner who was to assume the family's noble samurai name deserted her.

Immigrants from Japan became more adaptive, as they sought to invest in American opportunities and committed themselves to strategies and tactics of intergenerational mobility. Family formation helped women develop power, security, and more freedom; they managed family politics, organized the household, and became more important as income earners. Through the evolution of family units, the Japanese community pushed toward new social possibilities with the demographic dividend of a new and large second generation of Japanese Americans, the Nisei.

The Korean community consisted predominantly of male laborers (Table 2-7) who also benefitted from the "picture bride" system. Nearly one thousand Korean "picture brides" migrated to Hawaiʻi from 1910 to 1924, while only about one hundred migrated to California. Bernice B. H. Kim, in a 1937 study of the Korean

Table 2-6. Pioneer Households of Asian Immigrants.

Households in Urban Areas, Hawaiʻi and U.S. Mainland (Part B)

Chinese	Percent
Honolulu, Kakaako	
Household Heads (N = 59)	
Married, Spouse in United States	27.1
Single	30.5
Married, Spouse in China	37.3
Widowed	3.4
Divorced	1.7
Male	86.4
Female	13.6
White Collar	27.1
Skilled	6.8
Semi-skilled	40.7
Unskilled	1.2
Housewife	13.6
Unemployed	1.7
Honolulu, McCully	
Household Heads (N = 338)	
Married, Spouse in United States	30.9
(Average of Years Married = 14.2 years)	
Single	30.2
Married, Spouse in China	34.0
(Average of Years Married = 15.3 years)	
Divorced	0.3
Male	86.4
(Average Age = 40.9 years)	
Female	13.6
(Average Age = 31.9 years)	

(continued)

Table 2-6. Pioneer Households of Asian Immigrants. (*continued*)

Professional	0.6
White Collar	4.7
Skilled	0.9
Semi-skilled	6.5
Unskilled	31.1
Housewife	14.5
Retired	0.3
Household Property	
Owns Home	1.9
Owns Home Free of Mortgage	21.4
Owns Home with Mortgage	1.0
Rents Home	58.3
Owns Farm Free of Mortgage	2.9
Rents Farm	14.6

Japanese	**Percent**

Honolulu, Kakaako

Household Heads (N = 358)	
Married, Spouse in United States	68.7
Single	17.2
Married, Spouse in Japan	6.7
Widowed	5.6
Divorced	1.7
Male	65.1
(Average Age = 34.6 years)	
Female	13.6
(Average Age = 33.4 years)	
Professional	0.6
White Collar	10.3
Skilled	8.4
Semi-skilled	34.9
Unskilled	12.8
Farmer	0.3
Housewife	32.1
Unemployed	0.6

Honolulu, McCully

Household Heads (N = 244)	
Married, Spouse in United States	77.9
(Average of Years Married = 11.0 years)	

Single	9.8
Married, Spouse in Japan	7.0
(Average of Years Married = 13.8 years)	
Widowed	5.3
Male	86.4
(Average Age = 37.8 years)	
Female	13.6
(Average Age = 31.6 years)	
Professional	1.2
White Collar	5.3
Skilled	9.8
Semi-skilled	18.4
Unskilled	31.6
Farmer	8.6
Housewife	23.4
Retired	0.4
Unemployed	0.8
Unknown	0.4
Household Property	
Owns Home	0.8
Owns Home Free of Mortgage	44.9
Rents Home	54.2

Los Angeles, Gardena

Household Heads (N = 843)	
Married, Spouse in United States	20.2
(Average of Years Married = 5.4 years)	
Single	79.9
Married, Spouse in Japan	0.1
(Average of Years Married = 20.0 years)	
Male	89.9
(Average Age = 30.3 years)	
Female	10.1
(Average Age = 28.9 years)	
White Collar	0.5
Skilled	0.1
Semi-skilled	0.2
Farmer	19.9
Farm Laborer	78.4
Nursery Man	0.1
Housewife	0.7

(*continued*)

Table 2-6.   Pioneer Households of Asian Immigrants. (*continued*)

Household Property	
Rents Home	5.6
Owns Farm Free of Mortgage	1.1
Rents Farm	93.3

PART B. *Source: U.S. Census, Manuscript Schedules, 1910.*

Table 2-7.   Korean Male Laborers in Hawaiian Islands, 1904.

Hawaiian Islands	N
Ewa Plantation (Island of Oʻahu)	343
Hawaiian Sugar Co. (Island of Kauaʻi)	292
Hawaiian Commercial & Sugar Co. (Island of Maui)	195
Olaa Plantation (Island of Hawaiʻi)	164
Waialua Plantation (Island of Oʻahu)	229

Source: Bernice B. H. Kim, "The Koreans in Hawaii" (master's thesis, University of Hawaii, 1937), Table IV, p. 101.

community in Hawaiʻi, found large age differences between Korean husbands and their "picture brides." Researchers have taken her findings and postulated that age differences had a destabilizing effect on marriages, giving the Korean community an unusually high divorce rate in the period from 1914 to 1926. Nevertheless, the Hawaiian Korean population was able to construct a community based on families and integration in agricultural labor and ethnic small businesses. Korean immigrants began to settle throughout the Hawaiian Islands and achieved sufficient population density to form enclaves on sugar plantations where they replaced Chinese and Japanese laborers who were leaving the fields for better jobs in small towns and cities.[36] In Hawaiʻi, the Korean population, like the Chinese and Japanese, developed a core solidarity and would move quickly out of the plantations. Hyung-chan Kim, a leading historian of Korean Americans, has shown that in Hawaiʻi a small population of Korean immigrants built a cohesive community with organizations, institutions, and intergenerational family life, whereas on the mainland prior to the 1950s "a real community was never able to evolve."

In Hawaiʻi, immigrants from the Philippines arrived later than other immigrants from Asia and persisted in initial plantation settlements longer. Their enclaves in the early twentieth century were marked by an almost complete absence of women and family life. The sex ratio was among the most imbalanced of any immigrant group in history. In Hawaiʻi in 1935, the population of single adults was composed of 29,413 males and 366 females, which produced a sex ratio of 80 to 1. The few wives, mostly Tagalogs and Visayans, came to Hawaiʻi as field laborers.

Since Filipinos were the latest to arrive of all the Asian immigrants, the movement to urban jobs and livings came at the end of an ethnic "queue" and involved competing with pre-established Chinese and Japanese small businesses.

On the mainland, immigrants from the Philippines were dependent on the annual cycle of transient farm labor migration which periodically destabilized and dissolved communities and their institutions. They were not integrated into the core labor force of large urban centers, where racial restrictions in construction and industrial jobs excluded them. Many Filipino immigrants made great efforts to obtain English language skills and education by attending Americanization and adult night classes that provided a path to more opportunity. In the Central Valley counties of California where many Filipino laborers worked in the fields, hundreds could be found in English and Americanization courses, which were often taught by highly dedicated and sympathetic teachers such as the remarkable Bernice Wood (Figure 2-5a). Filipino immigrants did not establish an effective mechanism for chain migration, such as the "picture bride" system used by Japanese and Koreans. Like early Chinese rural settlements, the communities of immigrants from the Philippines were fluid and impermanent, due to the lack of family formation. The gender proportions, still heavily unbalanced at 14 to 1 in 1930, impeded building a permanent community based on families and intergenerational succession. Additionally, anti-miscegenation laws prevented intermarriage as a way of starting families.[37]

The Asian Indian population also displayed an extremely imbalanced sex ratio. Well over 90 percent of annual immigrant arrivals were men. The predominance of men in the labor force (Figure 2-5b) could be seen in the settlements

Figure 2-5. (a) Class photograph of Filipino students in Americanization class taught by Bernice Wood, an innovator in immigrant education in Turlock, Modesto, and Hughson areas of California's Central Valley.

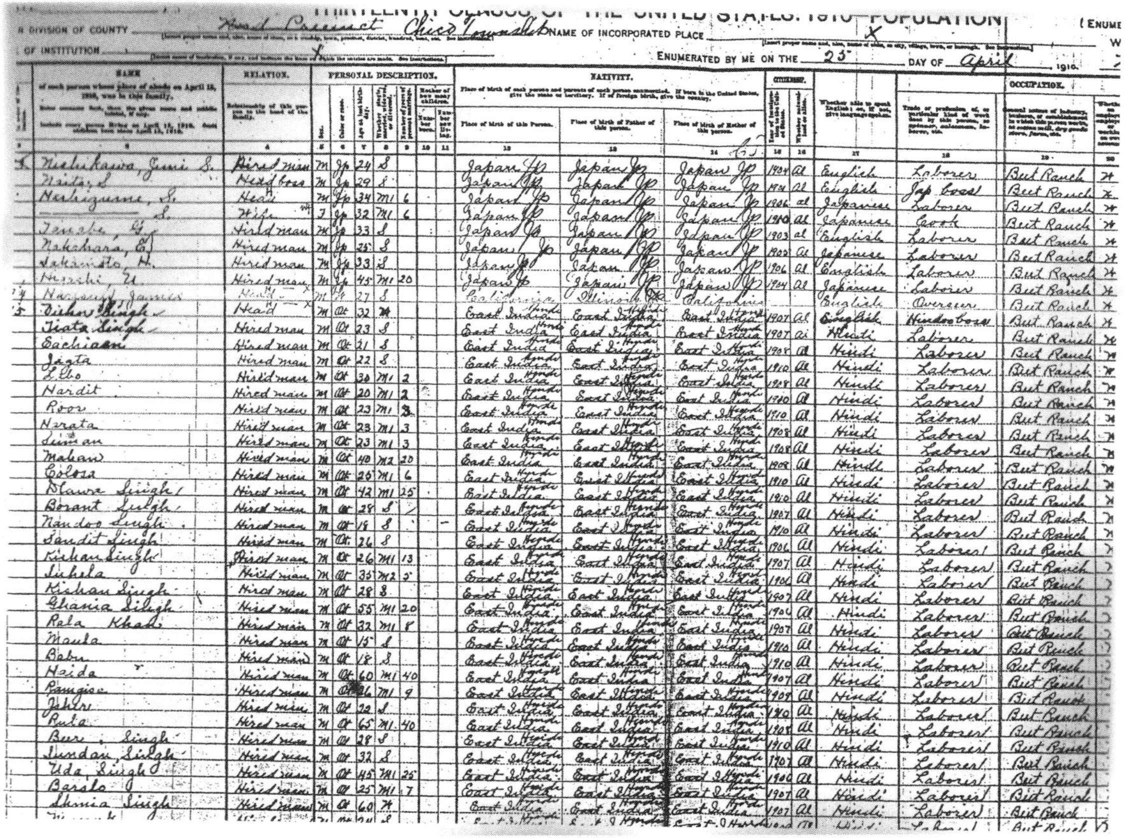

Figure 2-5. (b) 1910 U.S. Census manuscript schedules, Beet Ranch, Chico, California.

they formed in rural California. On a beet ranch (farm) in Chico near Yuba City in northern California, an enumerator working on the U.S. Census of 1910 recorded dozens of male laborers (many with Sikh names) living together, whose place of birth was listed as "East India" and whose mother tongue as "Hindi."

As a consequence of having few families and high return migration, the Indian population in the United States declined steadily. The 1910 population was 5,424. By 1930 it was 3,130, and in 1940 it had declined to 2,405. The small size of the Indian colony in the United States, coupled with the inability to recruit marriageable women, produced a rapidly shrinking and nearly vanishing ethnic community.

EARLY CHINESE COMMUNITIES AND HOUSEHOLDS IN THE U.S. MAINLAND

The demographic importance of the sex ratio of Chinese American communities is illustrated by juxtaposing the Hawaiian with the U.S. mainland pattern. In Hawai'i where the sex ratio was less imbalanced and more favorable to family formation, Chinese American society developed a sizable group of second-generation, or American-born, Chinese earlier than Chinese communities on the mainland. Seventy-three percent of the Chinese in Hawai'i were American born, as early as 1930, while as late as 1940 only 52 percent of the mainland Chinese population were American born. The early rise of a Chinese American second generation in Hawai'i speeded up group acculturation in that area. The fictional character of detective Charlie Chan lived in Honolulu and had a highly Americanized son he called "number one son." Because Hawai'i was a racially more tolerant society than the mainland, the Chinese were able to intermarry with the local population. In 1913, in a sample of 121 Chinese men who married in Hawai'i, half took non-Chinese wives, most of them native Hawaiians.

In the United States mainland, the more imbalanced Chinese sex ratio impeded the process of generational succession. The Americanizing influence of a large second generation upon the community was missing. In Hawai'i, by contrast, where the Chinese formed families and a second generation sooner, Chinese Americans were regarded as the most socially mobile and acculturated of immigrant groups. The contrast between Hawai'i and the mainland suggests that the demographics of intergenerational succession played a role in the relatively lower and less visible rate of early acculturation of the mainland Chinese population.

The different demographic transitions to family life in the Japanese and Chinese immigrant populations can be compared to patterns among English settlers in colonial America. In colonial New England, this transition was intense and rapid, much as it was for the Japanese immigrants of the far west. The Japanese migratory demography resembled to a degree that of the seventeenth-century Puritan colonists: both populations had a favorably balanced sex ratio and often migrated in conjugal units or families in the making. Among Chinese immigrants, by contrast, the sex ratio was very skewed toward male preponderance, which slowed down the rate of family formation and intergenerational succession, much as was found among English settlers in seventeenth-century Virginia. As historian Sucheng Chan has stated, early Chinese immigrant communities with small numbers of families were "not normal in either a demographic or a social sense, they failed to continue in existence beyond the natural life-spans of their members."[38] While the Chinese continued to work in farming, they were unable to establish permanent communities in nearly all areas in which they settled.

Manuscripts recorded by federal census takers show that the households of the first immigrants from China usually consisted of young men. These individuals were either bachelors or married men whose spouses remained at home in China. Few Chinese women appeared in the households recorded in the census. The customary duty of a wife to stay with her mother-in-law to maintain her husband's family line, as well as the cost of maintaining a married couple overseas, prevented wives from joining their husbands. It was difficult for a poor laborer to bring along his family when he could barely care for himself. After 1882, the Chinese Exclusion Act prevented any wives or single females from joining the men. For these reasons all-male partnership households and lodging houses formed the basic unit of group life in Chinese communities and predominated in both urban and rural areas (Figure 2-6).

From a transnational perspective, Chinese immigrants were in a functional role that made them members of two households at once. Through remittances they supported their family members in southern China and continued a relationship with them that was transnational. Concurrently, as members of a household of immigrant partners "abroad," they contributed to the upkeep of their local collective. Sucheng Chan has argued that maintaining a family in China, where the cost of living was lower than in the United States, was an economic advantage to the Chinese immigrants.[39]

Chan's comparisons of data recorded in the 1880 and 1900 U.S. censuses on Chinese families cast light on the demographic dynamics of Chinese rural enclaves. In the Sacramento-San Joaquin delta region in 1880, sixty-five out of eighty-five Chinese households, a solid majority, consisted of farmer partners who lived with no more than four laborers. Thirty-six of the eighty-five households had no laborers. The farmer partners were leasing farmers, while farm laborers who lived with the partners most likely were serving an apprenticeship. They probably hoped someday to save up enough money to lease their own farms. The early Chinese rural household was basically a collective and roughly egalitarian partnership arrangement among immigrant males. The all-male households of rural areas had a counterpart in the small number of all-female households whose several members were often involved in prostitution.

Beginning in 1880, more households with conjugal units began to appear in California. It is important to remember that women comprised in 1880 only 5 percent of all Chinese. The growing proportion of married Chinese women represented only a small number of women, but it was rising: 29 percent of the 317 women in the Southern Mines, 30.8 percent of the 439 women in the Northern

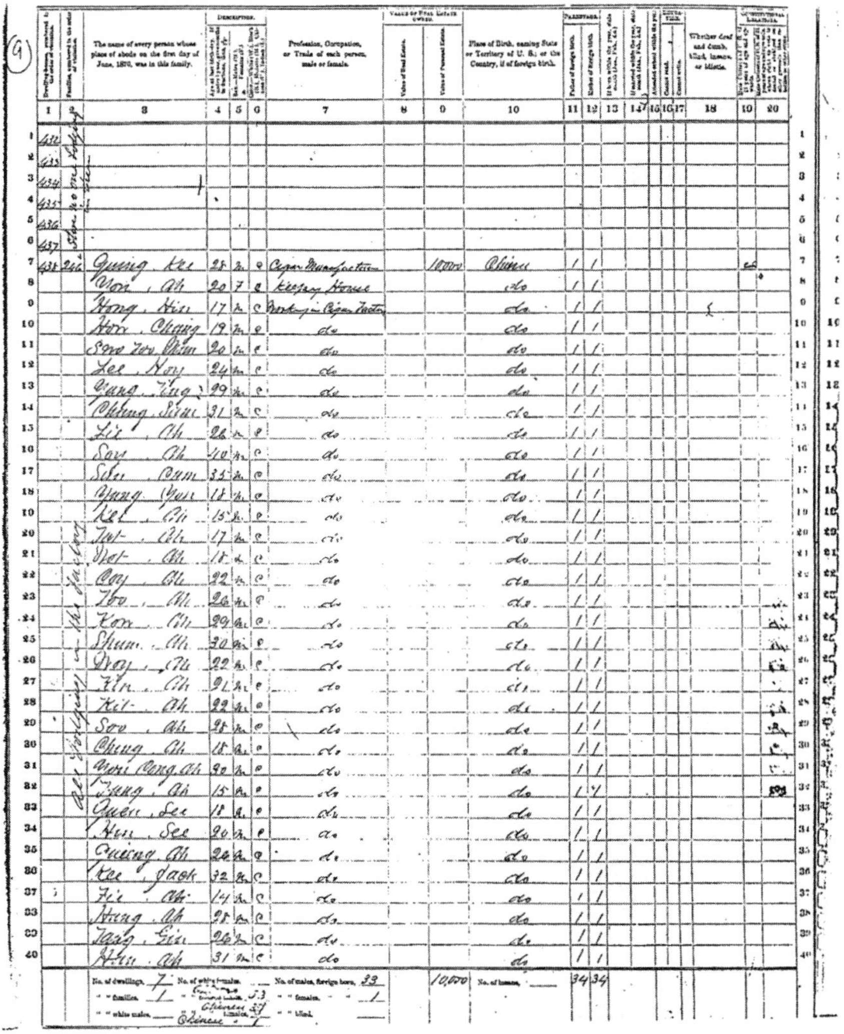

Figure 2-6. 1870 U.S. Census manuscript schedules, Chinese immigrants: Lodging House, San Francisco cigar factory.

Mines, 41.8 percent of the 225 women in the Sacramento Valley, and 35.7 percent of the 157 women in the San Francisco Bay Area were enumerated as wives. By 1900, the percentage of women who were wives in the Northern Mines, the Sacramento Valley, and the San Francisco Bay Area increased respectively to 44.6 percent, 49.5 percent, and 46.5 percent. Concomitantly, the proportion of prostitutes declined from 1880 to 1900 in the Northern Mines from 47.8 percent to 16.0 percent, in the Sacramento Valley from 31.6 percent to 11.6 percent, and in the San Francisco Bay Area from 22.9 percent to 14.5 percent.

By 1900, significant changes had occurred in the organization of the Chinese household in rural California (Tables 2-8a, b; Map 2-1). The size of the Chinese farms had become larger, requiring more manpower and making the households less egalitarian. Fewer partners shared in the control of the enterprise, and more laborers worked for the small group of partners. While the percentage of married women rose, they still composed a tiny number, and their children were a very small proportion of the Chinese population. U.S.-born Chinese—the second generation—were few and far between. In 1880 only 1 percent of the Chinese population had been born in America; even in 1900 only 10 percent of all Chinese were American-born. First-generation institutions and a patriarchal worldview still largely dominated Chinese communities.

A bird's eye overview of the geographic distribution of the first generation of Chinese Americans in the 1850s and 1860s reveals that the typical immigrant community was situated at the rural work outpost—the mine, plantation, or railroad line. San Francisco housed less than 10 percent of the Chinese population, while California's mining districts had the vast majority.

Table 2-8a. Farm Laborers and Laborers in Farmer's Households by Nativity, Selected Counties in San Francisco Bay Region, 1900.

	Alameda	Contra Costa	Monterey	Sacramento	Solano
Percent Chinese	12.7	11.3	17.6	24.9	10.5
Percent Japanese	14.0	10.3	26.2	13.6	17.7
Percent American	37.6	49.5	41.8	38.0	47.2
Percent European (Britain, Ireland, Germany, Portugal, Italy, Canada) & Other	33.6	28.5	14.0	23.5	24.6
Percent Mexican	0.1	0.4	0.4	0	0

Source: Sucheng Chan, This Bittersweet Soil: The Chinese in California Agriculture, 1860–1910 (Berkeley: University of California Press, 1986), Table 27, pp. 314–315.

Table 2-8b. Land Tenure by Ethnic Groups in the Sacramento River Delta (circa 1900–1910).

	N of Farms	Acreage Leased
Chinese	48	11,516
Japanese	112	17,597
Portuguese	40	4,545
Italian	60	12,985
Other	45	11,301

Source: Reports of the Immigration Commission, Vol. 24, Immigrants in Industries, Part 25, Table 8, p. 328.

Rural Chinese communities formed and vanished, reformed and re-vanished with the cycle of work and migration. When the mine ran out or the railroad line was completed they moved on to the next job or drifted to the Chinatowns. The call of filial duty to return home to China meant the abandonment of businesses and jobs. Vulnerability to harassment and violence also caused Chinese departures. The rural communities based on farming were as evanescent as those based on mining or construction work.[40] Chinese farmers and laborers who had

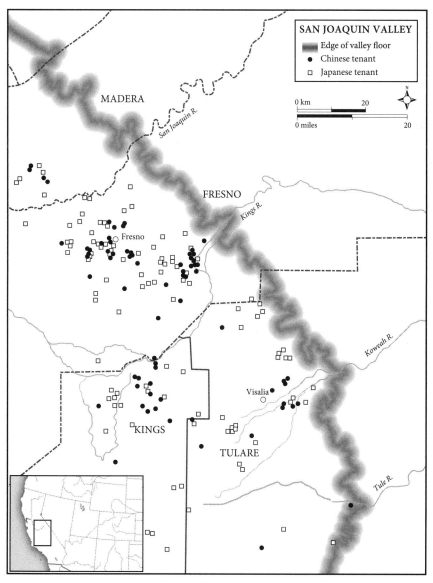

Map 2-1.   San Joaquin Valley, 1900–1920.

pioneered the Sacramento River delta managed to hold on until the turn of the century. Eventually they were surrounded by new neighbors, Americans and immigrants from Japan, Britain, Ireland, Germany, Portugal, Italy, and Canada, who competed economically and eventually displaced them.[41]

In both city and country, Chinese immigrants were cut off by the informal barriers of extreme cultural distances and racial differences. In the more organized polities of the large cities such as San Francisco, a host of legal restrictions on residence and employment reinforced the division between whites and Chinese. Chinese communities were treated as separate, self-governing enclaves, and the Chinese were excluded from the American polity by being banned from American citizenship. The statesmen of Chinatown were the merchant elite, whose wealth gave them power, prestige, and leadership of mutual benefit associations that could exercise coercive control over members.[42]

Anti-miscegenation laws made the compartmentalization of the Chinese community tighter, closing off intermarriage as an avenue of primary assimilation. The imbalanced sex ratio greatly limited marriages among Chinese. A cross-racial family system that mediated between Chinese and whites or other minority races (a characteristic of Hawai'i) did not develop in the far west United States.[43] (Another group of Asian immigrants, Sikh laborers from India, facing a shortage of co-ethnic women and anti-miscegenation laws, intermarried with Mexican wives (Table 2-9b), and Chinese men in New York City intermarried (Table 2-9c) but Chinese men in California did not take this route to family life.)

Lacking families as the building block of the community, a future generation would be very limited in size, and this would greatly affect the character of the community. The cultural orientation of the community—lifestyle and worldview—was traditional and controlled by older male interests. The demographic dominance of the first generation ensured their leadership over institutions and cultural life.

Table 2-9a.   Demographic Conditions for Marriage among Asian Immigrants.

Asian Immigrant Sex Ratios in California, 1870–1930

	Number of Men per 100 Women				
Year	Chinese	Japanese	Asian Indian	Korean	Filipino
1870	1,172	312			
1880	1,832	1,620			
1890	2,245	933			
1900	1,124	1,736			
1910	1,017	563			
1920	529	171		261	1,307
1930	299	138	1,572	168	1,552

Source: Karen Isaksen Leonard, Making Ethnic Choices: California's Punjabi Mexican Americans (Philadelphia: Temple University Press, 1992), Table 3, p. 23.

Table 2-9b. Demographic Conditions for Marriage among Asian Immigrants. Marriages of Sikhs in California, with Number and Rate of Interracial Marriages, 1913–1949

	Spouses						
	Hispanic (Mexican)		Anglo		Other		Total
Counties	N	%	N	%	N	%	N
Yuba, Sutter, Sacramento, San Joaquin	45	50.6	25	28.1	19	23.3	89
Fresno, Tulare, Kings	38	76.0	11	22.0	1	2.0	50
Imperial, Los Angeles, San Diego	221	92.5	12	5.0	6	2.5	239

Source: Karen Isaksen Leonard, Making Ethnic Choices: California's Punjabi Mexican Americans (Philadelphia: Temple University Press, 1992), Table 5, p. 67.

Table 2-9c. Demographic Conditions for Marriage among Asian Immigrants. Marriages of Chinese in New York City, with Number and Rate of Interracial Marriages

Years	Number of Marriages Involving Chinese Persons	Number of Interracial Marriages	Percent Interracial Marriages
1908–12	18	10	55.5
1920–24	49	27	55.1
1925–29	127	51	40.2

Source: Shepard Schwartz, "Mate Selection among New York City's Chinese Males, 1931–1938," American Journal of Sociology 56 (May 1961): 562–568.

Acculturation and social mobility usually increased with generational succession, so assimilation rates in the Chinese community were slowed by the absence of a sizable second generation. The Chinese community dwindled steadily in size. In 1890, the Chinese population in the United States was 107,000, but by 1920 it had shrunk to 62,000.

Extreme ostracism in the United States, however, did not mean that the social structure of Chinese communities was inert or static everywhere at the primary level of family life. Creative intermarriage patterns developed, showing that Chinese immigrants had an adaptive strategy to start families despite pressures against intermarriage and the enormous sex ratio imbalance in their communities. In New York City's Chinatown, Chinese men married non-Chinese women, among whom were many women of European ancestry. In Hawai'i, Chinese male immigrants intermarried with Hawaiians of indigenous and settler families.

ECONOMIC ACTIVITY

From the 1850s to 1870s, mining constituted the scaffold of the far west regional Chinese economy, giving it form and structure (Map 2-2; Figure 2-7).

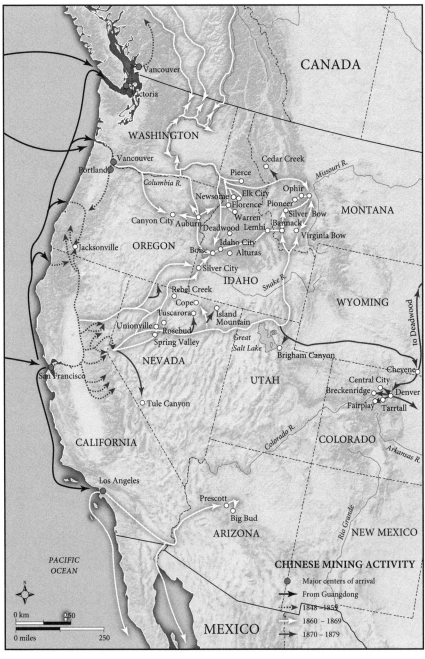

Map 2-2. Chinese mining activity in the American West.

Figure 2-7. Chinese and white miners in California, early 1850s.

Mining allowed the majority of Chinese to start at a point of independence in the economy, and not to be restricted to the urban job market. From the 1850s to the mid-1860s, California's mining districts had 80 percent of the Chinese population. Mining was a primary sector that generated a secondary economy that was ethnically defined and autonomous. The building blocks of the secondary economy consisted of retail businesses located in small, dispersed hinterland Chinatowns.

This commercial network revolved on the San Francisco Chinatown. The merchants of San Francisco's Chinatown shipped goods to the stores and miners in the backcountry.[44] Fishing employed a fifth of the Chinese in San Francisco and was closely tied into Chinatown's food provisioning business. Other key economic dimensions of San Francisco's Chinatown were a mass manufacturing economy employing industrial wage labor, a service economy providing laundering, domestic service, and food preparation, an internal consumer economy of commerce in food, clothing, and imported goods, illicit industries involving drugs, gambling, and prostitution, and legitimate forms of entertainment such as the popular Chinese theater.

The Chinatowns of the hinterland were linked to this economic center in San Francisco, which sustained their survival and development through long-distance commerce. Thus, a floating population of workers from far-off mines, farms, and construction sites entered and exited hinterland Chinatowns continuously, enabling these settlements to develop a thriving commerce in goods and provisions.

The mining industry that had been the key stimulus to far-flung Chinese settlements began to decline in the 1870s. The Chinese population in the California mining region shrank from a majority to a minority of the state's Chinese population. Many Chinese miners drifted back to San Francisco where they had entered the country. These men sometimes worked in railroad construction projects and agriculture as intermediate employment before resettling in the big city. Back in San Francisco, they constituted a pool of low-wage labor desperately looking for jobs, who were competing with new immigrants arriving in the 1870s.

Out-of-work Chinese miners and immigrants, however, appeared in San Francisco precisely at the time that industrialists were looking for new sources of labor. By 1870, 75 percent of San Francisco's Chinese worked for white employers or Chinese firms with a white clientele. Thus, the bulk of incoming Chinese workers were integrated with the larger economy as industrial wage workers, and were absorbed chiefly into low-skilled positions in cigar-making and machine-based industries: woolen mills, cotton mills, paper mills, shoe factories, and garment factories (Table 2-10).

As a result of rural-to-urban migration, the Chinese working class of San Francisco grew while industrial manufacturing was eroding the labor dominance of whites rooted in the old artisan trades. Chinese workers competed with white workers for jobs in the new mass manufacturing industries, while they kept sending remittances back home, and paid off loans incurred in transporting and provisioning themselves.[45] Nevertheless, by the 1890s white workingmen had largely displaced the aging and China-bound Chinese from the field of industrial occupations.

Chinese immigrant businessmen in San Francisco did not have the resources to compete long-term with American corporate enterprises and to establish self-sustaining industrial-scale employment for their countrymen. Within one generation, the San Francisco Chinatown population was reshuffled around an old

Table 2-10.   Chinese Male Immigrants in Factory Work: San Francisco, 1870.

Age, Years	Cigar Factory (Percent)	Slipper Factory (Percent)
0–9	0	0
10–14	7.7	6.8
15–19	43.0	37.9
20–24	27.4	31.0
25–29	11.6	6.8
30–34	5.9	10.3
35–39	2.0	6.8
40–49	2.0	0

PART C. *Source: U.S. Census, Manuscript Schedules, 1870.*

economic axis—the small business economy, the major field left to the Chinese. Growth in the Chinatown economy came in ethnic groceries, importing, restaurants, laundering, domestic service, and the vice business that catered to single male laborers. The crucial condition for the rise of new small ethnic businesses was the limited competition with white workers and white businessmen. Historian June Mei noted that the people of Chinatown turned "into a predominantly petite bourgeois population." The Chinese bourgeoisie remained stable within its circumscribed world and hired the remnants of a shrinking Chinese working class. The patterns of economic change of San Francisco's Chinatown were reflected in other Chinese communities as well. By 1920, of 46,000 Chinese in the U.S. labor force, 26,000 worked for laundries and restaurants and 7,000 worked as clerical and sales personnel. This occupational shift was an outgrowth of the consolidation of the Chinese population in urban centers. By 1910, 76 percent of the Chinese population resided in cities. Moreover, this concentration appeared chiefly in the largest cities and was concurrent with the decline of smaller Chinese communities. The Chinatowns of Butte, Montana; Denver, Colorado; Salt Lake City, Utah; Boise, Idaho; and Rock Springs, Wyoming dwindled markedly. Meanwhile, Los Angeles, New York City, San Francisco, and Boston experienced an upsurge in the Chinese population. Los Angeles' Chinatown grew from 1,200 in 1910 to 4,700 in 1940, New York City's from 4,600 to 11,000, San Francisco's from 10,600 to 17,800, and Boston's Chinatown grew from 200 in 1890 to 1,300 in 1940.[46]

By the early twentieth century, the Chinese population that had not returned home or died off was concentrated in ethnically defined urban employment. The small businesses were employment agencies for entire family units. Historian Henry Tsai has drawn a picture of households in which "Young children carried packages for customers or unloaded goods while older brothers and sisters served as clerks or cashiers."[47] The new Chinatown economy enlarged and intensified itself through family collectivism and role instrumentalism. The family-based small-business economy was gradually replacing the laborer-household based economy and was energized by the growing Chinese populations in the big cities and towns.

URBANIZATION AND CLASS
FORMATION IN HAWAI'I

Within one generation of their arrival in Hawai'i, Asian laborers on the plantations began to migrate to towns and cities all over the islands. In Hawai'i, the Chinese were the first Asian immigrants to arrive[48] and were the first to accumulate the resources and skills to leave the plantations. They moved to urban centers such as Honolulu on O'ahu and Hilo on the Big Island as quickly as possible and practical.

Before the 1890s, when Chinese immigrants had constituted the main labor force on the sugar plantations, plantation communities experienced life through a dialectic of accommodation and resistance to white planter control and industrial regimentation. Under a system of paternalistic domination, the Chinese knew that their independence and autonomy would not be achieved unless they left the plantations. Enterprising immigrants who sought to establish life prospects outside the plantations used a device familiar on the mainland—male partnership agricultural households. With these households, Chinese workers moved to their own land where they initiated and dominated the rice growing industry of Hawaiʻi. They swiftly expanded into farming taro, pineapples, bananas, coffee, tobacco, and garden vegetables. They also introduced numerous Chinese flowers, fruits, and vegetables which flourished in the Hawaiian climate, so similar to that of the immigrants' native Guangdong Province. Until the first years of the twentieth century, they also played major roles in hog and poultry raising, in bee culture, and in the fishing industry. The pioneering farmer outlivers eventually moved to towns near the plantations among other ethnic groups, particularly the Portuguese and Hawaiians. Some started their mercantile careers at the entry level of vegetable peddler. Many worked as humble boiled peanut vendors on the streets of Honolulu neighborhoods such as Moilili and Chinatown before graduating to the ranks of shopkeepers. Of the 692 firms listed in the Honolulu business directory in 1886, 219 were Chinese-owned.[49]

When the United States annexed Hawaiʻi in 1898, the Chinese exclusion laws ended the flow of Chinese immigrants which the Hawaiian monarchy had already been limiting. In 1896 some 5,000 Chinese entered Hawaiʻi; ten years later only 106 came. For the next four decades new arrivals were too few to play a major role in the development of Hawaiʻi's Chinese community. The population remained between 21,000 and 29,000 until restrictions against Chinese immigration were lifted during World War II.

The tapering of immigration ended high population turnover and reforeignization. As the agricultural laborers of the late nineteenth century retired, departed, and died, and those remaining turned to commercial occupations, the Chinese became Hawaiʻi's quintessential urban ethnic group whose primary economic impact was in business enterprises. In 1900, 32 percent of Hawaiʻi's Chinese lived in Honolulu; by 1930 the proportion had more than doubled to 71 percent. While the sex ratio on the mainland was 19 to 1 in 1900, it was 7 to 1 in Hawaiʻi. By 1920, the sex ratio in Hawaiʻi was only 2 to 1.[50] Also, the Chinese in Hawaiʻi formed families through racial intermarriage, which was not allowed on the mainland. The Chinese of Hawaiʻi thus developed extensive family life earlier than the Chinese in the United States mainland and had a substantial second generation achieving rapid social mobility and acculturation. Supported by resourceful families, an Americanized second generation was a demographic dividend that propelled the ascent of the Chinese community.

The Hawaiian Chinese were probably the first Asian American community to use the education of children extensively and instrumentally for pursuing economic and social advancement. From 1910 to 1940 the Chinese had a higher percentage of 16- and 17-year-olds attending schools than any other ethnic group in Hawaiʻi; in the mid-1920s almost 15 percent of schoolteachers in Hawaiʻi were

Chinese, entering a major avenue of social mobility and independence for second-generation Chinese women. By 1940 more than a third of gainfully employed Chinese were in professional or clerical work.

An opportunity structure in Hawai'i that was more open to Asians encouraged the formation of a Chinese upper class, a power elite, like that found in Hong Kong or Singapore. Chinese-American entrepreneurs played a far larger economic role in the Hawaiian Islands than in the mainland. Filling a vacuum in Hawaiian society caused by a lack of a white and native Polynesian middle class, Chinese immigrants started small businesses quickly, and with substantial financial resources accumulated before World War II launched banks and corporations. The community's financial needs were met by the hui (the mutual-benefit fraternal association) and the Chinese-owned Chinese-American Bank (f. 1916) and Liberty Bank (f. 1922). In 1939 Chinese Americans owned 56 of 275 manufacturing establishments in Hawai'i. Particularly successful were the C. Q. Yee Hop interests, which by the late 1940s owned supermarkets and a slaughter house, developed real estate, and operated the American Brewing Company (f. 1933).

Within two generations of Chinese arrival in the United States and within one generation of their arrival in Hawai'i, the threads of social class had begun to pull apart from the threads of racial subcaste. A large lower middle class and a small upper class existed in both Hawai'i and the United States mainland. The process of upper class formation, however, reached fuller and faster development in Hawai'i, where less discrimination and the absence of a dominant white settler and native class provided more room for economic maneuver.

The Japanese community established the other major Asian ethnic pattern in upward social mobility in Hawai'i. They had been brought initially to serve as a racial balance to offset Chinese labor power on the plantations, and to replace the Chinese who had returned home or left the plantations for other parts of the islands. Although the plantation provided welcome opportunities to the adventurous sons and daughters from impoverished farming families in southern Japan, within a matter of years they were paving a road to leave the plantations. Thus, like the Chinese community, the Japanese community provided an example of rapid transition from rural residence to urban, which triggered intergenerational social mobility. The Japanese strategy for escaping the plantation involved usage of family instrumentalism as well as the all-male farming company as stepping stones to the urban economy. Along with risk-taking and intensive economic activity, they also saved money to develop a stake with which to leave the plantation and start small businesses.[51]

The Japanese had an exceptional drive to learn manual trade skills, and thus for many the skilled trades served as a route out of the plantation. It led to greater concentration in blue-collar employment than occurred among the Chinese. Although the Japanese field worker was an unskilled worker, he acquired mechanical skills from performing construction and repair jobs on plantation buildings such as the sugar mill and houses for workers. A glimpse of the "re-skilling" of the Japanese plantation laborer is provided by the recorded observations of a statistician who worked for the U.S. Bureau of Labor Statistics and described the Japanese worker as the possessor of technical aptitude and a high degree of industriousness. The statistician also noticed the opportunistic behavior of the Japanese: "Wherever a Japanese is given a position as assistant to a skilled worker or in a mechanical position, he becomes a marvel of industry, disregarding hours, working early and late, and displaying a peculiarly farsighted willingness to be imposed upon and do the work which properly belongs to the workman he is assisting." The statistician noticed the tendency of white dependency on Japanese labor to undermine the work habits of white workers. "A [white] carpenter wants a board and tells a Japanese to get it; then he finds it convenient to have the man saw it, hold it in place, nail it; and so unconsciously he gradually begins . . . to associate an idea of degradation with the manual parts of his craft. . . ." The statistician felt white workers in this way gave a precious opening in skilled employment to the ambitious Japanese worker.[52] Once equipped with marketable craft skills, many Japanese laborers left the plantations to find work in the outside economy, in the urban job markets of Honolulu, Hilo, Lihue, Kahului, and other growing cities.

The Japanese, who arrived in Hawai'i one generation after the Chinese, began to leave the plantations about a generation after the Chinese had moved out to the towns. The U.S. Census of 1910 provided a snapshot of the urbanization process as it affected the Chinese and Japanese at different stages. In 1910, 46 percent of the Chinese resided in urban centers, and 54 percent in rural places. By contrast, only 19 percent of the Japanese lived in urban areas, while 81 percent lived in rural locations. The clustering of Japanese in the country in 1910 was only an artifact of later arrival. In reality, they were moving into the urban districts as quickly as the Chinese, who had just moved earlier. By 1910, in the city of Hilo, Japanese who had moved off the plantation had achieved rates of home ownership comparable to the Portuguese, who as plantation foremen stood on a higher socioeconomic plane.

The accumulation of capital to start small businesses was a prime goal of the Japanese. In the early twentieth century, frugal Japanese workers were saving $2.10 out of their monthly wage of $14.60. Japanese plantation laboring families could save, in five years, $120 from the earnings of the head of the household and another $80 from the income of the spouse and child laborers. Family members performed in multiple economic roles to earn enough capital to leave the plantation. Mothers wove clothing out of discarded rice bags: one daughter of a plantation mother referred to her as the "rice bag champion." The Japanese tradition of female labor continued naturally as wives took their position besides their husbands as field laborers. Mothers would get up very early before dawn to make lunches sold for a few pennies. They would do laundry and prepare hot baths for workers and charge 25 cents a month. Children would hike to the post office to pick up mail for a penny.

Savings could be supplemented from a loan from the rotating credit association within the community, the "tanomoshi." With a few hundred dollars of capital saved and borrowed, enterprising individuals started retail grocery and dry-goods stores. The small mom and pop store became a standard Japanese business in Hawaiian towns and cities. Other entrepreneurs opened up barber shops, restaurants, garages, and construction businesses.

Occupational versatility and moonlighting were also vital supplements to plantation-derived skills and savings. Industrious immigrants put together creative combinations of jobs to maximize earnings. A Japanese who bought his own small sugar cane field also owned a store. A plantation worker who immigrated from Hiroshima started his own rice farm with hired Chinese laborers in the Hanalei River area of the island of Kauaʻi. Another man doubled as a proprietor of a dry-goods store and post-office clerk; a carpenter also raised poultry and hogs; a businessman moonlighted as a teacher. These immigrants created their own formulas for economic betterment, involving occupational versatility combined with a willingness to work overtime. The Japanese immigrant work ethic was continuous with the tradition of long hours of labor-intensive agriculture in Japan. Furthermore, multiple job holding had been typical of the occupational pattern of a frontier area in the American Pacific region. Labor shortages multiplied opportunities for work without regard to demand for specialization.

Utilizing these avenues for economic mobility, the Hawaiian Japanese moved in two generations from occupational concentration in unskilled rural labor to occupational diversity in both industrial and commercial employment. This mobility out of the plantation economy was made possible by the external demand for labor and commerce, and the more open opportunity structure for non-white races in the Hawaiian Islands. By 1910, the Japanese population of Hawaiʻi had started a mass migration from the country to the city. In Honolulu, the first American urban working class that was substantially Japanese American took shape. Concurrently, the Japanese began to compete in shopkeeping with Chinese merchants. According to Lawrence H. Fuchs,

> Between 1920 and 1930, the proportion of Japanese retail dealers and skilled and semiskilled workers leaped forward. There were more Japanese machinists, painters, glazers, varnishers, carpenters, and fishermen than there were of any other group. . . . Although there were only 237 Japanese retail dealers in 1896, by 1930 there were 1,835. Many believed shopkeeping to be one of the easiest stepping-stones to economic security, and by 1930, the Japanese were operating 49 per cent of the retail stores of Hawaiʻi.

The deepening roots of economic security made Hawaiʻi more attractive to Japanese immigrants as a permanent residence, while the cost of living in Japan rose higher to make return migration less appealing.[53]

Facing Asian labor and economic power, American white workers in Hawaiʻi, like their counterparts on the mainland, feared the competition of Asians. They successfully petitioned the Hawaiian territorial legislature to pass a law in 1903 stipulating that only citizens or persons eligible to become citizens could work on projects contracted by the territorial government. In Hawaiʻi, government construction projects were a major source of employment. This restriction curtailed the manual jobs available to Issei, but ultimately it only redirected the current of Japanese upward mobility. The outcome was to steer more Issei out of blue-collar work and into self-employment as storeowners or other small businessmen. Additionally, Japanese skilled workers turned their energies toward developing a stronger base of clientage in the private job sector.

Thus, despite the protectionist tactics of white workers, Japanese Americans entered the core of the working class and lower middle class in Hawai'i by World War II. The Japanese of Hawai'i can be seen as comparable to the Irish Catholic population of eastern Massachusetts in the early twentieth century. They were the largest ethnic group in the islands, about fifty percent of the plantation labor force during World War I and 40 percent of Hawai'i's population in the 1930s. Both groups resembled each other in their core demographic, blue-collar, lower middle-class, and political roles in their respective regions. They were the driving forces behind labor strikes, unionization, minority advocacy journalism, and religious diversity.[54] Their historical presence and collective actions exemplified the important role of "regional enclaves" and "local spaces" as "contradictory locations inserted, and insurgent," where outsiders pushed for change within the worlds of global capital and empire, as Rob Wilson and Arif Dirlik have argued.[55]

MIGRANT LABOR TO THE ETHNIC ECONOMY

The Japanese founding generation in the mainland United States was, like the first generation of Chinese immigrants, distributed between rural communities centered on farms, mines, and railroad junctions and urban colonies based on small ethnic businesses and service occupations. Unlike their Chinese counterparts, however, Japanese rural colonies achieved a degree of permanence and a threshold of continuing growth. They were also established in a more settled society where institutionalized law and order existed effectively. The mass migration of Japanese immigrants to the United States did not begin until the termination of Chinese labor immigration. When the Japanese arrived, they faced an imposing wall of discrimination, prejudice, and persecution already erected by the anti-Chinese movement. The denial of citizenship to the Chinese in 1882 was extended to the Japanese. Anti-Chinese segregation and anti-miscegenation policies also applied to the Japanese by the turn of the century. Japanese immigrants were threatened as new targets of the mob violence that had started against the Chinese. Building a Japanese American community in such conditions was an imposing challenge, but the immigrants braced themselves against the hardships and set about establishing economic and institutional foundations for permanent, growing enclaves. The Japanese entry into the mainland economy occurred through a more varied set of routes than those in Hawai'i, since they had arrived in a more diversified and developed regional economy. In 1910, over 6,000 Japanese were employed by the railroads as section hands, and another 3,000 worked in shops or on maintenance crews. Japanese immigrants also worked in canneries, lumber mills, and mining. In 1909, over twelve thousand were service workers employed as butlers, cooks, waiters, chauffeurs, and the like.[56] The Japanese houseboy became in California what the stereotype of the Irish Catholic servant "Bridget" was to Bostonians. Other Japanese established retail businesses but faced less favorable economic and social conditions than their countrymen in Hawai'i. They had a smaller and fragmented ethnic market because of the sparseness and dispersion of the Japanese population, and they encountered more discrimination from financiers, customers, and competitors.

Despite the diversity of the mainland occupational spectrum, 40 percent of Japanese immigrants on the mainland began their careers as agricultural laborers or migrant farm workers (Table 2-11). Over time, however, these Japanese laborers sought opportunities to become tenant farmers. Those who were able to accumulate sufficient savings then purchased their own farms, often in partnership with a white farmer or with other countrymen. They took wives and started families, and ran farms with a combination of hired labor and the labor of family

Table 2-11.   Ethnic Diversity in the Agricultural Economy, California.
Employees in Fresno County Agriculture, by Ethnicity

	Number of Vineyard Employees	Number of Employees in Fruit Packing Plants
Japanese	574	14
White	168	1,063
Chinese	119	
Italian	72	97
Asian Indian	55	
Mexican	50	13
American Indian	42	
Armenian	31	150
German-Russian	11	656

Tenure of Land by Japanese from 1904–1908, Fresno County

Year	Acres Owned	Acres Rented for Cash	Acres Rented for Crop Share	Total Acreage
1904	439	1,825	760	3,024
1905	1,095	3,633	907	5,635
1906	2,712	2,108	2,376	7,196
1907	4,099	1,796	3,322	9,217
1908	5,745	3,977	8,065	17,787

Source: Reports of the Immigration Commission, Vol. 24, Immigrants in Industries, Part 25, Table 11, p. 635.

members. Japanese enclaves formed one part in a mosaic of neighborhoods in areas that included immigrants from all over the world, as well as native-born white Americans. In the farming centers of California's central valley, such as Fresno, Stockton, and Merced, Japanese Americans lived among groups of fellow workers who were immigrants from Italy, Scandinavia, Korea, China, India, Mexico, and Armenia as well as American farmers from the midwest.

Until excluded by the Gentlemen's Agreement, Japanese immigrants supplied the unskilled laborers that manned the Japanese-owned or -leased commercial farms. These were usually younger male relatives or migrants from the home prefectures of established Japanese residents, and they displaced the remnants of the aging Chinese labor force. Often they were shifting from temporary industrial employment into the agricultural job market where they constituted a reliable and hardworking labor force for the fruit and vegetable farms.

Japanese American commercial agriculture became the most dynamic sector of the California farm economy by World War I. A study of Japanese American agriculture by Edna Bonacich and John Modell concluded, "Two major principles seem to be operating in the climb up to self-employment from these humble beginnings. They are thrift and community cooperation. . . . Thrift is shown in a willingness to work in the business as unpaid family labor, and in saving the proceeds of the enterprise for expansion rather than spending them on consumer goods, such as luxurious housing. [A researcher found] that 'the farm home of a Japanese, even of a wealthy farmer, is far below that of a home of a white man owning a similar piece of ground or of similar wealth.'" In addition to the "Spartan" frugality of the Japanese American farmer, the study also noted, "Community cooperation, too, was evident in many aspects of Japanese American business. It played a role in the accumulation of capital, in the acquisition and treatment of labor, in the passing around of other resources, in the development of vertical integration, and in the control of competition between Japanese firms. Family, prefectural, and ethnic ties provided the basis for this cooperation."[57]

Community cooperation was made necessary by racial ostracism and discrimination. Many desirable jobs outside the ethnic economy were unavailable to Japanese immigrants. Discrimination, or the threat of it, encouraged developing economic resources with fellow Japanese, including arrangements for pooling capital. The Japanese farmers of Turlock, for example, were known for the operation of innovative farm cooperatives.[58] The surrounding climate of anti-Japanese prejudice pressured new arrivals into a strong interdependency and commitment to collective activity. Working with fellow countrymen, they could speak Japanese and be assured that their boss and their co-workers understood them, and respected their rights, customs, and needs.

The movement of Japanese along the path of upward mobility through the agricultural economy was rapid. In 1900, only thirty-nine Japanese farmers were recorded as resident in California in the U.S. Census, and they owned less than five thousand acres of land in total. By 1909, 6,000 Japanese farmed under various forms of tenancy, and their total holdings were more than 210,000 acres. The rapid ascent of Japanese farmers to major holders of farmland was a pattern repeated all over the state. In just five years, Japanese increased the acreage they owned in Fresno County over twelvefold and the total acreage they rented and owned by over fivefold.[59]

The entry of Japanese immigrants into competition with white agriculturalists provoked harsh legislative reprisals to contain their advances. The fulcrum point for this legislation was the status of Japanese immigrants as aliens ineligible for citizenship. In 1913, the California legislature passed the Alien Land Act, which barred aliens ineligible for citizenship from purchasing agricultural property and limited any lease they might hold to three years. In 1920, another Alien Land Act prohibited the Japanese farmer from bequeathing or selling agricultural property to another Japanese. Nevertheless, the Japanese found ways to circumvent discriminatory laws. Foreign-born farmers registered their deeds with friendly white partners, under the names of their U.S.-born children (who were American citizens), or through other U.S. born Japanese who possessed American citizenship.

With the aid of these circumventions, the aggregate amount of land under Japanese ownership actually grew after the enactment of the anti-alien land laws. In 1920, the Japanese controlled over 450,000 acres of California's superior farmland and produced 10 percent of the state's crops in annual dollar value. Michi Weglyn wrote as follows about the important role of the Japanese immigrants in the development of California agriculture:

> [Although] the Japanese minority comprised only a minuscule 1 percent of the state's population, they were a group well on their way to controlling one-half of the commercial truck crops in California. Centuries-old agricultural skills which the Japanese brought over with them enabled Issei farmers not only to turn out an improved quality of farm produce but also to bring down prices. The retail distribution of fruits and vegetables in the heavily populated Southern California area was already a firmly entrenched monopoly of Japanese Americans. . . . It was a common practice among the Issei to snatch up strips of marginal unwanted land which were cheap: swamplands, barren desert areas that Caucasians disdained to invest their labor in. Often it included land bordering dangerously close to high-tension wires, dams, and railroad tracks. The extraordinary drive and morale of these hardworking, frugal Issei who could turn parched wastelands, even marshes, into lush growing fields—usually with help from the entire family—became legendary.[60]

The Japanese farming economy intensified ethnic solidarity and was the economic propellant that fueled the demographic growth of the Japanese American community. With the rise in population, neighborhoods expanded and ethnic businesses catered to ever more clientele (Table 2-12).[61]

Japanese immigration was a force for the development and commercialization of the hinterland economy. As primary producers, Japanese Americans had added another link to the food-supply chain enabling the support of a larger urban population in California. With its increasing food supply, California's population grew over fourfold, from 1.5 million in 1900 to 7 million in 1940.

Table 2-12. Japanese Business Establishments in
Fresno City, 1909.

Banks	2
Provision stores	4
Fish dealers	4
Drug stores	2
Bicyle stores	2
Watch and jewelry stores	6
Restaurants (American meals)	5
Restaurants (Japanese meals)	15
Lodging houses	12
Barber shops	12
Bath houses	4
Laundries	5
Shoemakers	2
Moving-picture shows	2
Pool rooms	10
Miscellaneous	20

*Source: Reports of the Immigration Commission, Vols. 24,
Immigrants in Industries, Part 25, Table 12, p. 653.*

Despite labor propaganda, xenophobic journalism, and mass-media stereo-typing of the aggressive Japanese, white Americans began to recognize that Japanese immigrants displayed signs of positive adaptation to American life. This reaction occurred more often away from San Francisco and areas influenced by its labor politics. In Los Angeles, anti-Japanese xenophobia did not achieve the constant and high intensity found in the Bay Area, where lingering attitudes of the earlier anti-Chinese movement remained. Instead, in southern California, anxiety mingled with recognition of the accomplishments of Japanese immigrants to affect popular attitudes toward them as a group. Whites in Southern California were uneasy with the idea of an Asian minority taking an economic position close to them, but they did not angrily hate or despise Japanese Americans as a norm of reaction. Historian John Modell even found that "Indifference, rather than either contempt or hatred, usually characterized Los Angeles public opinion toward the Japanese Americans."[62]

In the greater Los Angeles area, the Japanese farming enterprise reflected a collaborative ethnic network that was dynamic and expanding over a wide geographic domain. In the early twentieth century, Japanese farmers started to become very active concurrently in multiple sectors of commercial agriculture throughout Los Angeles County (Table 2-13).[63] By 1920, there was one Japanese farm per thirteen Japanese men, women, and children in Los Angeles County. In 1940, the primary occupations for Japanese Americans in Los Angeles County were farming, food wholesaling, food retailing, restaurant work, food processing, hotel keeping, and gardening. This distribution of jobs indicated that the

Table 2-13. Types of Commercial Farming by Japanese in Los Angeles County, 1909.

City of Los Angeles, Newmark, Laguna, Montebello, Tropico, Glendale, Burbank, Arcadia, El Monte, Pasadena, Long Beach, Burnett, West Adams Street (Los Angeles), Green Meadow, Rowland, Watts, Compton

Products	N Farms	Acreage
Berries	199	1,228.5
Vegetables	157	2,639.5
Berries & vegetables	27	231.5
Nursery stock	2	11.0
Flowers	24	146.5
Chicken & pigs	11	51.0
Miscellaneous	22	406.0
Total	442	4,714

Source: Reports of the Immigration Commission, Vol. 24, Immigrants in Industries, Part 25, Table 18, p. 381.

Japanese had created a large vertically integrated ethnic economy powered by commercial farming. By the 1920s, the Japanese population of Los Angeles occupied a middle position in the social structure. It was anchored by concentration and cooperation in both primary production and marketing in agricultural enterprise. Wealthy Japanese wholesalers provided informal crop-loans to growers at the beginning of the season in exchange for future patronage. The shared economic activities and joint economic interests of Los Angeles Japanese fortified the bonds of ethnicity and community solidarity.[64]

Sociologist Ivan Light pointed out that Asian American ethnic economies can be compared with the black solidarity enterprises of Father Divine and Marcus Garvey. The Japanese ethnic economy was more enduring and expansive than these black economic initiatives, however, resembling more the "needle" trades of Jewish entrepreneurs. Ethnic cooperation succeeded in overcoming internal class divisions and powered self-sufficient growth within the Japanese American ethnic economy of Los Angeles in the early twentieth century.[65]

The positive relationship between commercial agriculture and the evolution of a multigenerational population was the key to making the Japanese American community of Los Angeles larger than any other in the United States mainland before World War II. The agricultural economy rested upon a structure of vertical integration that supplied jobs and services to the entire community. Food production, processing, and distribution made it possible to make a living in a society that denied the Japanese full opportunity for employment.

Japanese immigrants also pioneered commercial fishing in the Los Angeles area and made it a major part of the Japanese ethnic economy. Based in East San Pedro, Japanese fishermen created a thriving industry around which a large multi-faceted ethnic community developed (Table 2-14). A remarkable degree of

Table 2-14. Number of Japanese Stores and Businesses in East San Pedro, Terminal Island.

	Years	
	1900–1910	**1926–1930**
Hardware	0	4
Groceries	1	7
Restaurant	0	11
Fishing goods	0	3
Pool room	1	4
Apartment	0	6
Soda fountain	0	2
Physician	0	2
Hospital	0	2
Midwife	0	1
Dentist	0	1
Meat market	0	2
Dry goods	0	3
Barbershop	0	4
Shoe repair	0	1
Electrician	0	2
Bank	0	1
Book store	0	1
Drug store	0	1
Tailor	0	1
Newspaper	0	1

Source: Kanichi Kawasaki, "The Japanese Community of East San Pedro, Terminal Island, California" (master's thesis, University of Southern California, 1931), Table V, p. 17.

institutional completeness rapidly developed in East San Pedro as Japanese immigrants established enterprises that provided nearly every service a resident of their enclave needed.[66] A sociologist wrote a contemporary account describing a flourishing enclave linked to commerce and popular media from Japan:

> The Japanese in this community are engaged in twenty occupations. They are able to maintain a good economic standard of living. In this community they have created culture which is a combination of American and Japanese. . . . Half of the food-stuffs sold in the stores are imported from Japan. Each morning, a boy from each grocery store visits the customers' homes for orders and delivers the goods in the evening. Every grocery gives credit. At the end of each month statements are rendered and collections made.
>
> [The Japanese subscribe to the Japanese newspapers published in San Francisco and] local newspapers which are published in Los Angeles. These Japanese newspapers are the Rafu Shimpo [and] the Rafu-Nichibei of Los Angeles, and the Nichibei and the Shinsekai of San Francisco.

The adults read thirty-eight magazines, of which thirty are Japanese and eight are [in] English. Into the four hundred and fifty-nine families of this community there come, at a rough estimate, one thousand and three hundred copies of monthly periodicals. This means that an average of three monthly magazines are subscribed to by each family.

The ethnic economy became part of an intergenerational mobility agenda. The second generation, the Nisei, were the recipients of the fruits of the ethnic economy built by their parents. They and their parents believed that the savings accumulated would be used to invest in the mobility of the second generation through education, a strategy shared most notably by Chinese, Korean, Indian, and Jewish immigrants. The Issei who ran the commercial produce business, it was said, aimed to turn "lettuce into diplomas." With the financial and moral backing of the Issei, the Nisei attained high levels of schooling. Even in California, where anti-orientalism was historically ferocious, the public school establishment warmly regarded Japanese American students. They were consistently rated as among the group of superior students in the schools. Japanese youngsters who absorbed the values propagated by American educators believed they could gain society's acceptance by becoming exemplary students and expected that their future was to aspire to self-made success through education.

While, on the whole, the educational system treated them fairly, the external world was a different place. Outside of school, the Nisei found that discriminatory employment policies robbed them of the value of schooling. For example, Nisei education majors, fully teacher certified, were virtually unemployable as teachers in the very schools where they had been star pupils. The Nisei had inherited from their parents a powerful drive to succeed in the face of hardship, and then had gained from the schools an optimistic view of social mobility. Despite these positive factors, few of the maturing Nisei could find the jobs commensurate with their education. Instead they were forced to take jobs inside the interior economy of the ethnic community. College graduates were not hired in government, business, or education because of their race. One of the first Nisei graduates of UCLA from Hawai'i could only find employment as a gardener, houseboy, and farm laborer. Interviewing for a job, he was turned away by the prospective employer who justified himself by saying, "If I were in Japan, I would not be hired because I'm an American." He returned to Hawai'i to work for the University of Hawai'i agricultural extension. Other Nisei on the mainland had to settle for jobs in agriculture, groceries, restaurants, and oriental curio shops. The Nisei were the predecessors of today's educationally mobile Asian Americans, but they were a generation trapped by the patterns of racial discrimination of their era. One young Nisei described his situation in 1937, to which he was apparently resigned: "I am a fruit stand worker. It is not a very attractive nor distinguished occupation. . . . I would much rather be a doctor or lawyer . . . but my aspiration of developing into such was frustrated long ago. . . . I am only what I am, a professional carrot washer. . . ."[67]

The social and psychological strain of frustrated mobility permeated the rising generation in the Japanese American capital of Los Angeles. An Issei compared the Japanese community to "a bear cooped up in cage"; and a white outsider noted that the Nisei were "suffocating in Little Tokyo." The gains of the ethnic agricultural economy that enabled the Los Angeles Japanese community to expand demographically and secure its economic life could not propel the Nisei beyond the discriminatory barriers to their aspirations.

COMMUNITIES IN TRANSITION

In the United States, the Chinese and Japanese moved in the early twentieth century toward increasing ethnic solidarity and continuing marginalization in the institutional structures of the surrounding society. They were evolving into an American version of a global ethnic phenomenon known as middleman minorities, identified and theorized by sociologists Karl Marx, Georg Simmel, Max Weber, and Ferdinand Toennies. They and other social scientists have found many case examples of such groups including the Jews in Europe, the Chinese in Southeast Asia, Asian Indians in East Africa, Arabs in West Africa, and Armenians in Turkey. Although they varied in history and circumstances, the similarities they shared were their position as social buffers between indigenous often hostile masses and elite strata and displacement from primary production. As aliens ineligible for U.S. citizenship, the first generation of Asian Americans lacked political power and were dependent on elites of the dominant surrounding communities who controlled the levers of government. Their social exclusion was aggravated by the visible difference of race. Immigrants from Asia were limited in their access to marriage partners on the grounds of race nearly as much as blacks. Before the end of World War II, the state legislatures of Maryland, Mississippi, Missouri, Nebraska, South Carolina, South Dakota, Wyoming, Arizona, Nevada, Oregon, Utah, and California passed laws restricting the right of Asian immigrants to marry white spouses. These laws usually lumped Asians together with blacks as groups not permitted to intermarry with whites. Thus, South Dakota had a law stipulating that a white person was not allowed to marry Africans, Malayans, Koreans, and Mongolians. Some of these states drew the line only against intermarriage between white females and Asian males. For example, South Carolina permitted a white man to marry a Chinese woman, but a Chinese man was not allowed to marry a white woman.[68]

The Chinese and Japanese in the United States displayed some striking similarities but also notable differences when compared to typical middleman minorities. Their similarities were as follows. The economic roles of Chinese and Japanese in shopkeeping and service industries such as food provisioning and laundries were petit bourgeois, a lower-middle class economic type between the producer-owner capitalist class and the working class. Their patterns of group life involved continuing connection with homelands through shared information and cultural corridors, return migration, and the sending of remittances.

Chinese and Japanese set up separate language schools, practiced ancestor worship, sent children back to Asia for education, and stressed marriage within the group. For these immigrants, their mutual-benefit organizations, the Chinese hui and the Japanese kenjinkai (prefectural mutual-benefit association), provided collective assistance and protection, which gave the impression that "they took care of their own" without reliance on outside aid and thereby reinforced the image of group separatism. Chinese and Japanese immigrants, however, also had important differences from the middle-man minorities of classical sociological theories. For example, a substantial number of these Asian immigrants were primary producers, particularly in mining, agriculture, and fishing, and also in urban industrial manufactures. Perhaps most importantly, most members of the second and later generations were strongly motivated to assimilate into American life and determined to move beyond ethnic enclaves to mingle with the surrounding society.[69]

In Hawai'i, the demographic conditions and more open social structure limited the evolution of the Chinese and Japanese into middleman minorities. They constituted core groups of the middle class and working class of the entire community in which Asians formed a majority, and were integrated to a significant degree in mainstream social, economic, and cultural life. Importantly, they achieved political power through labor organizing and mass party politics. As groups they were not small, politically powerless, and isolated in the middle. They were major demographic forces that took over social and economic space from other groups, and even intermixed through intermarriage to produce a new multi-racial society.

In Hawai'i, class formation and economic integration shaped the core of the Chinese, Japanese, and Korean communities, paralleling to a degree patterns of social development found among European immigrant communities after two or three generations in eastern industrial cities (as recently described by historians Olivier Zunz for Detroit, and John Bodnar and Francis Couvares for Pittsburgh). In these cases, urban and class integration competed with ethnicity as determinants of social change. The cultural life and social identities of Japanese Americans in Hawai'i were more defined in the broader terms of regionalism and class, and not as strongly in terms of racial isolation and compartmentalization as experienced by Asian immigrants on the mainland. A recent study comparing ethnic intensity among the Seattle and Honolulu Japanese populations shows that the latter scored lower than the former, seeing themselves in terms of the local culture of the Hawaiian Islands rather than a minority ethnicity.[70]

In California, the geographic mobility of the Chinese and Japanese occurred in a multi-group pattern of ethnic and race relations. Residential patterns of the state's two largest Asian urban populations took shape in an ethnically and racially diversified and stratified social order that reflected the demographic history of California: the transcontinental migration of whites[71] and blacks, as well as immigration from Asia, Europe, and Latin America. Within this context, lawmakers focused in a uniquely restrictionist way on the rights of Asian immigrants and their descendants to acquire residential and agricultural property and were affected by their perception of American international relations with Asian countries.

The large communities of Chinese and Japanese in San Francisco and Los Angeles faced very limited opportunities for residential mobility. Anti-Asian prejudice that originated with the reaction to the first wave of Chinese immigration in the mid-nineteenth century carried over to affect subsequent Asian immigrant groups, especially Japanese immigrants. As a result of the anti-Asian discrimination in the Bay area and environs with respect to ownership of house lots and farmland that began with the arrival of the Chinese, many Japanese relocated to southern California where this type of unequal treatment was not as pervasive and harshly engrained.[72]

PLURALISM WITHOUT DEMOCRACY

In the early twentieth century, American law and custom limited the degree to which ethnic and racial groups could intermix or act together across racial lines. The dominance of the Anglo-Saxon core population was reinforced by hardening the public boundaries dividing immigrants and racial minorities from native whites. The result was a hegemonic pluralism in which American diversity patterns took their form from the Protestant Anglo-Saxon core's control over institutions that incorporated ethnic and racial minorities. It was a means of producing national order while compromising ethnic and racial democracy, a defensive reaction to the expanding diversity created by black emancipation, global immigration, and territorial expansion.

The exclusionary practices against Asians and Mexicans in the western states were injurious, but as minorities they were less affected than blacks in the racial-caste regime of the south. Federal courts annulled the most blatantly discriminatory local ordinances which were set up to restrict fields of employment for Chinese immigrants. Chinese and Japanese immigrants were able to find "demand" niches in the economy, enabling them to run small businesses that provided commercial or personal services. Even as "aliens ineligible for citizenship," they circumvented laws restricting possession of land to citizens by obtaining land that was held through their children or proxies. The movement to segregate Chinese and Japanese students was limited in the first decade of the twentieth century by political protest, international diplomacy, and the intervention of the federal government. The dual system of English standard and non-standard schools in Hawai'i displayed some racial mixing by the 1920s and fell into disuse by the end of World War II. Mexicans and Asians who lived in the southern states were reported by African American newspapers often to use "whites-only" accommodations and conveyances.[73]

The architects of hegemonic pluralism in which whites dominated were predisposed to see ethnic cultures as timeless, incommensurable, anchored in biological difference, and corresponding to a ranked global order of higher and lower races. The belief that immutable groups existed made it possible to conceive of schemes of ethno-racial sorting. The far western and territorial ethnic patterns of the United States hinged on multiracial categories of status separating whites, Latinos, American Indians, Asians, blacks, and Pacific Islanders.[74] The job of public policy was to classify and marginalize allegedly inferior groups. The oligarchy of newspaper and land barons of southern California ran a national advertising campaign to attract Anglo-midwestern settlers; the ads advertised Los Angeles as "the white spot" of America, implying a socially hygienic realm without minorities.[75] Discrimination and exclusion, enforced through racialized housing policy and employment barriers, were levers to move toward a future west coast society that would remain firmly aligned to the control and benefit of a white settler majority.

Notes

1. Hilary Conroy, *The Japanese Frontier in Hawaii, 1868–1898* (Berkeley: University of California Press, 1953), p. v.
2. Walter Nugent, *Crossings: The Great Transatlantic Migrations, 1870–1914* (Bloomington: Indiana University Press, 1992), Table 3, p. 14.
3. Evelyn Hu-DeHart, "Latin America in Asia-Pacific Perspective," in *"What Is in a Rim?: Critical Perspectives on the Pacific Region Idea*, 2nd ed. (Lanham, Md.: Rowman & Littlefield, 1998), ch. 11; Philip A. Kuhn, *Chinese Among Others: Emigration in Modern Times* (Lanham, Md.: Rowman & Littlefield, 1998), pp. 144–145.
4. This type of location was described by Robert A. Woods and Albert J. Kennedy in *The Zone of Emergence: Observations of the Lower Middle and Upper Working Class Communities of Boston, 1905–1914*, 2nd ed. (Cambridge, Mass., M.I.T. Press, (1962; 1969).
5. J. R. McNeill, "The End of the Old Atlantic World: America, Africa, Europe, 1770–1888," in Alan L. Karras and J. R. McNeill, *Atlantic American Societies: From Columbus through Abolition, 1492–1888* (London: Routledge, 1992), p. 246.
6. Evan Haefeli, "A Note on the Use of North American Borderlands," *American Historical Review* 104, no. 4 (October 1999): 1222–1224; David J. Weber, "A New Borderlands Historiography: Constructing and Negotiating the Boundaries of Identity" and Sylvia L. Hilton, "Identities and the Usable Pasts of Colonial Borderlands: Spanish Historians and the North Pacific Frontiers of the Spanish Empire" in Steven W. Hackel, ed., *Alta California: Peoples in Motion, Identities in Formation, 1769–1850* (Berkeley: University of California Press, and the Huntington Library, San Marino, Calif., 2010).
7. Kuhn, *Chinese Among Others*, p. 144.
8. Easurk Emsen Charr, *The Golden Mountain: The Autobiography of a Korean Immigrant, 1895–1960*, 2nd ed. (Urbana: University of Illinois Press, 1996), ch. 12–14.
9. Evelyn Hu-Dehart, "Latin America in Asia-Pacific Perspective," in Arif Dirlik, ed., *What Is in a Rim?*, ch. 11. Other works which provide a global view of the movement and settlement in Latin America of immigrants from Asia are Roshni Rustomji-Kerns (with Rajini Srikanth and Levy Mendoza Strobel), *Encounters: People of Asian Descent in the Americas* (Lanham, Md.: Rowman and Littlefield, 1999); Daniel M. Masterson (with Sayaka Funada-Classen), *The Japanese in Latin America* (Urbana: University of Illinois Press, 2004); Lane Ryo Hirabayashi, Akemi Kikumura-Yano,

and James A. Hirabayashi, *New Worlds, New Lives: Globalization and People of Japanese Descent in the Americas and from Latin America in Japan* (Stanford, Calif.: Stanford University Press, 2002).

10. Ralph Mann, *After the Gold Rush: Society in Grass Valley and Nevada City, California 1840–1879* (Stanford, Calif.: Stanford University Press, 1982), p. 183.

11. James Loewen, *Mississippi Chinese: Between Black and White* (Cambridge, Mass.: Harvard University Press, 1971), ch. 1.

12. Xinyang Wang, *Surviving the City: The Chinese Immigrant Experience in New York City, 1890–1970* (Lanham, Md.: Rowman and Littlefield, 2001), pp. 25–28; Renqiu Yu, *To Save China, to Save Ourselves: The Chinese Hand Laundry Alliance of New York* (Philadelphia: Temple University Press, 1992), pp. 8–12.

13. Madeline Yuan-yin Hsu, *Dreaming of Gold, Dreaming of Home: Transnationalism and Migration between the United States and South China, 1882–1943* (Stanford, Calif.: Stanford University Press, 2000), pp. 40–43.

14. Hsu, *Dreaming of Gold, Dreaming of Home*, p. 2.

15. Conroy, *The Japanese Frontier in Hawaii*, p. v; Henry Yu, *Thinking Orientals: Migration, Contact, and Exoticism in Modern America* (New York: Oxford University Press, 2001), pp. 5–6.

16. Vivek Bald, *Bengali Harlem and the Lost Histories of South Asian America* (Cambridge, Mass.: Harvard University Press, 2013).

17. United States, Eighty-first Congress, Second Session, Senate, Committee on the Judiciary, Report No. 1515, *The Immigration and Naturalization Systems of the United States* (Washington, D.C.: U.S. Government Printing Office, 1950), p. 78.

18. Mario T. Garcia, *Desert Immigrants: The Mexicans of El Paso, 1880–1920* (New Haven: Yale University Press, 1981), ch. 8–10; Samuel Truett, *Fugitive Landscapes: The Forgotten History of the U.S.-Mexico Borderlands* (New Haven, Conn.: Yale University Press 2006); Katherine Benton-Cohen, *Borderline Americans: Racial Division and Labor War in the Arizona Borderlands* (Cambridge, Mass.: Harvard University Press, 2009); Rachel St. John, *Line in the Sand: A History of the Western U.S.-Mexico Border* (Princeton: Princeton University Press, 2011). A bibliographic essay on the historiographic themes addressed by these works is Geraldo Cadava, "Historians Explore the Borderlands: A Rapidly Developing Field," *The Immigration and Ethnic History Newsletter* XLV, no. 1 (May 2013): 1, 8.

19. Charlotte Brooks, *Alien Neighbors, Foreign Friends: Asian Americans, Housing, and Transformation of Urban California* (Chicago: University of Chicago Press, 2009), pp. 1, 7.

20. Frederick C. Luebke, *European Immigrants in the American West: Community Histories* (Albuquerque: University of New Mexico Press, 1998), pp. viii-xv.

21. Peter R. Decker, *Fortunes and Failures: White Collar Mobility in Nineteenth-Century San Francisco* (Cambridge, Mass.: Harvard University Press, 1978), pp. 171–177, 196–215; Albert L. Hurtado, *John Sutter, A Life on the North American Frontier* (Norman, Oklahoma: University of Oklahoma Press, 2006), ch. 1, 5; Patrick J. Blessing, *West Among Strangers: Irish Migration to California, 1850–1880* (Ph.D. dissertation, UCLA, 1981), ch. 1; Jules Tygiel, *Workingmen in San Francisco, 1880–1901* (New York: Garland, 1992), Table 3.2, pp. 97–98; Marcus Lee Hansen, *The Mingling of the Canadian and American Peoples* (New Haven: Yale University Press, 1940), pp. 204, 249–250; Helen Alma Hohenthal et al., and John Edwards Caswell, ed., *Streams in a Thirsty Land: A History of the Turlock Region* (Turlock, Calif.: City of Turlock, 1972; 2008), ch. X, XV.

22. Decker, *Fortunes and Failures,* pp. 81–84, 114–115; Ava F. Kahn, ed., *Jewish Life in the American West: Perspectives on Migration, Settlement, and Community* (Los Angeles and Seattle: Autry Museum of Western Heritage, Los Angeles, in Association with University of Washington Press, 2002), pp. 9, 18, 25, 44, 48, 53, 54, 64, 68, 91, 92.

23. *Reports of the Immigration Commission, Volume 24, Immigrants in Industries, Part 25: Japanese and Other Immigrant Races in the Pacific Coast and Rocky Mountain States* (Washington, D.C.: U.S. Government Printing Office, 1911), p. 565; Table 2, p. 579.

24. Kathleen Weiler, *Country Schoolwomen: Teaching in Rural California, 1850–1950* (Stanford, Calif.: Stanford University Press, 1998), p. 90.

25. Hohenthal et al., *Streams in a Thirsty Land,* pp. 72–131, 148–149. Also see reference in Valerie J. Matsumoto, *Farming the Home Place: A Japanese American Community in California, 1919–1982* (Ithaca, N.Y.: Cornell University Press, 1993) to estimates of ethnic populations from Betty Frances Brown, "The Evacuation of the Japanese Population from a California Agricultural Community" (master's thesis, Stanford University, 1944); "Merced, California and the San Joaquin Valley" (reprint of article in *Emanu-El,* San Francisco, November 22, 1895, p. 10), *Western States Jewish Historical Quarterly* 5, no. 1 (1972): 61.

26. *Reports of the Immigration Commission, Volume 24, Immigrants in Industries, Part 25,* Table 13, p. 659; Weiler, *Country Schoolwomen,* pp. 100–106.

27. Hohenthal et al., *Streams in a Thirsty Land,* ch. X–XIX.

28. Matsumoto, *Farming the Home Place,* pp. 25–31.

29. Manuscripts in the Nisaburo Aibara collection, Special Collections and University Archives of the Vasche Library, California State University, Stanislaus.

30. James A. Henretta, "The Morphology of New England Society in the Colonial Period," *Journal of Interdisciplinary History* 2 (1971): 379–398.

31. Oscar Handlin, *The Uprooted: The Epic Story of the Great Migrations that Made the American People* (Boston: Little, Brown, 1972), 2nd Ed., p. 317; Gregory R. Woirol, *In the Floating Army: F. C. Mills on Itinerant Life in California, 1914* (Urbana: University of Illinois Press, 1992), pp. 5–12.

32. Computed from U.S. Census Bureau, *Chinese and Japanese in the U. S., 1910* (Washington, D. C.: U. S. Government Printing Office, 1914), Table 54, pp. 26–29; Table 26, p. 14.

33. Ronald T. Takaki, *Pau Hana: Plantation Life and Labor in Hawaii, 1835–1920* (Honolulu: University of Hawaii Press, 1983), pp. 129–131, 145–152, 153–176.

34. Sylvia Junko Yanagisako, *Transforming the Past: Tradition and Kinship among Japanese Americans* (Stanford: Stanford University Press, 1985), pp. 8–9. Also see S. Frank Miyamoto, *Social Solidarity of the Japanese in Seattle* (Seattle: University of Washington Press, 1939, 1981), Part III; Linda Tamura, *The Hood River Issei: An Oral History of Japanese Settlers in Oregon's Hood River Valley* (Urbana: University of Illinois Press, 1993), Preface; Yukiko Kimura, *Issei: Japanese Immigrants in Hawaii* (Honolulu: University of Hawaii Press, 1988), ch. 1.

35. For the relation of genealogy and diaspora, see Engseng Ho, *The Graves of Tarim: Genealogy and Mobility across the Indian Ocean* (Berkeley: University of California Press, 2006), Part II.

36. Bernice B. H. Kim, "Koreans in Hawaii" (master's thesis, University of Hawaii, 1937), Table IV, p. 101.

37. H. Brett Melendy, "Filipinos," in Stephan Thernstrom, ed., *Harvard Encyclopedia of American Ethnic Groups* (Cambridge, Mass.: Harvard University Press, 1980), p. 360.

38. Sucheng Chan, *This Bittersweet Soil: The Chinese in California Agriculture, 1860–1910* (Berkeley: University of California Press, 1986), p. 386.

39. Chan, *This Bittersweet Soil*, pp. 328–329.

40. Chan, *This Bittersweet Soil*, pp. 386–399.

41. *Reports of the Immigration Commission, Volume 24, Immigrants in Industries, Part 25*, Table 8, p. 328.

42. Betty Lee Sung, *Gold Mountain: The Story of the Chinese in America* (New York: Macmillan, 1967), p. 240; Thomas Sowell, *Ethnic America: A History* (NewYork: Basic Books, 1981), p. 139.

43. Milton R. Konvitz, *The Alien and the Asiatic in American Law* (Ithaca, N.Y.: Cornell University Press, 1946), pp. 231–232.

44. Paul Ong, "Chinese Labor in Early San Francisco: Racial Segmentation and Economic Expansion," in Genny Lim, ed., *The Chinese American Experience; Papers from the Second National Conference on Chinese American Studies* (San Francisco, 1984), pp. 91–92; Chan, *This Bittersweet Soil*, pp. 58–86.

45. June Mei, "Socioeconomic Developments Among the Chinese in San Francisco, 1848–1906," in Lucie Cheng and Edna Bonacich, eds., *Labor Immigration Under Capitalism: Asian Workers in the United States Before World War II* (Berkeley: University of California Press, 1984), pp. 378–392.

46. U.S. Census, *Chinese and Japanese in the U.S., 1910*, Table 57, pp. 33–35. Also see Rose Hum Lee, "The Decline of Chinatowns in the United States," *American Journal of Sociology* Vol. 54, No. 5 (March 1949): 422–432.

47. Shih-shan Henry Tsai, *The Chinese Experience in America* (Bloomington: Indiana University Press, 1986), p. 105.

48. Adam McKeown, *Chinese Migrant Networks and Cultural Change: Peru, Chicago, Hawaii 1900–1936* (Chicago: University of Chicago Press, 2001), p. 33.

49. Lawrence H. Fuchs, *Hawaii Pono: A Social History* (New York: Harper and Row, 1961), ch. 3.

50. McKeown, *Chinese Migrant Networks*, pp. 32–33.

51. Robert Bellah, in *Tokugawa Religion: The Cultural Roots of Modern Japan* (New York: The Free Press, 1957), pp. 194–197, has described the modern Japanese population as having an ethic of economic productivity that was a byproduct of religion in the Tokugawa Era.

52. William Petersen, *Japanese Americans: Oppression and Success* (New York: Random House, 1971), p. 23.

53. Fuchs, *Hawaii Pono*, pp. 117, 123.

54. Masayo Umezawa Duus, *The Japanese Conspiracy: The O'ahu Sugar Strike of 1920* (Berkeley: University of California Press, 1999), ch. 2–4.

55. Rob Wilson and Arif Dirlik, *Asia/Pacific as Space of Cultural Production* (Durham, N.C.: Duke University Press, 1995), p. 8.

56. Petersen, *Japanese Americans*, pp. 28–29.

57. Edna Bonacich and John Modell, *The Economic Basis of Ethnic Solidarity: Small Business in the Japanese American Community* (Berkeley: University of California Press, 1980), pp. 47–48.

58. Nisaburo Aibara collection, Special Collections and University Archives, Vasche Library, California State University, Stanislaus.

59. *Reports of the Immigration Commission, Volume 24, Immigrants in Industries, Part 25*, Table 11, p. 635.

60. Michi Weglyn, *Years of Infamy: The Untold Story of America's Concentration Camps* (New York: Morrow Quill Paperbacks, 1980), p. 37.

61. *Reports of the Immigration Commission, Volume 24, Immigrants in Industries, Part 25*, Table 12, p. 653.

62. John Modell, The *Economics and Politics of Racial Accommodation, 1900–1942 (Urbana: University of Illinois Press, 1977)*, p. 2.

63. *Reports of the Immigration Commission, Volume 24, Immigrants in Industries, Part 25*, Table 18, p. 381.

64. Bonacich and Modell, *The Economic Basis of Ethnic Solidarity*, p. 4.

65. Ivan H. Light, *Ethnic Enterprise in America: Business and Welfare among Chinese, Japanese, and Blacks* (Berkeley: University of California Press, 1972).

66. Kanichi Kawasaki, "The Japanese Community of East San Pedro, Terminal Island, California" (master's thesis, University of Southern California, 1931), Table V, p. 17; Olivier Zunz, *The Changing Face of Inequality: Urbanization, Industrial Development, and Immigrants in Detroit, 1880–1920* (Chicago: University of Chicago Press, 1982), ch. 7.

67. Taishi Matsumoto, "The Protest of a Professional Carrot Washer," *Kashu Mainichi* (April 4, 1937), cited in Modell, *Economics*.

68. Konvitz, *Alien and the Asiatic in American Law*, pp. 231–232.

69. Bonacich and Modell, *The Economic Basis of Ethnic Solidarity*, pp. 13–19.

70. Harry H. L. Kitano contrasts the Hawaiian Japanese pattern of local community with the mainland Japanese middleman minority in "Japanese Americans: The Development of a Middleman Minority," in Norris Hundley, Jr., ed., *The Asian American: The Historical Experience* (Santa Barbara: ABC-CLIO, 1976).

71. James N. Gregory, *American Exodus: The Dust Bowl Migration and Okie Culture in California* (New York: Oxford University Press, 1989), ch. 2.

72. Brooks, *Alien Neighbors, Foreign Friends*, pp. 27–28.

73. Lawrence H. Fuchs, *The American Kaleidoscope: Race, Ethnicity, and the Civic Culture* (Hanover, N.H.: Wesleyan University Press, 1990), ch. 7.

74. Nathan Glazer, "The Politics of a Multiethnic Society," in Lance Liebman, ed., *Ethnic Relations in America* (Englewood Cliffs, N.J.: Prentice-Hall, 1982), p. 133; Mae Ngai, *Impossible Subjects: Illegal Aliens and the Making of Modern America* (Princeton: Princeton University Press, 2004), pp. 3–9.

75. Brooks, *Alien Neighbors, Foreign Friends*, ch. 2.

THREE

TRANSPLANTATION AND TRANSCULTURATION

"The telling fact, however, is not that the immigrant colony maintains its old-world cultural organization, but that in its new environment it mediates a cultural adjustment to its new situation."[1]

Robert E. Park and Ernest W. Burgess, *The City*

Asian immigrants were innovators of techniques for transplanting and adapting assets from their homelands to their new settlements in the American far west. They effectively transferred skill sets and social capital for building careers, families, and communities through transnational corridors connected to their places of origin. Asian immigrants turned their enclaves into outposts for homeland practices and traditions that continued to be useful, but they had a practical attitude about combining them with new life strategies learned from their American surroundings.

Asian immigrants created a new diversity of the public sphere by founding institutions dedicated to their community life. They established hundreds of houses of worship for Buddhist, Shinto, Confucian, Taoist, Sikh, and Christian faiths that brought an ethical and civilizing spiritual influence to raw frontier areas. Chinese temples, often called "Joss" houses (a term that was a distortion of the Portuguese word for god, "Deos"), were central institutions in Chinese communities. Temples "constituted an important part of the social landscape in Chinese communities," according to historian Yong Chen, even in small, remote Chinatowns in the far west. San Francisco Chinatown had ten joss houses in the late nineteenth century. One of the earliest temples was established in Spofford Alley and dedicated to the "boddhisatva" (a type of saint intercessor) Guan Yin, a female deity who was derived from the Hindu deity Avalokitesvara. This deity's journey from temples in India to the streets of San Francisco's Chinatown reflected the intertwining of Buddhism and migration in global history.[2] Waverly Street was named "Queen-of-Heaven Street" by Chinese residents, after a female deity brought from southern China who supported sailors and the art of navigation.

The fraternal organizations of Chinatown, the hui, and the stores of merchants maintained their own religious shrines on their premises.[3] The Hawaiian Islands alone had nearly one hundred Buddhist temples. The skyline of Honolulu became crowded with the facades and roofs of Indian-inspired, stupa-like Buddhist churches and Shinto shrines with their distinctive wooden gateways.[4] The Chinese American community established the first Christian Chinese Church on King Street close to downtown Honolulu and a Chinese cemetery in the Manoa Valley near the University of Hawaiʻi campus.

The keystone that extended transnational cultural connectivity across the generations was the Asian language school with regular enrollments, faculties, and classrooms (Table 3-1). The Hongwanji Buddhist temple of Honolulu's Pali neighborhood operated a full-scale parochial high school with instruction in the Japanese language and a curriculum taught by faculty educated in Japan. Japanese language schools of Hawaiʻi in small rural communities at times had students from European, Polynesian, and other Asian backgrounds because they provided proper schooling where educational opportunities were rare (Figure 3-1). The parents wanted their children to be educated in a proper school even though they were taught to learn the Japanese language.

The Japanese Benevolent Society, a philanthropic organization of the Japanese American community, built a Japanese hospital in the Kapalama neighborhood of Honolulu in 1900 called the Japanese Charity Hospital. It originally provided free care to Japanese immigrant plantation laborers who were displaced by a fire in Chinatown. With thirty-eight beds, this facility treated patients in a setting with Japanese-style food, hygiene, and furnishings. The Japanese Charity Hospital expanded its services to meet increasing demand and relocated in 1917 to a Honolulu suburb.

Asian immigrants kept homeland culture flowing into their neighborhoods by establishing newspapers, radio stations for news and entertainment, theaters, and musical groups. Chinese and Japanese immigrants moved quickly to create national-language community newspapers. The number of Chinese-language newspapers published in the United States grew from two in 1880 to ten in 1930; Japanese-language newspapers increased from two in 1900 to sixteen in 1930.[5] The advent of radio broadcasting provided a new source for receiving popular culture from the homeland. In Los Angeles, the San Francisco Bay area, and the Central Valley of California, eager listeners tuned in to the broadcasts of Japanese-language radio stations. They hired Japanese broadcasters and disc jockeys to provide the news, music, and radio shows of the homeland. The stations KGMB and KGU supplied a similar service to the Japanese American radio market in Hawaiʻi, which had the largest listening audience in the islands.[6]

Like immigrants from Germany in the American midwest, Japanese immigrants had a taste in their new communities for European classical music, which was already popular in Japan. In the Japanese enclave of East San Pedro, California, dozens of families owned and played pianos and violins for home entertainment and for the cultural enrichment of their children, while also

Table 3-1.   Language Schools in Hawaiian Islands, 1920s.

Language Schools Showing Schools, Teachers, and Pupils by Islands December 31, 1926

Schools	No.	Teachers			Pupils		
		Male	Fem.	Total	Male	Fem.	Total
Hawaiʻi	60	83	63	146	3600	3496	7096
Maui	29	33	34	67	1934	1756	3690
Oʻahu	60	141	93	234	8416	7569	15985
Kauaʻi	21	31	16	47	1283	1233	2516
Molokai	2	2	—	2	48	42	90
Lanai	1	1	—	1	40	39	79
Totals	173	291	196	497	15321	14135	29456

	1924–25	1925–26
Number of licensed schools	78	84
Chinese	10	13
Korean	10	11
Japanese	58	60

Language Schools, Showing Enrollment by Grades, December 31, 1926

	Haw.	Maui	Kauaʻi	Molokai	Lanai	Honolulu	Rural Oʻahu	Totals
Kindgtn.	393	85	—	—	—	399	71	948
1	1256	758	659	28	15	2229	1004	5949
2	1018	647	431	17	25	1557	888	4583
3	956	600	301	12	20	1433	680	4002
4	812	364	236	14	4	1306	478	3214
5	759	337	253	9	5	936	417	2716
6	695	349	239	7	5	993	459	2747
7	495	232	196	3	4	873	352	2155
8	451	211	165	—	1	756	246	1830
9	162	67	30	—	—	426	107	792
10	74	37	2	—	—	265	27	405
11	25	3	1	—	—	46	9	84
12	—	—	3	—	—	28	—	31
Totals	7096	3690	2516	90	79	11247	4738	29456

Source: Territory of Hawaii, Department of Public Instruction, Bienniel Report, 1925–1926.

keeping up their skill on the "shaku-hachi" and "yodo bue," traditional Japanese instruments. In Honolulu, children of Chinese and Japanese immigrants by the droves took lessons in Western classical instruments and performed works by

Figure 3-1. Japanese language school students in rural Kaua'i with students of different ancestries in back row.

Western composers in youth orchestral groups. The student orchestra of the University of Hawaii featured Asian American musicians such as the violinist known as R. Tamashiro. Pianist Yuriko Yamamoto played at a reception for Madame Tamaki Miura, an opera singer from Japan, and Helen T. and Dorothy Morita formed a singing and piano duet. The Nuuanu YMCA of Honolulu provided a regular venue for young Asian American performers who were accomplished in European classical music.[7]

The novelty of the phonograph brought up-to-date popular culture from Japan into the homes of Japanese immigrants. A visiting sociologist found that "the Japanese want to hear the Japanese songs which are popular in Japan at the present time, and the phonograph is the most convenient way to satisfy this desire." Interviews with Japanese immigrants in San Pedro, California, drew comments that showed the phonograph to be the preferred entertainment medium of the foreign born.[8]

"We know all kinds of popular songs which are being sung in Japan recently. You know why? Because the phonograph brings them to us."

"In my experience the best musical invention is the phonograph, because it creates a harmonious family atmosphere for us."

"We spend a considerable amount of money for records every month, but never feel that we spend our money in a foolish way."

"I cannot understand American songs, therefore, I do not enjoy listening to them. But, oh, Japanese songs! Do you feel that way?"

"Right now [the phonograph] is for my husband and me rather than our child."

The phonograph that supplied the music of the home country also brought American popular songs into the living room. According to a Japanese parent,

> "It is hard to get the children to stay home after supper; I am never troubled to do so since we bought our phonograph. Of course I bought a number of English records for them."

The rise of a trans-Pacific circuit for live theater provided perhaps the most exciting vehicle for bringing homeland cultural models and ideal-type behavior to Asian American communities. In the growing Chinatowns of the mainland, theaters that provided venues for performances of traditional Chinese music and plays also served as community centers for informal socialization (Figure 3-2a). Surveying the immigrant theater in San Francisco Chinatown, which was established by the first wave of Chinese in the Gold Rush years, historian Yong Chen provided a vivid description of this institution as follows:

> For the immigrants theatergoing meant re-experiencing a host of cultural traditions. Besides historical events, gods from Chinese folk religion were often featured in the drama, and sometimes statues of them stood in the theater hall to "witness and preside over the performance." . . . As early as 1852 a regular Chinese dramatic company started to perform "pieces in their native language." In 1853 another

Figure 3-2. (a) Stage and interior of the Chinese Theater on Jackson Street, San Francisco, c. 1885.

theater was opened. The 1870s was a golden period for the immigrant theater. In September 1875 there were eleven Chinese troupes in San Francisco, each of which had 28 players. The names of these players printed in the Chinese newspaper indicate that a number of them were women. In the late 1870s and early 1880s the Chinese American community supported four regular theaters. . . .

An English visitor to the Chinese immigrant theater noted that the dramas performed often combined historical themes with moral messages and instructions.[9]

As Asian Americans gained social mobility in Hawai'i, they patronized movie theaters that were a far cry from the makeshift tent shows of silent film first started on the plantations.[10] In Honolulu's Chinatown, the Chinese Theater opened in 1903 and was rebuilt in 1920 to show movies from China. The Toyo Theater for Japanese cinema which opened nearby was designed architecturally to replicate the mausoleum shrine of the first Tokugawa shogun in Nikko, Japan (Figure 3-2b). Every week, immigrant parents took their children to the movies to view noble samurai warriors (portrayed by actors like Ichikawa Utaemon and Okouchi Denjiro) and lady-like heroines inspiring patience and endurance (portrayed by Takamine Hideko). Movies that would have affirmed the cultural orthodoxy of the homeland achieved a new meaning in America where Asian Americans felt socially marginalized and unrepresented in American popular culture. Kung fu schools with their fiercely devoted boxer fighters, and the loyal samurai band who fought to the last man defending the castle became inspiring models of manly valor; the samurai wife and woman warrior (portrayed by Misora Hibari) were symbols of feminine strength and virtue.

Figure 3-2.   (b) The Toyo movie theater of Honolulu.

NETWORKS FOR SOCIAL CAPITAL

Asian immigrants met the challenge of transplanting traditions of mutualism—highly developed interdependent social relations among individuals that supported collective well-being—to a new and isolating environment in the Pacific far west. Traditional Chinese mutualism which was practiced in homogeneous home communities had to be adapted to work with immigrants from a diversity of regions in south China, each with local dialects and cultural traditions. Regional identity was interwoven with occupational differentiation in Chinese American communities, producing sharp divisions by customs and wealth. The merchant class stood above the small shopkeepers and craftsmen who formed the middling stratum. The laboring classes tended to come from a range of districts both urban and rural in south China. Particular regional subgroups dominated certain occupations, for example the Hakka in barbering and the San-yi people in wholesaling, the garment industry, and other manufacturing enterprises in Chinatowns.[11]

Chinese immigrants continued to think of themselves in terms of the particularistic communities from which they had emigrated. Tensions existed between the rural Cantonese and the urban Cantonese, and between all the Cantonese and the Hakka. Different communities spoke in distinctive dialects. Many rural Cantonese were speakers of the Toisanese dialect, while the urban Cantonese spoke the standardized version of Cantonese. The Hakkas had migrated from the north of China several centuries before Chinese immigration to the United States started and spoke a dialect related to Mandarin. Hakkas were especially numerous in Hawai'i, where they composed 25 percent of the Chinese population; in the mainland United States they made up 10 percent of the Chinese.

Mutual benefit fraternal societies known as "hui" formed on the basis of district, dialect, and kin groupings. They resembled overseas transplantations of "hometown" associations in China that evolved and changed to meet new communal needs in America. The most powerful hui in the United States were the Six Companies of San Francisco which grew out of a complex series of consolidations of smaller hui. The Six Companies provided reception and hospitality to newcomers and registered the names and addresses of Chinese in the United States. A comparison of their enumerations to the U.S. federal census suggests that Chinese immigrants in the nineteenth century were probably significantly undercounted. For example, in 1876 the Six Companies' rolls showed a total Chinese population of 160,000, while the U.S. Census of 1880 showed only 105,000.[12]

For Chinese immigrants, the Six Companies served as their political leadership and judicial arbitrator. They functioned as a type of quasi-government for a community made up of immigrants who had been denied American citizenship and a mainstream political role and public status. They settled disputes within the Chinese community and gave legal representation in disputes between Chinese and members of the surrounding society. In the minds of ordinary laborers, the Six Companies embodied the familiar institutional justice and political wisdom of the Chinese homeland, while they also represented the Chinese in American courts of law and local civic affairs.

Another mutual aid association, the tong, became a rival of the hui in the Chinatowns. Unlike the huis, the tongs were based on voluntary ties, not previous roots or places of origin. Those who often sought tong membership had existed on the social margins of the Chinese community and appreciated the tong's role as a rough democratizing influence. Historian H. Mark Lai explained:

> Membership in a tong was based on a fraternal principle that accorded the same treatment to every member and disregarded social status, clan ties, or locality or origin. Formed for mutual aid and protection, the tongs appealed especially to those who lacked money and influence, did not belong to a powerful clan, had some grievance, or were alienated from the established social system. Their rivalry with the clan and district associations included an element of rebellion against domination by affluent merchants.[13]

The Japanese Association was the protective civic organization of immigrants from Japan, the Issei (the first generation). Each local Japanese community had a Japanese Association. Because these local organizations had similar structures and functions, a member of a Japanese Association in Pocatello, Idaho, who moved to San Francisco could easily fit into a Japanese Association there. Association membership was restricted to men, and their leaders were usually those Issei who had achieved the greatest economic success in the community. Holding office was prestigious, and elections were fiercely competitive. The Associations raised funds, sponsored picnics, provided interpreters, participated in American patriotic parades, cared for cemeteries, and supplied a variety of social welfare services. They were especially concerned with upholding the reputation of the Japanese as good and loyal citizens in the U.S., and they functioned as an informal constabulary in the community.

In addition to the Japanese Associations, the Issei formed ascriptive "kenjinkai" prefectural organizations, such as the Hiroshima kenjinkai, which included as members all immigrants from that particular prefecture. They organized churches—Buddhist, Shinto, and Christian—with all-Japanese congregations, religious youth clubs, and women's auxiliaries, and they established Japanese language schools. Kenjinkai provided study and hobby groups for activities such as flower arranging, cooking, martial arts, and fishing derbies."[14]

MUTUALISM AND COMMUNITY DEVELOPMENT

Based on associational life in their native districts, various mutual-benefit organizations of Chinese and Japanese immigrants in their new communities were templates for maintaining the cultural orientation of the homeland. Familiar values of justice and honor were preserved in the operating procedures of these societies. Confucian, Buddhist, Shinto, and Taoist ideas about values, customs, and behavior survived in these institutions. The organizations formed a society that was a welcome haven of protection and friendship in an often hostile and lawless frontier country.

Equally important were the workings of the mutual associations as vehicles for responding in an organized fashion to new economic opportunities in the wage labor market and the field of business enterprise.[15] Chinese and Japanese immigrants counted on the trust and reliability of associational members as employees and partners. Chinese hui and Japanese organizations known as "tanomoshi" became informal pooling arrangements of individual members' capital that served as a source of credit and loans. Members of the hui and tanomoshi borrowed money from the pooled savings of all members on a rotating basis, which they utilized to finance small business enterprises.

The hui and tanomoshi institutionalized the principle of collectivism in the social relationships of economic activity.[16] For example, messages of the secretaries of the kenjinkai read as follows:

> "[Indigents] were the ones who never joined any organizations, such as the Japanese Association, kenjinkai, trade association, or social club. They were not members of any religious organizations. They were transients who . . . spent money for their own pleasures. They never helped anybody when they were young and able; they were so selfish that they could not make friends in their lives. . . . It seems to be that [indigents] are the people who have the wrong attitudes toward life and society. . . . Always [indigents] were people who despised the works of the association and laughed at those who are members. . . . Yes, members [of the ken organization] help one another as far as they can. But it is strange enough that members never get in financial trouble."

External societal forces strengthened the imperative to economic mutualism among Asians. Mutualist association was required because there was little opportunity for advancement in the external fields of industrial labor and employment in white-owned businesses and uncertainty about obtaining services from mainstream banks and insurance companies. The Chinese and Japanese, who lacked the access to mainstream opportunities and services available to European immigrants, were greatly dependent on the internal services of the ethnic community, on its economy and its institutions. It should be noted, however, that European immigrants also utilized kin and ethnic ties to organize mutualist benevolent societies. For example, a study has shown that in a sample of New York City immigrant groups, over two-thirds of Russian, Bohemian, and Austrian wage earners, and nearly a third of Italian and German wage earners, belonged to ethnic "lodges" for mutual assistance; about one-half of Polish, Scandinavian, Irish, and Bohemian heads of families in Chicago in 1919 belonged to fraternal associations that provided life insurance. But these European ethnic groups had broader avenues for employment and business services than Asian immigrants, who had to rely on the internal collective supports of the Asian community.[17]

The mutualist practices of Asian immigrant associations demonstrated the utility of ethnic social relations as social capital in overcoming what political scientist Robert D. Putnam has called "dilemmas of collective action," by "facilitating coordinated actions" and "civic engagement" with community life. As immigrants, they brought a preexisting collectivist social construct for coordinating group activity. Putnam has noted, "Voluntary cooperation is easier in a community that has inherited a substantial stock of social capital."[18]

TRANSCULTURAL SPACES

Immigrant enclaves became experimental spaces of transplantation, modification, and innovation for migrating cultural heritages and skill sets. The Asian thrift ethic and work ethic transplanted and invigorated by new challenges were a source of community pride. On Hawai'i's plantations, immigrant families started household production of clothing. Japanese wives who were skilled seamstresses sewed everyday work and household garments; the most skilled sewed fine fabrics into attire for the plantation owner's family. Artisanal skills brought into immigrant communities had major effects on the surrounding built environment. Japanese carpenters constructed and repaired plantation housing and facilities and raised industrial structures such as the famous aqueduct north of Hilo on the "big island" known as the "Onomea high cane flume" which was pictured in tourist postcards (Figure 3-3). They produced finished carpentry, making furniture such as the "safe," a storage cabinet found in every plantation laborer's home.

In Hawai'i and in the far western United States, Chinese immigrants brought their experience with techniques for farming and mining. Coming from southern China, where hilly agricultural land and water control had been shaped by collective efforts for generations, they built up arable land areas in the plantations of Hawai'i and in the intersection of the Sacramento and San Joaquin Rivers in California. Chinese miners who flocked to the California Gold Rush adapted skills, learned in farming in China and in nearby regions where Chinese laborers had previously worked in mining, to the excavation and extraction techniques of mining in the American far west.

Figure 3-3. Onomea high cane flume.

Situated at an interoceanic crossroads, the Hawaiian Islands became an active ground for the process of transculturation between the civilizations of the Atlantic and Pacific basin. In his study of the "colonial crucible" of Latin America, John Charles Chasteen has provided a description of transculturation as "the formation of new and distinctive" cultures, "fusions of two or more elements" in "kaleidoscopic combinations" that emerge gradually from a "give-and-take process." "Imagine transculturation," Chasteen posited, "as a thousand tiny confrontations and tacit negotiations taking place in people's daily lives, always within the force field of hierarchy and domination." He noted, "The people on top are usually able to impose the broad outlines of things . . . with those below contributing subtle aspects more difficult to police from above: style, rhythm, texture, mood." As in colonial Latin America, transculturation in the Hawaiian Islands was imbedded in a continuous process of contested interaction involving indigenous people and newcomers.[19]

The settlers from the Atlantic region brought new customs, styles, and artifacts that syncretized the local island culture. The Portuguese made "malasada" (fried dough) and "pao dulce" (sweet bread) into staples of local foodways. The cowboy subculture of Hawaiian cattle ranches was created by Spanish-Mexican "vaqueros" brought in to train locals who called them "Paniolos," a nickname that was a corruption of "espanole" or "Hispaniola." The Hawaiian ukulele, a kind of miniature guitar used in musical performance and dance, developed out of the "cavaquinho" brought by Portuguese immigrants. Music produced by the slack-key guitar sprang from a fusion of Hispanic and Polynesian elements into new forms of instrumentation and music.[20]

Missionaries, plantation owners, and ranch owners introduced elements of New England architectural style to the built environment of the Hawaiian islands. The cattle magnate John Palmer Parker built his ranch home in the "saltbox" style found in communities of coastal Massachusetts. The Reverend Asa Thurston worked with Hawaiian Christians to erect the Mokuʻaikaua Congregational Church in Kailua-Kona on the "big island" of Hawaiʻi, designed to have the exterior and interior form of a classic Congregational church of a small New England town. (See Chapter 1, this volume, Figure 1-3.) The building materials, however, completely reflected local Hawaiian environs. A visitor's guide to this historic site provides a vivid description of a construction that combined New England architecture with Hawaiʻi's natural ecological assets:

"Someone has described the interior of the church as an ohia forest, for all the posts and beams are of a native Hawaiian tree species called ohia. . . . The pews, the pulpit, wooden screens and railings are constructed out of another indigenous tree known as koa, sometimes referred to as Hawaiian mahogany. The church walls are of lava rock cemented together by mortar made by mixing sand and lime. The lime came from burnt and crushed coral. Natives gathered the coral from the sea. . . . For years the native fishermen have used our church steeple [112 feet high] as the most prominent landmark. The designer of the church . . . decided well the arrangement of the building, for the ocean breeze, which comes from the west, literally flows through the entire length of the church, providing a natural air conditioning system."

Perhaps the most pervasive daily aspect of transculturation was the "pidgin" English spoken by all who lived in Hawaiʻi, which developed from the social atmosphere of the labor gangs of the plantations. The Portuguese "luna," or overseer, played a key role in cobbling together "pidgin," which was first used in communications with laborers from China, Japan, Korea, and the Philippines. A new local vernacular arose from the combination of a vocabulary of basic English words with terms drawn from the Hawaiian language, Portuguese, and other immigrant languages. It quickly became the everyday parlance of Hawaiʻi, a rough, lower class Pacific version of Swahili.

Transculturation also reconfigured the public and civic culture of Hawaiʻi. Modern Hawaiian institutions emerged from the vision of Hawaiʻi as a place to be civilized by Protestant Christianity and Western education. It was fitting that when James Michener wrote his best-selling novel, *Hawaii*,[21] in the 1950s, he was inspired by a visit and stay in Walpole, New Hampshire, to frame the backdrop to his saga in terms of the calling of New England missionaries.[22] New England had played a large role in creating the imagined Pacific image of Hawaiʻi since the days when the first Congregationalist missionaries embarked from Boston on voyages to the Kona coast of the "Big Island" and the crews of whaling ships set sail from New Bedford for Lahaina, Maui.[23] Transplanted Yankee religious elites successfully proselytized the indigenous Hawaiian people and made them into a Christian community in less than a century. They also laid the modern foundations of Hawaiian education by fostering public school systems based on the common school of Massachusetts and Connecticut and by sponsoring independent schools modeled on New England preparatory schools.

Settlers in Hawaiʻi from the Atlantic region also learned to adapt to a new and unfamiliar environment being created by the transculturative relationships among themselves and their Asian and Polynesian neighbors. An experimental and innovative attitude held the key to success in the Hawaiian Islands. For example, his ability to assimilate to Hawaiʻi's multicultural styles enabled John A. Burns, an Irish Catholic newcomer from Montana, to become the trusted political mentor to Japanese American leaders and other local politicians whose support he needed in the drive for Hawaiʻi statehood in 1959 and his successful run to become Hawaiʻi's first popularly elected Governor. Over several generations, transculturative processes working at various levels of local life produced a trend toward cultural unification. The diverse settler communities of Hawaiʻi came to share a common diet and culinary style. New Englanders, Europeans, and Hispanics from the Atlantic world witnessed the new sights of Asian neighbors tending ducks, wet rice, soybean, and "oriental" produce, and Hawaiians farming taro and fishing with a spear and net. They found surprising, strange, and sometimes repugnant the food-preparation styles and dishes from the Pacific such as mashed taro root ("poi"), rice balls ("musubi"), noodle soup ("saimin" and "udon"), tofu, dim sum ("manapua"), fish cakes ("kamaboko"), "barbecue" meat, curry, pickled cabbage ("kimchee"), pickled onion ("rakkyo"), and pickled radish ("takuan"). But through myriad experiences of sampling and sharing each other's food, the various communities of Hawaiʻi would develop a common taste and culinary style called "local food." A breakfast would consist of American-style sunny-side up eggs, Portuguese sausage ("chorizos"), and Chinese fried rice; while lunch might include "spam musubi" made from a ball of boiled Japanese rice topped by a slice of American spam held in place by a wrapping of Japanese or Korean roasted, dried seaweed.[24] As recent studies have demonstrated, foodways and food production have revealed a great deal about the social history of ethnic interactions.[25]

The cumulative, unifying effect of the continuous transculturation of Atlantic and Pacific elements diffused through the multiple facets of the everyday world in the Hawaiian Islands. Newcomers from the outside became familiar with Hawaiian bark-cloth ("tapa") garments, Japanese farming implements, and footwear such as flip-flops ("zori") and platform shoes ("getta"). They grew accustomed to the presence of the mongoose, myna bird, bulbul bird, shama bird, ti plant, mango, and banyan tree—all imported from South Asia and ubiquitous in the everyday environment.[26] Newcomers from Atlantic communities encountered an Asia-Pacific–built environment in the Buddhist and Shinto temples, graveyards, tong society lodge houses, Japanese gardens, Hawaiian-style cottages, and a Protestant church in Honolulu built in form of a medieval Japanese castle. Their descendants in the twentieth century would see, within a few miles of downtown Honolulu, public statues of a Buddhist sage, the monarch King Kamehameha I (who unified the Hawaiian Islands), and Indian independence leader Mohandas K. Gandhi, a hero to the prominent Hawaiian Indian merchant, Gulab Watumull.[27]

The salience of transculturation in Hawai'i also had an important demographic byproduct in the form of widespread interracial marriage. Hawai'i's cross-cultural pluralism fostered a tolerant atmosphere for racially mixed marriages. People of European ancestry who came to Hawai'i from the United States, the other Americas, and Europe intermarried with indigenous Hawaiians and immigrants from Asia. In the 1920s, of marriages involving white males, 24 percent were interracial; and of marriages involving white females, 14 percent were interracial. By 1985, rates of intermarriage had risen higher: 38 percent of marriages involving white males were interracial, as were 28 percent involving white females.[28] Due substantially to interracial marriages involving whites, the U.S. Census of 2000, which enumerated multiracial populations for the first time, revealed that Hawai'i had by far the highest proportion of multiracial people of any state. The proportion of "the Two or more Races Population" in Hawai'i was 21.0 percent; while the next highest states were Alaska with 5.4 percent, California with 4.7 percent, and Oklahoma with 4.5 percent. (The national proportion of multiracial people was 2.4 percent.) These statistics bore out why Hawai'i was called the melting pot of races in the twentieth century.[29]

The pattern of modern Hawaiian history can be seen as the beginning of a new interoceanic world in which the western hemisphere came to share a wide interconnecting framework of collective life with countries in Asia. As the Hawaiian Islands became a local site for the intermingling of elements from the Atlantic, Pacific, and Indian Ocean worlds, it grew into a platform for multiplying and intensifying interregional exchange processes, a geographic accelerator for new worldwide movements of trade, population, and capital. As the Atlantic world extended its influences through economic, migratory, and ecological corridors that shaped a gradually integrating Pacific region in the nineteenth century, the Pacific world concurrently penetrated into the Atlantic through mass migration and trade. A key pattern in this Pacific-to-Atlantic movement was the influx of Chinese, Japanese, and Indian immigrants who settled throughout North America, South America, and the Caribbean basin. Canada, the United States, Mexico, Cuba, Trinidad, Peru, Chile, Guyana, and Brazil became home to sizable populations of workers and merchants from China, Japan, and India. By providing labor and transoceanic commercial contacts, Asian immigrants were crucial in the development of these Atlantic societies.[30]

Asian American communities functioned as safe vantage points in transnational space for Asian reformers and revolutionaries to learn about the West and plan the political reform of their homelands. European ethnic communities in the United States had also functioned as havens for displaced political leaders. Carl Schurz, a refugee from the repression of the Revolution of 1848, became the spokesman and first citizen of German America and dreamed of a reformed modern Germany from American shores; Leon Trotsky, the Russian revolutionary leader, sojourned in New York City while planning the future transformation of his motherland. For Chinese leaders such as Liang Qichao and Sun Yat-sen, Chinese American communities in Honolulu and San Francisco were safe havens for studying Western institutions and exploring how they could be applied to the modernization of China. An open letter from Sun Yat-sen to the Chinese community of Hilo, Hawai'i was written on September 14, 1904 to advance the transnational political mobilization of Chinese immigrants (Figure 3-4). Sun exhorted as follows:

> "Comrades in Hilo, each of my benevolent brothers. I have received the August 21 letter and am very happy to learn that you comrades are persisting in your revolutionary pursuit, disregarding hardships. This certainly makes me feel optimistic about our future. . . . It is my hope that all the comrades will exert themselves in the pursuit and mobilize the masses. I urgently ask you to increase the momentum to support the cause."

In California, students, journalists, and community leaders in the enclaves of immigrants from India established a base abroad from which they launched new political efforts opposing British colonialism. Under the leadership of Har Dayal and Sohan Singh Bhakna, they organized into the Ghadar Party, which published the "Hindustan Ghadar" newspaper in Urdu and Punjabi and operated in a transnational corridor of political mobilization (Figure 3-5). Calling for Indian independence and anticolonial militancy, the newspaper was shipped to India with immigrants returning home and was suppressed by British colonial authorities. Korean intellectuals nurtured hopes for the overthrow of Japanese colonial hegemony in their country. Pak Yong-man edited the *United Korean Weekly* in Hawai'i and tried to recruit a paramilitary cadre of independence fighters. Syngman Rhee studied and worked in the United States until he returned to Korea to

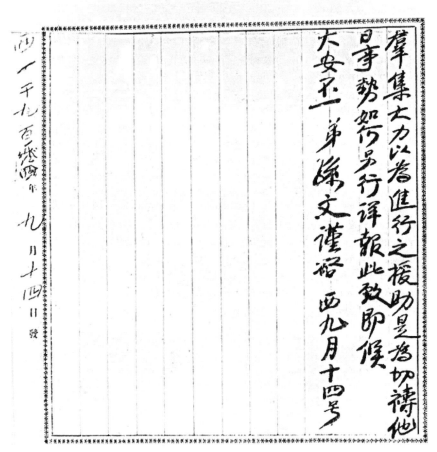

Figure 3-4. Open letter by Sun Yat-Sen, calling for transnational mobilization of overseas Chinese to seek independence for China.

become its first president in 1948. Ahn Chang-ho devised strategies for a gradual-ist transition from Japanese to Korean power. These leaders were cosmopolitan statesmen-intellectuals, marginal men who were citizens of the world. While they propagated their vision of the future of a reformed and independent home nation, communities of their countrymen asserted new public identities in the transnational spaces of local settlements in the U.S. (Figure 3-6a, b).[31]

A transoceanic perspective reveals the intensifying involvement of members of outpost societies in negotiating and advocating the political redevelopment of

Figure 3-5. Ghadar newspaper (Urdu) Vol. 1, No. 22, March 24, 1914, San Francisco, California.

colonized homelands. This transnational mobilization pursued in diasporic spaces by displaced political leaders showed how movements from home and abroad converged across oceanic regions to promote collaborative efforts for the independence and modernization of states under external domination.

Figure 3-6. Displaying public identity in the transnational spaces of America:
(a) The Sikh Temple (Gurdwara) in Stocketon, c. 1920, the first in North America;
(b) Korean American family displaying U.S. and Korean Flags.

THE CIVIC COMMUNITY OF SCHOOLS

Ethnic cultures in the United States have been compared to a kaleidoscope of old fragments resetting themselves into new and unexpected patterns under surrounding assimilation pressures.[32] Historian Timothy L. Smith noted that immigrants generally felt "learning new patterns of correct behavior" was a key "to their sense of well-being" as they built new lifeworlds in the wake of "the acts of uprooting, migration, resettlement and community-building."[33] Nowhere in the country were Asian immigrants and their descendants more creative and effective in handling the concurrent needs of entering the mainstream and of maintaining a different ethnic life than on the Pacific coast and the islands of Hawaiʻi. As a Polynesian kingdom, U.S. territory, and state, Hawaiʻi was a prototypical site for intercultural encounters and exchanges involving Asian immigrants. They could live with assimilating self-adaptation and still rededicate themselves to a unique heritage. Asian immigrants utilized the experimental spaces of new settlements that allowed them to find innovative ways to merge with the wider community while maintaining ethnic life. Asian American cultures were living, changing resources that grew in the new openings created by migratory movement and displacement.

The institutional development of schools in the U.S. Territory of Hawaii during the 1920s demonstrated how public education created a new space in which the expectations of American citizenship were learned by the children of immigrants. The major educational issues in Hawaiʻi were in large measure defined by the felt need to assimilate the children of Asian immigrants. The educational system was transformed as Asian immigrants established new families and produced a rapid increase of the school-age population. Katherine M. Cook, Chief of the Division of Special Problems in the Office of Education, wrote:

> "Many of Hawaii's elementary—and intermediate-school problems began with and had their roots in the phenomenal increase in enrollment which set in about 1900 and continued as the flood of plantation-laborers which had been flowing inward in ever-increasing numbers during the preceding decades reached school-age. Many young men who had come in earlier as unmarried laborers, young Japanese men in particular, had by that time acquired picture brides and rapidly increasing families."[34]

In 1920, a survey by the Office of Education was published that called attention to the crowded classrooms of elementary schools which sometimes held as many as fifty to sixty pupils. The *Hawaii Educational Review*, the chief organ of communication among Hawaiʻi's educators, was filled with lamentations about the shortage of teachers and facilities.[35] One teacher complained, "The demand for special help in English is so great it is impossible for one teacher to meet it."[36]

Cook noted that "demands for schoolrooms and teachers taxed the resources of the Territory beyond their possibilities" and accounted for a high drop-out and retardation rate between 1910 and 1930, but she noted that "health, character training, and citizenship" were conveyed in class. She spoke of public education as "the basic means through which . . . many different peoples learn to live together with common ideals and purposes." Her view of educational objectives accorded with those expressed by other spokespersons for Hawai'i's schools. Educational policy in Hawai'i was a response to Asian immigration in which Americanization, citizenship training, and economic usefulness grew into principal programmatic objectives. In the December 1919 issue of the *Hawaii Educational Review*, Ruth C. Shaw of the Territorial Normal School proclaimed, "The great task of mingling the brown, and the white, and the yellow and turning out American citizens, falls in a very large measure upon the public school teachers."[37] She concluded her article with an evocative summation of the ways in which the public school served the cause of Americanization:

> "Instruction in civil government, hygiene, arithmetic, geography, and sewing is good Americanism: the inculcation of patriotism through song, picture, poem and dance is good Americanism; and the flag upon the schoolhouse is also good Americanism. . . . Thus it is for each teacher of Hawaii to grasp every opportunity offered by the course of study and to exert every influence to make the children of Hawaii good future citizens of the United States."

The public school also provided extracurricular experiences for acculturation. A key device for molding student behavior to accord with American norms was the school cafeteria. Cook observed, "Cafeterias as they function in Hawaiian schools are directed toward the promotion of better standards of living, gradual and natural adjustment to American social usages . . . and the like." A bulletin published by the Department of Public Instruction read:

> "[At] lunch service, when properly and completely carried on, the child of foreign parentage has opportunity for constant practice of simple customs and ordinary social procedures so important in the everyday future life of the child. . . . Some of these social customs are 1) washing hands before eating; 2) sitting at a table or desk and eating slowly and in an orderly manner; 3) engaging in conversation of a pleasant nature during mealtimes; 4) proper use of tableware and simple tablemanners and courtesy at mealtime."[38]

The extracurriculum afforded by the cafeteria would complement health education courses, which sought to provide instruction in proper personal hygiene and awareness of public health.

Another goal set by the schools of Hawai'i was to make their pupils economically useful. Katherine M. Cook reported that the junior high schools, because most students terminated their education there, stressed "the ability to make good in some type of productive labor." Cook sometimes sounded like a lobbyist for the pineapple and sugar growers, urging that the school be "in part responsive to the particular situation in Hawaii whose individual system demands unskilled and low-cost workers wholly of agricultural variety." An economy which imported agricultural laborers from Asia demanded that public schooling be made relevant to industrial needs.

From the first arrival of New England missionaries, the leaders of the educational establishment in Hawai'i were predominantly white, middle-class, and Protestant. During field research in Hawai'i, Professor Allison Davis of the University of Chicago Education Department, the first African American to receive a tenured professorship at Chicago, found that the "great emphasis upon the more formal types of curricula of teaching, and of methods of study has been maintained primarily by the dominant group of older white teachers, who are devoted to the ideals of 19th century education, as represented by the New England preparatory school and the College of the day."[39]

The public system of education was bifurcated into a higher and lower track defined by compentence in "standard English." During his field research in Hawai'i, Professor Davis learned that "the average Japanese-, Chinese-, or Filipino-American adolescent speaks or understands three languages: a foreign language, English, and pidgin." Standard English usage was utilized as a means of academic sorting and tracking that tended to reinforce social and economic divisions. Davis pointed out that since ability in standard English was a measure of acculturation and relatively high socioeconomic standing, "The real function of the Standard schools, therefore, is largely *to sort pupils according to social classes.* . . . By definition . . . all whites are middleclass. . . ." From inception, the Standard English schools mainly enrolled white students and the most acculturated members of the various ethnic groups. Davis observed that of the non-whites, the children of Chinese Americans, the most economically successful Asian ethnic group, composed the largest share of students in Standard schools. However, children of the less acculturated and less economically mobile Japanese Americans were much more likely to be assigned to Non-Standard schools, despite the fact that they were "the most conscientious and studious ethnic group in the schools." Japanese American parents were vocal in protesting this language-based system of tracking. Finally, in 1947, the Territorial Legislature voted to repeal the law that had originally created the dual-track public school system.[40]

The language issue also led to the rise of an extensive private school network. Private schools were sponsored by parents who arrived from the mainland who worried that their children would grow up in a linguistic environment dominated by foreign languages and a pidgin form of English speech. Upper-class and middle-class white parents were concerned about the corruption of their children's linguistic and learning habits by contact with tri-lingual classmates. They responded by supporting private schools such as Punahoa and Iolani (strongholds of white Protesant elitism), St. Louis College, Sacred Heart Academy, St. Andrew's Priory, and the Mid-Pacific Institute (Table 3-2).

The elite private system of schools became Hawaiian equivalents of New England preparatory schools. Most of their graduates continued to college on the mainland. It perpetuated a class system in which whites were in a favored position. But, during his research visit in 1947, Davis found that the Chinese, Japanese,

Table 3-2.   Student Ancestry in Honolulu Secondary Schools and Territory of Hawaii, 1929

	Sacred Heart Academy (Girls)		St. Louis College (Boys)		Punahou School		McKinley High School		Territory of Hawaii Population
	N	%	N	%	N	%	N	%	%
Hawaiian	1	0.1	18	3	—	—	35	1	9
Part-Hawaiian	56	—	132	25	63	18	240	10	12
Portuguese	67	—	148	28	5	0.1	82	4	11
Puerto Rican	—	—	1	—	2	2	—	—	3
Spanish	3	0.2	4	0.1	2	—	6	0.2	0.5
Other White	36	21	60	11	243	68	232	9	16
Chinese	8	5	126	24	33	9	640	27	7
Japanese	1	0.1	30	6	8	2	1005	43	37
Korean	1	0.1	1	—	—	—	71	3	1
Filipino	1	0.1	5	0.1	—	—	20	0.8	3
Others	9	0.2	—	—	6	0.2	0.1		
Total	173	531	355	2339					

Source: Compiled from Miles E. Cary, "A Vitalized Curriculum for McKinley High School" (master's thesis, University of Hawaii, 1930), Table IX, p. 27 and Table X, p. 28.

and Korean Americans of Hawai'i were rapidly ascending to the top levels of the public system and were beginning to enroll their children in private schools.

A third set of educational institutions consisted of foreign-language schools in which Japanese language schools predominated. Japanese Americans made up over one-third of Hawai'i's population, and a large proportion of parents sent their children to Japanese language schools. The Japanese language schools became a center of controversy, much as German language schools or Irish Catholic parochial schools on the mainland. Their very existence challenged American educators, who worried about a competing national and linguistic culture that many Japanese Americans felt a strong duty to preserve. The *Senate Journal of the Territorial Legislature* recorded appeals in the form of letters from Japanese immigrant parents in Kaua'i to preserve Japanese language schools as an important form of educational opportunity.[41]

From the grammar schools of Honolulu to the plantation schools of Hanamaulu on Kaua'i, the American public school classroom was a place where teachers found that most of their students had foreign ethnic origins. A student from an immigrant family remembered her sixth grade teacher, recently arrived in Hawai'i from the mainland: "Everything we did or said seemed to irritate her."[42] The life of the schoolroom was interwoven with the life of a surrounding society being transformed by immigration.

The community built by immigrants in their neighborhoods was complemented by a new civic community created by the public schools.[43] The waves of immigrants in the early twentieth century produced the greatest challenge yet seen to the ability of the public schools to create a common culture for all Americans. Economic growth under industrialism produced new inequalities that widened social distances, and it generated enclaves whose enclosure, it was feared, limited wider communication with the surrounding society. The spreading mass culture of consumerism, lifestyle, and entertainment produced special problems of youthful distraction and deviancy. Escapist and hedonistic self-absorption eroded youngsters' capacity for public responsibility, family bonding, moral consciousness, and independent judgment. Educators and social reformers worried that these trends threatened to block the formation of a healthy civic identity among youth.[44]

Professional educators believed that society could be reformed by building a revitalized civic community in the public schools. Their new model of schooling was called progressive education, an offshoot of the social-reform movement of progressivism that grappled with the effects of rapid social change and the multiplying divisions created by immigration, industrialism, and urbanization.[45] Progressive educators attempted to socialize new generations into a new community of progressive citizens, to compensate for what they saw as the weakening of the family and community. In order to create a civic community, progressive schools tried to bring children of immigrants and natives together through study, play, and school service.[46] Educational philosopher John Dewey instructed that the progressive school would provide the student "an opportunity to escape from the limitations of the social group in which he was born."[47] When the children of immigrants came into the classroom, their teachers expected them to leave behind the identity of the home and neighborhood and behave like "Americans."

The general impact of the public school on immigrant families was felt in the complex patterns of social and cultural adjustment that schools introduced. The public school was a decompression chamber from both the peer culture of the street and the first-generation world of tradition. It provided an institutional space in which new cultural connections could form through mutual learning and group activity. In a single elementary classroom in Los Angeles in 1920 were Mexican, black, Japanese, Jewish, and "Anglo" students who were there to learn one history, one civics, and one linguistic tradition in English. Students read textbooks focusing on the institutions and political history of the nation and studied an iconographic gallery of great men and women who were presented as heroic role models. Teachers believed that revering national symbols and mythic figures was the path to a sense of belonging to the newly adopted country and would make a youngster a good American citizen.[48]

The experience of Japanese American students at William McKinley High School, the first public high school in Honolulu, revealed the central role of public education in the social history of Hawai'i's largest immigrant community. The children of Japanese immigrants made up close to a majority of its students.[49]

The editors and writers of the campus newspaper, *The Pinion*, many of whom were Nisei or of other Asian ancestry, paid homage to American ideals and the great symbolic role models of American history. On a deeper level, its journalistic style revealed how second-generation immigrant students were forming and claiming an egalitarian ethnic American identity based on inclusive principles of democracy and citizenship. Student writers clarified the civic meaning of school elections, activity programs, and athletics for their student readers. As McKinley High School's journalistic voice, *The Pinion* described how the Nisei students were taking on American ways. Essay contests, oratorical contests, lectures, student government, and service programs were vehicles for teaching patriotism, citizenship, and democratic values.[50]

McKinley High School teachers moved toward indoctrinating patriotic attitudes, and the Nisei of McKinley, like other high school students in the 1920s, appeared to accept this "values education" willingly and even with a notable degree of ardor. They publicly and privately expressed positive feelings about their daily life in school and showed fondness for courses in history, literature, and social studies that introduced them to the world of official American culture. They appeared to feel that through attending the high school they could gain a greater degree of access to American life. What mattered greatly to the Nisei about McKinley's education was that it aimed at including them in America in a democratic spirit. An op-ed writer for *The Pinion* declared idealistically:

> "All citizens have equal rights. The phrase is upheld by every student in high school. . . . With the students of different races, the class works and studies just as well as any class in any high school on the mainland. . . . No teacher has the impression that because of a student's color or race he should get a certain amount of attention. The teacher too thinks that every student has equal rights to learn. . . . [The students] are as friendly as if they were of the same race. . . . Not a thing about racial disadvantage is discussed by the students. As long as their friendship prevails among the students and there is no antagonistic feeling there will be no racial problem to solve in McKinley high school."[51]

The foreign-born generation of Issei and the American-born Nisei generally were open-minded about acculturation into the surrounding public world. The *Nippu Jiji*, one of the principal Japanese community newspapers, described the Japanese community of Hawai'i as a cradle of internationalization, as a place where the currents of East and West, of Japan and the United States, mingled fruitfully. Its publisher, Yasutaro Soga, editorialized about the cultural transformation visible in the community among the Japanese born, and particularly among the American born. Soga observed, "Even at the present time, the ideas, modes of living, habits of dressing, and kinds of foods of Japanese [in Hawai'i] are a great deal different from those of their fellow nationals in Japan." Soga was sure that "ethnic feeling" would continue, but in cosmopolitan Hawai'i, he reminded, "You may want the Japanese spirit but the Japanese spirit must be an Americanized Japanese spirit."[52] As a weekly newspaper with an English-language section, the *Nippu Jiji* was a medium for the development of a Japanese-American community voice that bridged cultural and generational differences.

Beneath the public surface of felicitous acculturation, however, was a residual layer of cultural incongruity and conflict. A set of student autobiographies submitted to McKinley's English classes in 1926 provided a glimpse of this sphere of personal experience.[53] In these highly personal essays, the Nisei expressed critical and approving views of Japanese customs and complained about the lack of understanding of these ways exhibited by "haoles," the white citizens of Hawai'i, as well as by other racial groups. Moreover, they recognized a distance between their ethnic Japanese world and the public world, which sometimes caused much ambivalence and even anguish.

The Nisei asserted a strong pride in the ethical traditions of Japanese culture. They admired moral qualities they saw as characteristic of the Japanese. These included, they said, honesty, respect for elders, politeness, sincerity, and a deep sensitivity to obligation. Although they ardently supported the need to learn proper American English, they also placed high importance on learning Japanese in the language schools established in the local community. The Nisei who attended these institutions pointed out that learning Japanese facilitated communication and understanding between themselves and their elders. One student explained that without effective linguistic contact, a cultural gap would grow and impair relationships with their parents.

In some instances, the students complained about unfair treatment by American teachers, most of whom were white and from the mainland in the 1920s. One student criticized the practice of English-skill grouping for keeping Japanese segregated from whites. Another student stated that equality for the Nisei was guaranteed only in commercial and economic areas but never in social and political activities. The students most troubled by the possibility of unfair treatment said they wished at times they were members of another race.

Nevertheless, the general response of the Nisei to encounters with prejudice was to become more demonstrative of their public image as American citizens. As one student remarked, "We are true Americans and we must prove that we are true Americans." McKinley High School was a vehicle for this action because it offered many ways to express and symbolize American identity. Students looked upon the patriotism they displayed in the high school as an assertion that they belonged in America. This was a deeply felt need, as one student explained, for they worried that "white people do not consider American-born Japanese as Americans . . . they confuse largely . . . their native tongue [and] nationality." By demonstrating their American identity, the Nisei students laid claim to their equal rights. "I am an American citizen so I think I should have equal rights as others," declared one student.

Many students struggled to harmonize both American and Japanese values in their lifestyles and self-image. Some students expressed embarrassment or discomfort over what they saw as antiquated or alien Japanese customs. The most intense complaints were about strict parental control and discipline. They resented the efforts of their fathers and mothers to police social and leisure time, to restrict the rights and freedoms of daughters, and to arrange marriages. The Nisei were acutely aware of the existence of a contrasting "American way" of less elder-dominated and more open family life. Many young people indicated that they wanted to incorporate Americanized customs when they started their own families. While a few felt sharply torn between the two cultures, most of the students were confident of functioning successfully as American citizens who were still ethnically Japanese.

The Nisei believed that their Japanese American heritage equipped them to be part of a democratic melting pot. The students who espoused Americanism in the public school proclaimed that they were American citizens of Japanese heritage. The Nisei interpreted the characteristic features of their ethnic heritage as a set of high ideals congruent with the values of American life. Endowed with this dual identity, the educated members of the new generation could overcome racial divisions by showing that Japanese Americans were as good Americans as anyone else.[54] Accomplishing this project would not be easy, but the imperatives were strong. One student noted:

> "Here in Hawaii today, the 'melting-pot' of the nations, we are confronted with numerous problems. To us especially, the American citizens of Japanese parentage, there are numerous problems facing us. We are trying to adjust our cultural and racial heritages to meet the civilization and political institutions of the land of our birth. Being physically and mentally Japanese, and Americans only by place of birth and formal community education, the problems of doing away with racial clashes so that these islands may continue to be one of the most successful laboratories of racial associations, is no easy task. The successful accomplishment of this object is so important to the world, and to Hawaii and the peace of the Pacific, that I, as an American citizen of Japanese parentage and as a member of the second generation, shall ever strive for it, and shall contribute my share in such as a loyal citizen."

Other students expressed a deep fervor for promoting the common good of both their adopted and their ancestral country. In their autobiographies, they summoned up all their eloquence to declare their dedication to this objective. One student even went so far as to assert that if he could realize this objective he could die with a sense of fulfillment. Another student vowed, "We are the younger generation, upon whose shoulders are placed the responsibility and duty to distinguish ourselves as ideal American citizens, and at the same time, to pay obedience and respect due our Japanese parents, to create understanding and good fellowship between the East and the West, thus establishing the foundation of the realization of World Wide Brotherhood." In another autobiography, a student felt that working to harmonize the relations of Japan and the United States was not only a personal cause but an international mission that Hawai'i was uniquely positioned to serve. This task would be of the highest interest to the entire world: "As Hawaii, the crossroad of the Pacific, is our native land and upon which dwells our promising future, all eyes of the Pacific countries will be focused upon us to observe how well we carry out and fulfill our heavy responsibilities." These idealistic and hopeful sentiments mirrored some of the themes of cosmopolitan internationalism and peaceful expansionism popular in Japan from the 1890s to the early 1920s.[55]

As Japanese Americans equipped with knowledge about both America and Japan, these students looked forward to becoming cultural liaisons who would build better relationships between the two countries. The most articulate and high-minded of the educated Nisei felt that this was the greatest service they could render as American citizens. The views of these Nisei students of their life-worlds should not be overgeneralized, but there was a common thread woven into the autobiographies. It was the self-image of new Americans who had adapted to what they perceived as the best qualities in American culture while cultivating what they saw as the best features of their ancestral culture, to produce a new cosmopolitan, more egalitarian, global culture.

The McKinley High School experience occurred at the geographic and social margins of American life, but it probably had parallels with the educational experiences of the second generation in the Polish, Jewish, Italian, Greek, and German enclaves of the United States. Observing the education of Japanese Americans in Hawai'i, a commentator noted, "The theory that the Oriental mind is essentially different from the Occidental mind no one who teaches in Hawai'i would consider for a moment."[56] In McKinley High School, educational experiences guided the movement from a particularized identity based on ethnic origin to broader forms of collective identity based on institutional community and membership.[57] The civic communitarianism and social trust exhibited in McKinley High School has been described by the political scientist Robert D. Putnam as "bridging" social capital, a set of investments in social relationships that overarch group boundaries.[58]

In Honolulu, the Nisei elite emerged from McKinley High School with a vision of remaking the world on positive lines that included universal citizenship, equal opportunity, religious ecumenicalism, intergroup tolerance, and ethnic pride. As second-generation Japanese who were ethnic outsiders, they were acutely aware of the obstacles and challenges lying in the way of realizing their vision. Nevertheless, through civic acculturation they endeavored to transform their lives and change American society in Hawai'i to establish a democratic pluralism that rose above the bounds of race.

The institutional culture of universal citizenship portrayed in *The Pinion* shaped the bonds of civic community in the second generation. McKinley High School created a peer network in which students helped each other see citizenship as a transracial status that would bring them into the American mainstream. It also introduced ideological motifs with the potential to be appropriated for political mobilization.[59]

McKinley High School influenced the political worldview of the many future leaders of the Japanese American community who matriculated there. Through schooling, the Nisei learned a new language of political democracy that created civic connections among new Americans of Japanese ancestry. In their rise to power in the Democratic Party in Hawai'i and their backing of statehood for Hawai'i, the Nisei leaders mobilized politically through these networks.[60] The commemorative volume assembled by alumni and alumnae, *A Hundred Years: McKinley High School, 1865–1965*, pointed out the conjunction between the civic lessons learned at McKinley and the attainment of statehood for Hawai'i. It contained excerpts from the "centennial day" speech by Hawai'i's first elected governor, John A. Burns, who described McKinley's key role in teaching Hawai'i's post-war generation that they were part of a democratic civic community. Burns described how McKinley had "a very great deal to do with making democracy more meaningful in Hawaii."

Burns singled out for special recognition "the many courageous superintendents and principals and teachers" who "steadfastly fought" for the right of Hawai'i's children to learn about the relevance of the Declaration of Independence and the Constitution. These educators, according to Burns, "managed to inject" the "American idea" into their teaching. For example, McKinley's principal before World War II, Dr. Miles E. Cary, had managed the high-school's curriculum to motivate a student so that he "will want to change his environment." Thus, Burns recalled, after the war, many of McKinley's graduates, who were the children of immigrants, set out to change their environment to give themselves and their parents "a stronger voice in their destinies." Hawai'i's achievement of statehood in 1959 revealed that they were largely successful in this endeavor. Burns pointed out that "the distinguished McKinley alumni" had a central role in the changes that made Hawai'i an "integral and essential part" of the United States, changes that had helped to bring about not "merely the realization of Statehood," but the further realization of the equal citizenship they learned about in McKinley's classrooms, "the full appreciation of all of us in Hawaii that we all enjoy full American rights."[61]

As educators systematized teaching in order to mold the "rising generation," they came into conflict with some immigrant parents who were suspicious of the public school's efforts to compel attendance and to enforce conformity to unfamiliar values upon their children. The Japanese and Chinese of Hawai'i and the Pacific coast, like Irish and German Catholics of the northeast and midwest in the United States, worried over the potential for cultural coercion from the public school. They resorted to founding separate parochial schools or language schools where their children could receive training consistent with ancestral beliefs and traditions. As the historian Peter Sahlins discovered about culture on European frontiers, contests over cultural boundaries revealed that local identities and loyalties possessed an "oppositional character" and "remained constantly shifting."[62]

The American public school marked a cultural and generational boundary that was inconceivable in many homelands of Asian immigrants. Young immigrants and the children of immigrants had experiences within the public-school classroom that contrasted sharply with those of foreign-born parents whose habits and values were framed by a village in Hiroshima, a farm in Canton, or a shop in Manila. Nevertheless, in the view of many schoolteachers, their students did not progress fast enough or far enough. The result was that the public school was often unsatisfactory to both educators bent on Americanization and immigrant parents anxious about preserving traditions. Still, this ambiguous and partial resolution—frustrating and unfulfilling as it may have been to many—may have been the best result for insuring a pluralism that was democratic and open.[63] The public schools of the Progressive era were laboratories for exploring ways to bring together the children of immigrants in new social and civic relationships through academics combined with group activities. These students participated in an experiment in building institutional communities that crossed the boundaries of ethnicity.[64]

CULTURAL CHANGE AND EXPRESSION

Cultural change accelerated among the children of immigrants and created new, hybrid cultural modes.[65] The wedding ceremonies of second-generation Japanese Americans in Hawai'i of the 1920s were the product of the "combination of customs," according to a Japanese community newspaper. It pointed to the creative adaptations that were usually found in the wedding ceremonies taking place in the Hongwanji Buddhist temple in Honolulu. Guests of a half dozen races witnessed ceremonies where the "burning of incense and the striking of gongs lend an oriental atmosphere to the ceremony, but it is the old favorite, the march from Lohengrin, that heralds the approach of the bride and her party."[66]

In everyday life, the second generation attempted to gain popularity, recognition, and respect through creative and competitive self-expression. They sought to customize their personal styles and tastes in music, dress, amusement, recreation, and comportment through cultural idioms taken from movies, radio, and spectator sports. A Hawaiian civil servant described how the sons and daughters of proper Japanese parents adapted to the popular trends of the 1920s. David Akana of the Territorial Birth Registration Bureau witnessed how teen-aged Chinese and Japanese children gave themselves "English names." A sociologist reported that Akana attributed these alterations to the absorption of American popular culture. "Oriental flappers and sheikhs search for names that will be better suited to the dash of American sport clothing," and so "the names of Yoshi, Yuki, and Haru become reincarnated into Elsie, Daisy, and Rose."[67] "Kan-kan Musume," a hit song of postwar Japan, was modified by the Japanese American listeners of Hawai'i so that the opening line of the original Japanese lyrics was turned into "Anna go Hawai'i."

The constant percolation of new cultural ingredients in ethnic lifeworlds was described in the recollections of Aiji Tashiro, a Nisei generation son of Japanese immigrants in 1934:

"[I] sat down to American breakfasts and Japanese lunches. My palate developed a fondness for rice along with corned beef and cabbage. I became equally adept with knife and fork and with chopsticks. I said grace at meal times in Japanese, and recited the Lord's Prayer at night in English. I hung my stocking over the fireplace at Christmas and toasted 'mochi' at Japanese New Year. The stories of 'Tongue-cut Sparrow' and 'Momo-taro' were as well known to me as those of Red Riding Hood and Cinderella. . . . On some nights I was told bedtime stories of how Admiral Togo sent a great Russian fleet down to destruction. Other nights I heard of King Arthur or from *Gulliver's Travels* and *Tom Sawyer*. I was spoken to by both parents in Japanese and English. I answered in whatever was convenient or in a curious mixture of both."[68]

Over a half-century later, a journalist described the cross-cultural experiences of countless ethnic Americans like Aiji Tashiro to draw an important lesson about American identity. "Many things are possible in America, but the singleness of identity is not one of them," he noted. The "dream of liberalism was not the multicultural society"; it was "the multicultural individual" and "in America the dream came true."[69] Immigrants often resisted or were unconscious of cultural change, but it proved inescapable in the American mass culture. Historian Oscar Handlin described the typical immigrant who wills "not to change," but "change comes" as "new words and ways insidiously filter in."[70]

Cultural expression and social history were connected much as a twin set of lamps, revealing together what each singly would not have the power to illuminate about ethnic experience. The literature created by Chinese immigrants and their descendants in America built an expressive framework that charted the consciousness of group identity and group culture in the earliest immigrant community from Asia. The literary culture created in the Chinese American community represented a robust example of the fertile interaction between social history and group consciousness. Chinese Americans continuously produced, over a century and a half, an extensive literary tradition whose richness and vitality have been exhibited by the popular works of authors such as Jade Snow Wong, Maxine Hong Kingston, and Gish Jen.

The social-demographic coordinates of Chinese American group history formed a guiding map to the changing modes of Chinese American popular culture and literary expression. The stories, thoughts, and feelings imbedded in Chinese American life were linked to the evolution of individual and family migration that were strategized by immigrants under transnational conditions. A multigenerational history of Chinese immigrant families often involved the transnational impacts shaped by historical swings in U.S. admissions policies. American immigration policy has altered the social and demographic configuration of the Chinese American population, and therefore its cultural patterns, arguably more than for any other group of immigrants. The immigration control policies of the late nineteenth century first facilitated transient labor migration from China, then it excluded all Chinese laborers and treated Chinese immigrants as permanent aliens barred from U.S. citizenship. Until the early twentieth century, the Chinese American community rested preponderantly on a largely male, foreign-born working class. Compared to European immigrant communities, it fell behind in the formation of families and a large second generation, and was not culturally "refreshed" by new mass immigration due to the policy of Chinese exclusion that lasted until World War II. U.S. immigration policies since the 1960s have reopened immigration from China and, as a result, a different immigrant community with a new cultural background has been piggy-backed on top of the residual, shrinking community left from the "old" Chinese immigration. Historian Haiming Liu summarized the history of one Chinese American family to demonstrate how these shifts in policy affected family life. "Rather than a straightforward, one-way trip from one side of the Pacific to the other," Liu pointed out, "the Chang family history was a long, complicated transnational circular migration during which family members constantly considered factors that might affect their life and what strategies to adopt for the best of their future."[71]

A transnational and international perspective was built into the Chinese immigration experience and was essential for situating the Chinese American community and its expressive cultural life. Utilizing an expansive definition of literature that included familiar forms of fiction and nonfiction with journalism and various public and informal writing, historian Xiao-huang Yin has turned the study of ethnic literature toward primary documents with sociological and institutional implications, in this way revealing the active, transnational dimensions of ethnic life. The writings by Chinese immigrants in the Chinese language reflected an entire realm of collective life—the subculture of the foreign born— that has hitherto been rendered only partially visible because Chinese American social history has been studied by many scholars without a sophisticated knowledge of the Chinese language or Chinese homelands.

The unfolding picture of Chinese American culture produced by Yin is one of subtle and multiform tensions between individual identity and collective identity. Authors employed their writings for different, often contradictory purposes, as they sought to work out these tensions in various historical circumstances. Authors divided into different groupings that reflected the changing sociological contexts of their lived experiences. Chinese immigrant pioneers who made entreaties for tolerance, educated Chinese who sought to improve the public image of China and its people, second-generation Chinese who provided a personalized vision of assimilation and ethnic Americanization, and journalists who kept alive international information networks made for a robust diversity of writers who formed a contentious society of public discourse and debate.

Parallels existed between the experiences of identity negotiation and formation of Chinese Americans and other ethnic Americans. Chinese American tastes in writing and performing arts shifted with new aspirations for self-expression caused by inter-generational succession, much as in European immigrant communities (Figure 3-7a, b). Yin finds evidence for similarities between the Chinese and Irish immigrants' frustrations over the lack of a strong homeland, between the Chinese, Irish, and Jewish immigrants' preservation of ethnic and religious particularisms, between the intense appetite among Chinese and Russian immigrants

Figure 3-7. Shifting Chinese American expressions in performing arts: (a) Scenes of Charlie Low's Forbidden City nightclub, San Francisco Chinatown; (b) "When does Charlie find time to look at his floor shows?—Every time you see Charlie Low he's in the company of such interesting people you wonder how he finds time to stop looking into faces and concentrate on his glamorous Forbidden City revues. The celebrities posed with him this time are Jane Wyman and Ronald Reagan of the movies. The show that's entertaining the visitors is one of the celebrated all-Chinese revues with Dorothy Sun and Mary Mammon as highlights."

for ethnic journalism, and between Chinese and Jewish immigrant self-identity and mutual identification. The Chinese also constituted one of the first major waves of immigrants in the new American republic, arriving in large numbers about the same time as the Irish Catholic and German immigrants, during the third quarter of the nineteenth century. Like the immigrants from Europe, they played crucial roles in regional and economic development and aroused fierce nativistic feelings. However, the experiences of alienation and racial inequality forced the group life of Chinese Americans to take a sharp turn toward an evolutionary pathway that would set it apart from European immigrant communities.

In their writings, Chinese Americans grappled with insecurity, intergenerational tensions, and, above all, their "other-directedness." The strategic nature and educative function of the literature sprang from the Chinese social position as a minority group with a target audience, an all-important condition for determining the content and tone of writing. Chinese American authors writing in English were usually quite conscious of racial perceptions and interracial typecasting. They felt concern about how their writings would be received by a broader, non-Chinese reading audience and thereby affect relations between the Chinese as a minority group and the majority population. Chinese writers in America who wrote in the Chinese language, by contrast, were able to write with more freedom from these strategic considerations, as well as the dictates of "box office" conscious publishers urging authors to employ saleable themes and character stereotypes in the market of American publications.

The interlinkage of popular culture and generation appeared in the expressive cross-over performing arts and entertainment showcased in San Francisco Chinatown's famous Forbidden City nightclub, which attracted many white customers to its shows. The Forbidden City provided a stage for aspiring Chinese American singers and dancers performing in what musicologist Michael Feinstein has called American standard popular song and music.[72]

GENERATIONS ON THE MARGINS

Notwithstanding persistent gender imbalance caused by policies that excluded new Chinese immigrants, communities based on families grew steadily, and in many urban Chinese communities—particularly in Honolulu and San Francisco—a sizable second generation had developed by the early twentieth century. In small and scattered Chinese American enclaves, isolated members of the second generation faced a more challenging task of connecting with each other.[73]

The second generation in Asian American communities was marked off sharply from the first generation in terms of legal status and cultural orientation. As the first American-born Asian generation its members possessed American citizenship. But the second generation still faced the challenge of biculturalism within the framework of racial and cultural difference. Acculturation to "American" ways potentially involved a difficult personal distancing from traditional core ethnic values. The challenge was complicated by the ethical imperatives of familism, which required the repayment of the sacrifices of parents and the need to respect their ways. The steps toward the alien culture of white American society called into question the second generation's loyalty to the proud customs of their forebearers.

The autobiography of Jade Snow Wong, *Fifth Chinese Daughter* (1950), explored the experience of growing up as a second-generation Chinese American. It became widely read at its publication and for many decades remained one of the foremost autobiographies written by an Asian American. It appealed to many readers as a Chinese American version of a self-made success story in which the author describes her roots in a poor, struggling family in San Francisco's Chinatown and her ascent to educational honors and literary fame. When *Fifth Chinese Daughter* was published, it quickly gained a large reading audience and a degree of celebrity. Learning that the new book had a positive and popular reception, officials at the U.S. State Department realized that in the Cold War it could help boost the image of the United States as a country of opportunity for Asian immigrants. The State Department sponsored her on a speaking tour of Asia in 1953 and arranged to have *Fifth Chinese Daughter* translated into several Asian and European languages.[74]

Jade Snow Wong's autobiography was a vivid work of literature that described with deep feeling and sensitivity the cultural challenges she faced and her responses. Her personal story's power derived from an open and detailed account of conflict with her parents over the traditional lifestyle and goals they had set for her, and her concurrent attraction to the influence of the surrounding society, particularly the public school and college. Jade Snow Wong experienced life through dual worlds. At home, she was strongly bonded with her parents and her eight siblings, but at school and outside the Chinese community, she found herself drawn to new cultural tastes and standards, and most importantly a new horizon of ambition. Despite her parents' initial discouragement of her new activities and personal goals, Jade Snow Wong persevered, graduated from nearby Mills College with honors in 1942, and ultimately gained the approval of her parents. As an educated woman and a writer, she had found the path to keep her together with her family and to maintain ties with her Chinese identity in innovative ways. Jade Snow Wong had accomplished being ethnic, while becoming American—a lived experience that many second-generation Chinese Americans and other Asian Americans found relevant to their own lives.[75] By and large, the family bonds that crosscut generational divisions were able to withstand the stresses of these contradictory demands.[76]

In contrast to the gradual emergence of the Chinese second generation, the Japanese second generation grew in a relatively massive and sudden spurt in the early twentieth century. They were labeled the "Nisei" (Japanese for the second generation) by their parents, who were uniquely conscious of generational membership as a feature of personal identity and of a transnational genealogy that would link them to the homeland as part of a diaspora. A sociologist noted, "Japanese are the only ethnic group to emphasize geo-generational distinctions by a separate nomenclature and a belief in the unique character structure of each generational group."[77] The Nisei had parents, the Issei, who had been shaped by the strong Westernizing policies and ideologies of Meiji Era Japan and were imbued with an outlook receptive toward Western influences and acculturation to new experiences. The Issei had made a commitment to America and tolerated and even encouraged the acculturating behavior of their children, the Nisei. The early mutualist associations of the Japanese Issei stressed support for the wider society's values and traditions. The Nisei who came of age during the years between World War I and World War II and their children, the Sansei (third generation), augmented Issei institutions with a highly evolved peer group culture that centered on American sports and recreational associations, social organizations like clubs and sororities, and service organizations such as the Boy Scouts and Girl Scouts. Second-generation Japanese encountered two sets of role models: one in the family and ethnic community and the other in the surrounding mass and institutional culture. Exposed to two extremely different cultural worlds in a time of Anglo-conformity, the Nisei coped with growing up in a complex cultural and psychological space of feeling and thinking "American" according to external norms while being reared by Issei parents who imparted Japanese traditions.

American popular culture helped to bridge the gap with Issei parents. The radio, for example, proved to be a device for bringing immigrant parents into the world of the second generation. In interviews with a sociologist, Japanese parents made the following revealing comments about the impact of radio in the home.[78]

> "My children wanted us to buy a radio since they began attending high school. . . . At the supper table they teased us into buying a radio, so we bought this radio for them. Every Saturday afternoon their friends came here and listened to the football broadcasting. I don't know anything about football; but I enjoy to see their excitement when something happens in the game. Since we bought the radio for my children, all their friends have become my friends."
>
> "I like the radio better than the phonograph now. I cannot understand English songs but I enjoy listening to the music."

Because of their exposure to modern American mass culture and their receptiveness to it, the second generation had to sort out different, often contradictory, ideal-type qualities of physical attractiveness, personal conduct, and lifestyle. One of the great changes in the intimate behavior of the household was the American-born generation's adoption of the habit of wearing shoes in the home, which was unthinkable in the Japanese homeland, where it was seen as very unsanitary and impolite. Adjusting American popular lifestyles, role models and trends to the youthful tastes of second-generation Japanese Americans produced new social innovations. One way of coping with racial and cultural difference was to replicate external institutions in the ethnic community, to make the ethnic community a complete, self-contained point of reference. This enabled the creation of a level of competitive equality based on similar physical and behavioral qualities. Japanese youths organized themselves into all-Japanese athletic leagues and teams. Popular beauty contests such as the Nisei Week pageant were held within the Japanese American community.[79]

Despite their parents' support for acculturation and assimilation, the Nisei, like the Chinese second generation, often found themselves in conflict with parents who operated through authoritarian prescription rather than flexible negotiation. Nisei frequently complained about working for Issei employers who were rigid, harsh, and uncommunicative. But they could not escape the Issei control of family and community, and racial barriers prevented them from fulfilling their aspirations in the outer society. Some felt trapped in a foreign community after having been exposed to mainstream individualist ideals and aspirations. Milton Murayama's novel, *All I Asking for is My Body* (1975), captures the tension between the Nisei and Issei in Hawai'i. Two of the characters are brothers, Kiyoshi and Toshio, who question the idealized filial role presented to them. Their father, a plantation laborer, has accumulated a large debt, and they are pressured to mortgage their futures by working to help him pay it off. Their parents exhort Kiyoshi and Toshio with inspirational stories of loyal, self-sacrificing samurai in Japan, but they are unsatisfied with this prescribed path and protest. Murayama's story showed how American-born Japanese could find it troubling to submit to parental wishes and rebelled against what they perceived as subservience.[80]

The Nisei generation had learned in public school about individual equality, democracy, and personal rights. Many were inspired by their lessons in the ideals of liberty and democracy to challenge external norms. Racial discrimination seemed only to redouble their efforts to make America and its institutions reflect their ideals more fully. The young Nisei were filled with dreams of a more egalitarian America, cultivated by sympathetic public school teachers. The Nisei expounded on American ideals and heroes in *The Pinion* (Figure 3-8), the student newspaper of McKinley High School in Honolulu, called "Tokyo High" because of its preponderant number of Japanese American students. In essays and editorials, they expressed their admiration for Abraham Lincoln as a racial liberator, as well as for the humble origins of his greatness; they admired George Washington because he was a revolutionary who fought for liberty. They learned a new political language in student journalism—lofty, idealistic, and sometimes irreverent—that would be leveraged in their later lives in public efforts to create a more democratic and inclusive Hawai'i of the future.[81]

On the mainland, the Japanese American Citizens League (JACL) became the official voice of the Americanization ideology in the second generation. The power of its rhetoric drew from the transition between the first and second generations; the average age of its early members was in the twenties. It resonated with youthful idealism in which the JACL used Americanism as both a positive and a defensive ideology. Mike Masaoka, a Nisei spokesman, wrote a creed expressing gratitude and faith in America that functioned also as a contribution to the language of racial equality.[82] Masaoka's creed requested equal treatment irrespective of race: "I am firm in my belief that American sportsmanship and

GEORGE
WASHINGTON
(1732- 1799)

ALL ARE EQUAL AT McKINLEY; SPIRIT NOT COLOR, COUNTS

With approximately two thousand three hundred students in McKinley high school, ninety percent are of different races than that of the Caucasian. And yet there is no racial problem in the school. Of course this is an unusual thing to happen. You might ask how do the students of the different races get along together in the school? A proper answer would be that they are mostly American citizens. All citizens have equal rights. This phrase is upheld by every student in the high school.

There is no question of whether a student of the white race or the yellow race is the proper person for a certain office. For instance, the president of our student body this year is a Japanese. As long as he keeps up with his work there will be no question of taking him out of the office until his term expires. The policy of McKinley high school is to choose the most efficient student to that position.

Figure 3-8. McKinley High School *Pinion*, February 19, 1926.

attitude of fair play will judge citizenship and patriotism on the basis of action and achievement, and not on the basis of physical characteristics." Masaoka wrote with a future-oriented vocabulary. JACL political rhetoric proposed an agenda for the future based on hope and faith in reason. Asian journalists and politicians in Hawai'i also spoke for Asian Americans to shape a public discourse with an invigorated emphasis on racial equality. They called for the overcoming of racial difference, of a transracial, integrationist equality such as the early NAACP advocated. This type of Americanism was a device for constructing a kind of public platform that Nisei, not whites, could control and use for an ethnic self-presentation they could define with both assertive and defensive effects. It was a means of taking control to a significant degree of their political relationships to the external society. [83]

The structures of social and legal inequality deployed against Asian Americans reached a new cumulative density before World War II. They formed a far-reaching set of obstacles: anti-Asian restrictive immigration and naturalization policy; anti-alien laws on property ownership, occupation, and public welfare; anti-miscegenation laws; exclusion of Asians from civil service and labor unions; private discrimination in the housing market; exclusion in private businesses, public accommodations, and sociable institutions. Asians were also divided among themselves and could not ally to defend themselves effectively. Intergroup divisions were exacerbated by Chinese, Korean, and Filipino reactions against the incursions of Japanese imperialism in their homelands. The imposing social challenges facing all Asian Americans was whether their communities could be sustained under anti-Asian restrictionism and social discrimination, whether they could make socioeconomic and political advances under these conditions. Asian Americans worried about prospects for having permanent and growing communities that would be accepted in the surrounding society.[84]

The relocation to internment camps of the Japanese American population of the Pacific coast region was a turning point in the history of the largest Asian American ethnic group in the mid-twentieth century. This forced displacement was a form of deportation, which government authorities justified as necessary to protect the country against possible subversion, that produced great losses of property and educational investments and resulted in collective stigmatization. Japanese relocation in the United States was also part of an international phenomenon: governments in Latin American countries deported their Japanese immigrant populations to the United States for incarceration in the same relocation sites intended for Japanese Americans from Los Angeles and San Francisco (Figure 3-9a, b).

The experiences of mass internment, however, indirectly produced conditions that accelerated the rise of a mobile, dynamic second generation. The Nisei came of age in this moment of crisis and moved to the forefront of the Japanese American community, assuming unforseen new roles. Nisei soldiers fought and died for democracy in all Japanese combat regiments that received awards for exceptional valor. Many internees obtained passes to leave the camps if they moved east, away from the high-security zone of the west coast. In 1943, 17,000 Japanese Americans became re-settlers in the midwest and on the east

Figure 3-9. Japanese relocation in the United States. (a) Naturalization ceremony in Seabrook, New Jersey on June 23, 1953 involving Japanese immigrants who had been relocated from the U.S. Pacific coast and Japanese immigrants deported from Peru. (b) M. S. Gripsholm, Swedish ship that transported Japanese deportees from Peru to the United States.

coast. When the war ended, other internees who went east, instead of back home to the west coast because they feared a backlash also joined them. In places such as Chicago, they found new economic and social opportunities opening up that had been denied them in California.

But the majority returned to the west coast. To their surprise, anti-Japanese feeling abated with the ending of the war. With the defeat and occupation of Japan, the fears and hostilities aroused by the perceived Japanese threat began to subside, and so did hatred toward Japanese Americans as enemy nationals. In this atmosphere of transition and change, Japanese Americans began to rebuild their communities in the new post-war California. It was not to be the same community as before World War II. Instead of a part-foreign, tradition-oriented community dominated by the first-generation Issei, it was an assimilating community led by American-born Nisei citizens. The years after internment flowed into a period in which the Japanese American community reached out for wider contacts with the surrounding society and institutions.

Most importantly, California and the rest of the country were changing in unprecedented ways. New people from other regions poured into the "Golden State" after World War II. For the most part, they had not been steeped in the legacy of anti-orientalism that was a part of native Californian history. Together with many other groups they were ready to create a new west coast that would accommodate Asian Americans and other minorities in a more inclusive society. Californians in this new era discovered an agenda of future regional development based on the benefits of global migration, diversity, and innovation.

Notes

1. Robert E. Park and Ernest W. Burgess, *The City* (Chicago: University of Chicago Press, 1925), p. 146.
2. Jonathan S. Walters, *Finding Buddhists in Global History* (American Historical Association: Washington, D.C., 1998), ch. 4.
3. Yong Chen, *Chinese San Francisco, 1850–1943: A Transpacific Community* (Stanford, Calif.: Stanford University Press, 2000), pp. 135–136.
4. George J. Tanabe and Willa Jane Tanabe, *Japanese Buddhist Temples in Hawai'i: An Illustrated Guide* (Honolulu: University of Hawai'i Press, 2013).
5. Alfred M. Lee, *The Daily Newspaper in America: The Evolution of a Social Instrument* (New York: Macmillan, 1937), Table XXI, p. 734.
6. Shiho Imai, *Creating the Nisei Market: Race and Citizenship in Hawai'i's Japanese American Consumer Culture* (Honolulu: University of Hawai'i Press, 2010), pp. 61, 77, 91, 141.
7. *Nippu Jiji*, English language section (August 25, 1922; December 1, 1922).
8. Kanichi Kawasaki, "The Japanese Community of East San Pedro, Terminal Island, California" (master's thesis, University of Southern California, 1931), p. 168.
9. Chen, *Chinese San Francisco*, pp. 90–91.
10. Lowell Angell, *Theatres of Hawai'i* (Charleston, S.C.: Arcadia Publishing, 2011), pp.7–8, 28, 76–79.
11. Shih-shan Henry Tsai, *The Chinese Experience in America* (Bloomington: Indiana University Press, 1986), pp. 44–48.
12. U.S. Bureau of the Census, *Chinese and Japanese in the United States, 1910* (Washington, D.C.: U.S. Census Bureau, 1914), Table 53, p. 25.
13. H. Mark Lai, "Chinese," in Stephan Thernstrom, ed., *Harvard Encyclopedia of American Ethnic Groups* (Cambridge, Mass.: Harvard University Press, 1980), p. 222.
14. Harry H. L. Kitano, "Japanese," *Harvard Encyclopedia of American Ethnic Groups*, p. 564.
15. Adam McKeown, *Chinese Migrant Networks and Cultural Change: Peru, Chicago, Hawaii, 1900–1936* (Chicago: University of Chicago Press, 2001), p. 277.
16. Ivan H. Light, *Ethnic Enterprise in America: Business and Welfare among Chinese, Japanese, and Blacks* (Berkeley: University of California Press, 1972), pp. 9, 64–65, 93.

17. David T. Beito, *From Mutual Aid to the Welfare State: Fraternal Societies and Social Services, 1890–1967* (Chapel Hill: University of North Carolina Press, 2000), Tables 2.2, 2.3, pp. 22, 23; Oscar and Mary Handlin, *The Dimensions of Liberty* (Cambridge, Mass. Harvard University Press, 1961), pp. 127–128.

18. Robert D. Putnam, *Making Democracy Work: Civic Traditions in Modern Italy* (Princeton: Princeton University Press, 1993), pp. 167–171; Robert D. Putnam, "The Strange Disappearance of Civic America," *The American Prospect* (Winter 1996), pp. 34–48.

19. John Charles Chasteen, *Born in Blood and Fire: A Concise History of Latin America* (New York: W. W. Norton & Co., 2001), p. 74.

20. Gary Y. Okihiro, *Island World: A History of Hawai'i and the United States* (Berkeley: University of California Press, 2008), ch. 6.

21. James Michener, *Hawaii* (New York: Random House, 1959).

22. Christine Schultz, "One Perfect Summer Sunday," *Yankee Magazine* (August 1992), p. 123.

23. Hawai'i as part of imaginative discourse is discussed by Rob Wilson in "Blue Hawai'i: *Bamboo Ridge* as 'Critical Regionalism'," in Arif Dirlik, ed., *What Is in a Rim?: Critical Perspectives on the Pacific Region Idea*, 2nd ed. (Lanham, Md.: Rowman and Littlefield, 1998), pp. 325–349.

24. Debra Samuels, "Spam Goes Glam in This Japanese-American Snack," *Boston Globe*, February 20, 2013.

25. Historical studies have demonstrated the importance of food in understanding the immigration history of the United States. See Donna Gabaccia, *We Are What We Eat: Ethnic Food and the Making of Americans* (Cambridge, Mass.: Harvard University Press, 1998) and Hasia Diner, *Hungering for America: Italian, Irish, and Jewish Foodways in the Age of Migration* (Cambridge, Mass.: Harvard University Press, 2001).

26. Robert J. Shallenbergen, *Hawaii's Birds* (Honolulu: Hawaii Audubon Society, 1984), pp. 41–46, 83.

27. South Asian American Digital Archive http://www.saadigitalarchive.org/item/20110720–247 (August 1, 2014)

28. Eleanor C. Nordyke, *The Peopling of Hawai'i*, 2nd ed. (Honolulu: University of Hawaii Press, 1977; 1989), Table 3–10, p. 222.

29. Nicholas A. Jones and Amy Symens Smith, *The Two or More Races Population: 2000* (Washington, D.C.: U.S. Department of Commerce, U.S. Census Bureau, Economics and Statistics Administration, 2001), p. 3; David Hollinger discusses the growth of mixed-raced populations and identities in *Post-Ethnic America: Beyond Multiculturalism* (New York: Basic Books, 1995), pp. 41–43.

30. Evelyn Hu-Dehart, "Latin America in Asia-Pacific Perspective," in Arif Dirlik, *"What Is in a Rim?: Critical Perspectives on the Pacific Region Idea*, 2nd ed. (Lanham, Md: Rowman and Littlefield, 1998), pp. 253–272.

31. Sucheng Chan, "European and Asian Immigration into the United States in Perspective, 1820s to 1920s," in Virginia Yans-McLaughlin, ed., *Immigration Reconsidered: History, Sociology, Politics* (New York: Oxford University Press, 1990), pp. 50–52; Sucheng Chan, ed., *Chinese American Transnationalism: The Flow of People, Resources, and Ideas between China and America During the Exclusion Era* (Philadelphia: Temple University Press, 2006), pp. 198, 200; Sun Yat-Sen, "Open Letter to Followers in Hilo, *Hawaii*," in Arlene Lum, Ed., *Sailing for the Sun: The Chinese in Hawaii, 1789–1989* (Honolulu: Center for Chinese Studies, University of Hawaii, 1988), pp. 96–97.

32. Lawrence H. Fuchs, *The American Kaleidoscope: Race, Ethnicity, and the Civic Culture* (Hanover, N.H.: University Press of New England, 1990), p. 276.

33. Timothy L. Smith, "Religion and Ethnicity in America," *American Historical Review* 83(December 1978), pp. 1174–1175.

34. Katherine M. Cook, *Public Education in Hawaii* (Washington, D.C: U.S. Government Printing Office, 1935), pp. 15, 31, 38, 40, 54.

35. *Hawaii Educational Review*, see articles throughout Vols. 7–9, January 1919 to June 1922.

36. *Hawaii Educational Review* 8, no. 4, January 1920, p. 21.

37. *Hawaii Educational Review* 8, no. 4, December 1919, pp. 9, 26.

38. Department of Public Instruction, Hawaii, *General Practices, Menus and Recipes for the Cafeterias of the Public Schools* (Honolulu: January 1936).

39. Allison Davis, "The Public Schools in America's Most Successful Racial Democracy: Hawaii" (Chicago, 1947: unpublished paper), pp. 15, 16, 36.

40. *The Journal of the House of Representatives of the Twenty-fourth Legislature of the Territory of Hawaii, 1947* (Wailuku, Hawaii: Maui Publishing Co., Ltd., 1948), pp. 326, 342, 1288, 1319, 1581.

41. *Senate Journal*, Tenth Legislature of the Territory of Hawaii, Regular Season, 1919 (Honolulu: Honolulu Star Bulletin, Ltd., 1919), pp. 1107–1108, 1113–1115.)

42. Eileen H. Tamura, *Americanization, Acculturation, and Ethnic Identity: The Nisei Generation in Hawaii* (Urbana: University of Illinois Press, 1994), p. 94.

43. Lawrence A. Cremin, *The Transformation of the School: Progressivism in American Education, 1876–1957* (New York: Alfred A. Knopf, 1961), pp. 115–126.

44. Jacob A. Riis, *How the Other Half Lives* (New York: Charles Scribner's, 1890); David Nasaw, *Children of the City: At Work and at Play* (New York: Oxford University Press, 1985), chs. 2, 8–10; Jane Addams, *Twenty Years at Hull House* (New York: New American Library, 1960; 1910), pp. 170–182; John F. Kasson, *Amusing the Million: Coney Island at the Turn of the Century* (New York: Hill and Wang, 1978), pp. 100–101.

45. Merle Curti, *The Roots of American Loyalty* (New York: Columbia University Press, 1946), pp. 189–191; Cremin, *The Transformation of the School*, pp. 85–89; Lawrence A. Cremin, *The Genius of American Education* (New York: Vintage, 1965), pp. 6–7; 18–19; Marvin Lazerson, *Origins of the Urban School: Public Education in Massachusetts, 1870–1915* (Cambridge, Mass.: Harvard University Press, 1971), ch. 8.

46. Charles Merriam, *Civic Education in the United States* (New York: Charles Scribner's Sons, 1934), ch. 2; Merle Curti, *The Social Ideas of American Educators*, rev. ed. (Totowa, N.J.: Littlefield, Adams, 1968), pp. 574–580.

47. John Dewey, *Democracy and Education* (New York: Macmillan Co., 1916), pp. 93–96.

48. Eugen Weber, *Peasants into Frenchmen: The Modernization of Rural France, 1870–1914* (Stanford, Calif.: Stanford University Press, 1976), pp. 332–336.

49. Lawrence H. Fuchs, *Hawaii Pono: A Social History* (San Diego: Harcourt Brace Jovanovich, 1983; 1961), pp. 129, 286–290.

50. *The Pinion*, February 21, 1927, p. 1; March 8, 1927, p. 1; January 23, 1929, p. 3; February 26, 1929, p. 1; November 15, 1927, pp. 1, 3; December 18, 1925, p. 15; November 6, 1925, pp. 1, 4; December 16, 1927, p. 9; October 16, 1925, p. 2; October 23, 1925, p. 2; January 17, 1928, p. 3; March 8, 1927, p. 1.

51. *The Pinion*, February 19, 1926.

52. *Nippu Jiji*, June 19, 1922.

53. The student autobiographies are cited here by "MK" for McKinley High School and "WCS" for William Carlson Smith, the sociologist who collected them. See MK-174,

WCS. MK-101, WCS; MK-204, WCS; MK-173, WCS. For more detail on the student autobiographies and their authors, see Shiho Imai, *Creating the Nisei Market*, pp. 14–17.

54. See MK-102, WCS; MK-111, WCS; MK-125, WCS; MK-23, WCS; MK-25, WCS; MK-54, WCS; MK-43, WCS; MK-44, WCS; MK-45, WCS; MK-23, WCS.

55. Akira Iriye, *Pacific Estrangement: Japanese and American Expansion, 1897–1911* (Cambridge, Mass.: Harvard University Press, 1972), pp. 233–234.

56. Henry B. Restarick, "Americanizing Hawaii," *The Mid-Pacific Magazine* 7, no. 3 (March 1914): pp. 217–223.

57. Marcus Lee Hansen, "The Problem of the Third Generation Immigrant," in Dag Blank and Peter Kivisto, eds., *American Immigrants and Their Generations: Studies and Commentaries on the Hansen Thesis after Fifty Years* (Urbana: University of Illinois Press, 1990), pp. 192–193.

58. Putnam, *Making Democracy Work*, pp. 167–171; Putnam, "The Strange Disappearance of Civic America," *The American Prospect* (Winter 1996): 34–48.

59. Gary Gerstle, *Working-Class Americanism: The Politics of Labor in a Textile City, 1914–1960* (Cambridge, Eng.: Cambridge University Press, 1989), pp. 10, 177–187; idem, "The Politics of Patriotism: Americanization and the Formation of the CIO," *Dissent* 33(1986): 84–92.

60. George K. Yamamoto, "Political Participation among Orientals in Hawaii," *Sociology and Social Research* 43, no. 5 (May-June 1959): 359–364. Cf. "Spark Matsunaga: The Path to Understanding," *Japanese American National Museum Newsletter* (Summer 1990): 5; Fuchs, *Hawaii Pono*, pp. 129, 283–284, 286–290.

61. Henry Y. K. Tom, Linda Y. Furushima, and Paula T. Yano, *A Hundred Years: McKinley High School, 1865–1965* (Honolulu: McKinley High School Press, 1965), p. 7.

62. Peter Sahlins, *Boundaries: The Making of France and Spain in the Pyrenees* (Berkeley: University of California Press, 1989), pp. 111–112; Diane Ravitch, *The Great School Wars: New York City, 1805–1973: A History of the Public Schools as Battlefield of Social Change* (New York: Basic Books, 1983), ch. 4–5.

63. David B. Tyack, *The One Best System: A History of American Urban Education* (Cambridge, Mass.: Harvard University Press, 1974), p. 237; Reed Ueda, "American National Identity and Race in Immigrant Generations," *Journal of Interdisciplinary History* 22(Winter 1993): 483–491.

64. Cremin, *The Transformation of the School*, pp. 115–126; Oscar Handlin, *John Dewey's Challenge to Education: Historical Perspectives on the Cultural Context* (New York: Harper and Brothers, 1959), pp. 42–45; Arthur William Dunn, *Community Civics for City Schools* (New York: D. C. Heath and Co., 1921), p. 111.

65. Lizabeth Cohen, *Making a New Deal: Industrial Workers in Chicago, 1919–1939* (New York: Cambridge University Press, 1990), ch. 2–3.

66. *Japanese American News*, July 17, 1928, cited in William Carlson Smith, *Americans in Process: A Study of Our Citizens of Oriental Ancestry* (Ann Arbor, Mich.: Edwards Brothers, Inc., 1937), p. 240.

67. Smith, *Americans in Process*, pp. 247–248.

68. Aiji Tashiro in *New Outlook*, September, 1934. Quoted in Carey McWilliams, *Prejudice* (Boston: Little, Brown, 1944), p. 99.

69. Leon Wieseltier, "The Trouble with Multiculturalism," *New York Times Book Review* (October 23, 1991): 11.

70. Oscar Handlin, *The Uprooted*, rev. ed. (Boston: Little Brown, 1973), p. 175.

71. Haiming Liu, *The Transnational History of a Chinese Family: Immigrant Letters, Family Business, and Reverse Migration* (New Brunswick, N.J.: Rutgers University Press, 2005), pp. 11–12.

72. Gloria Heyung Chun, *Of Orphans and Warriors: Inventing Chinese American Culture and Identity* (New Brunswick, N.J.: Rutgers University Press, 2000), Introduction, ch. 1–2.

73. Stanford M. Lyman, ed., *The Asian in North America* (Santa Barbara: ABC-CLIO, 1977), pp. 120, 123.

74. Jade Snow Wong, *Fifth Chinese Daughter* (New York: Harper, 1950), p. 235.

75. Lowell Chun-Hoon, "Jade Snow Wong and the Fate of Chinese-American Identity," in Stanley Sue and Nathaniel N. Wagner, eds., *Asian Americans: Psychological Perspectives* (Palo Alto, 1973), pp. 125–135.

76. Tsai, *The Chinese Experience in America,* pp. 95–97.

77. Lyman, *The Asian in North America*, p. 121.

78. Kanichi Kawasaki, "The Japanese Community of East San Pedro, Terminal Island, California" (master's thesis, University of Southern California, 1931), p. 169.

79. Lon Kurashige, *Japanese American Celebration and Conflict: A History of Ethnic Identity and Festival, 1934–1990* (Berkeley: University of California Press, 2002), pp. 56, 146, 174–178.

80. Milton Murayama, *All I Asking for is my Body* (San Francisco: Supa Press, 1975); David Palumbo-Liu, *Asian/American: Historical Crossings of a Racial Frontier* (Stanford, Calif.: Stanford University Press, 1999), p. 408.

81. "All Are Equal at McKinley: Spirit Not Color Counts," *The Pinion*, January 19, 1926, p. 1.

82. "Japanese American Creed" (read before the U.S. Senate and printed in the *Congressional Record*, May 9, 1941).

83. Cf. Conclusion to the autobiography, Mary Antin, *The Promised Land* (Boston: Houghton Mifflin, 1912), pp. 357–358.

84. Bill Ong Hing, *Making and Re-Making Asian America through Immigration Policy, 1850–1990* (Stanford, Calif.: Stanford University Press, 1993), pp. 15–16.

FOUR

A GLOBALIST ERA

"A hundred years ago, immigrants arrived at Ellis Island . . . after a long ocean journey in steerage; now they emerge from the cabin of a jet plane. . . ."

"Indeed, contemporary immigration has a lot to do with America's political and economic penetration worldwide and the diffusion of a modern culture of consumption, a culture out of the reach of most people in developing countries."[1]

Nancy Foner, *From Ellis Island to JFK*

The tides of immigration have ebbed and flowed across the Atlantic and Pacific Oceans. After a long interlude of low immigration from the Great Depression to the post–World War II decade, the United States adopted global admissions policies in the 1960s that produced the resurgence of a mass influx. The new arrivals constituted a tremendous force for replenishment of the Asian American population and its international culture that had declined after many decades of anti-Asian exclusion policy.

The opening of admissions to global flows of immigrants occurred at a conjunction with a revisualization of the geographic position of the United States. Historian Susan Schulten has demonstrated the changes in the American "geographical imagination" after World War II, and their role in shaping a new perception of the relation of the United States to the world.[2] The standard maps of the Atlantic and Pacific Ocean rims were reconfigured seemingly to shrink distances between continents and to reflect transoceanic proximity (Maps 4, 5, 6, 7, 8).

An emergent consciousness of globalism influenced cartographic experts who in mass-market atlases portrayed countries and regions as virtual neighbors, closer together in transoceanic space than were depicted in early twentieth century maps.

The new immigrants from Asia challenged the historical structures of collective identity in communities across the country that had evolved with a scarcity of Asian immigrants. A bi-racial model of society based on black–white relations dominated southern states and also coincided with a long lack of any immigration there. In cities of the northeast and midwest that multiplied during the industrial revolution, a melting-pot social structure based on the assimilation of European immigrants defined the ethnic order. The historic dearth of Asians and Asian culture in the south, the northeast and upper midwest combined with an unprecedented surge in Asian immigration in the late twentieth century to produce a sudden challenge in these places to the self-image of communities and triggered a directional shift in the construction of collective identities based on race and ethnicity. It became evident both to newcomer Asians and to the established power structure of host communities that a move had to occur from a black–white dualistic paradigm of race relations, or a melting-pot model based on European immigrant assimilation, toward a new multiracial, multiethnic, and multicultural order suited to a new era of globalism and transnationalism.

The historic patterns of ebb and flow in international mass migration also provided keys to the intergenerational development of ethnic groups in the United States (Tables 4-1, 4-2). A prime example of this pattern was the case of European immigrants whose family structures took shape in the movement from plenitude of the foreign born under industrialization to dearth of the foreign born caused by restrictive immigration controls started in the 1920s, by the Great Depression, and by World War II. Historian Marcus Lee Hansen, in his famous essay, "The Problem of the Third Generation Immigrant" (1937), presented group evolution as a normative cycle of decline of identification with immigrant heritage and a return to it over the course of the first three generations of community development. Hansen's "law" conceptualized the history of collective and individual ethnic identity as linked sensitively to generational succession, and to a decline of immigration, the dearth of the foreign born, and the process of assimilation.[3]

In postwar America, large European immigrant groups formed in the industrial revolution shrank into small and aging communities. This situation of demographically declining ethnic communities began to change slightly with low levels of immigration from Europe, which brought foreign-born replenishment in the form of middle-class newcomers, and the "safety valve" of exogamous marriage that added part-ethnic persons of "multiple ancestry" (Tables 4-3, 4-4). This transition in group life produced a new ground for expressions of symbolic ethnic collective identity. The first ethnic studies programs in U.S. colleges were supported by students and faculty of Scandinavian heritages.[4] Soon after its founding by Danish immigrants who relocated from midwestern states, the town of Solvang in the Santa Ynez Valley of California's central coast established Atterdag College whose purpose was to educate students in their Danish heritage (Figure 4-1a, b, c). Among assimilated Irish Americans who were several generations removed from immigrant ancestors, culturally symbolic re-connections through heritage tourism and performing arts like step dancing and Gaelic folk music, achieved new popularity. The conditions of demographic decline of European immigrant communities provided opportunities for moving beyond old categories of Euro-American identity. In the wake of Communism in Poland, educated immigrants departed for American cities such as Chicago.

Table 4-1. Foreign-Born Persons in 1990 by Year of Admission, Selected Foreign-Born Populations, 1990.

	Foreign-Born[a]	Admitted Before 1980	Before 1980	After 1980
	N	N	Percent	Percent
Danish[a]	37,247	29,138	78.2	21.8
German[a]	806,936	713,164	88.4	11.6
Irish[a]	269,741	220,511	81.2	18.8
Italian[a]	643,203	586,801	91.2	8.8
Norwegian[a]	47,396	39,841	84.1	15.9
Polish[a]	408,504	208,044	50.9	49.1
Swedish[a]	58,675	45,542	77.6	22.4
Mexico[b]	4,298,014	2,153,095	50.1	49.9
Japan[b]	290,128	137,214	47.3	52.7
China[b]	529,837	246,179	46.5	53.5
Korea[b]	568,397	249,345	43.9	56.1
India[b]	450,406	199,551	44.3	55.7

[a]By ancestry.
Source: U.S. Bureau of the Census, 1990 Census of Population: Ancestry of the Population in the United States (1990 CP-3-2), Table 1.
[b]By country of birth.
Source: U.S. Bureau of the Census, 1990 Census of Population: The Foreign-Born Population in the United States (1990 CP-3-1), Table 1.

Table 4-2. Immigration by Country of Last Residence, Selected Decades of Twentieth Century.

	1901–1900	1931–1940	1951–1960	1981–1990
Denmark	65,285	2,559	10,984	5,370
Ireland	388,416	10,973	48,362	31,969
Italy	2,045,877	68,028	185,491	67,254
Norway	190,505	4,740	22,935	4,164
Sweden	249,534	3,960	21,697	11,018
Canada	179,226	108,527	377,952	156,938
Mexico	49,642	22,319	299,811	1,655,843
Japan	129,797	1,948	46,250	47,085
China	20,605	4,928	9,657	346,747
Korea	—	—	6,231	333,746
India	4,713	496	1,973	250,786

Source: U.S. Immigration and Naturalization Service, Statistical Yearbook of the Immigration and Naturalization Service, 1998 (Washington, D.C.: U.S. Government Printing Office, 2000), Table 2.

Table 4-3.   Foreign Born, by Education and Income, 1990.

| | Attended College: Foreign-Born Persons 25 Years and Over Admitted to U.S. 1980–1990 | | Family Income ($) | |
	Number	Percent	Median	Mean
Danish[a]	18,264	53.9	55,250	65,291
Irish[a]	22,030	60.6	42,480	53,843
Italian[a]	21,388	51.3	34,360	45,700
Norwegian[a]	3,601	80.9	49,471	58,037
Swedish[a]	6,016	72.2	50,011	64,685
Canada[b]	56,865	68.7	39,995	53,364
Mexico[b]	124,574	12.7	21,585	26,636
Japan[b]	77,336	78.6	47,034	59,194
China[b]	101,427	45.3	34,225	45,888
Korea[b]	117,190	52.1	33,406	45,394
India[b]	130,966	71.6	52,908	69,942

[a]By ancestry.
Source: U.S. Bureau of the Census, 1990 Census of Population: Ancestry of the Population in the United States (1990 CP-3-2), Tables 3, 5.
[b]By country of birth.
Source: U.S. Bureau of the Census, 1990 Census of Population: The Foreign-Born Population in the United States (1990 CP-3-1), Tables 3, 5.

Table 4-4.   Persons by Single and Multiple Ancestry, 1979.

	Percent of Persons Single Ancestry	Percent of Persons Multiple Ancestry
Danish	26.2	73.8
Irish	22.3	77.7
Italian, Sicilian	52.0	48.0
Norwegian	29.9	70.1
Swedish	24.9	75.1
Canadian	37.4	62.6
Mexican	88.1	11.9
Japanese	77.8	22.2
Chinese, Taiwanese	76.6	23.4
Korean	86.8	13.2
Indian	85.7	14.3

Source: U.S. Bureau of the Census, Current Population Reports, Series P-23, no. 116. Ancestry and Language in the United States: November 1979 (Washington, D.C.: U.S. Government Printing Office, 1982), p. 7.

Removed from the social life of Polish Americans whose ancestors arrived in the Chicago of the industrial revolution, these newcomers sought to avoid being labeled as neighborhood "white ethnics." They endowed themselves with a new identity as worldly innovators who were bringing a dynamic Polonia to America, a reflection of the transnationalism of a globalist era.[5]

Immigration from Asia over the half-century since the end of the national origins admissions system exerted a profound effect on collective identities in Asian American communities. In regions of the far west, especially in the Pacific coast states and Hawai'i, where Asian enclaves had deep historical roots, the new immigration from multiple Asian countries transformed the categories of the Asian American minority. Since the era when immigration from China and Japan towered over the flow from other Asian countries, being Asian American usually meant being Chinese American or Japanese American. This standard set

Figure 4-1. Founders of a California Danish immigrant town and their College for Danish Ethnic Studies; (a) Established in 1911 by Danish Americans from midwestern states, Solvang, California, began as a dream of three Danish immigrants: Professor P. P. Hornsyld, Reverend Benedict Nordentoft, and Reverend J. M. Gregersen. In this photograph taken with the land agent on the extreme left, they stood respectively in this order from left to right. They planned fund-raising to buy a large tract of land for farms, homes, churches, and (b) shops in historic Danish architectural style; and (c) Atterdag College for Danish ethnic studies built in 1914, directly behind the Solvang Lutheran Home, built in 1953.

Figure 4-1. *Continued.*

of Asian American identities was radically altered as historic Chinese and Japanese enclaves were outgrown by communities of newcomers from the Philippines, South Korea, India, Vietnam, Thailand, Laos, Cambodia, Bangladesh, and Pakistan. Being Asian American in California expanded in meaning to include Korean American, Vietnamese American, Asian Indian American, Hmong American, Thai American, Cambodian American, and Bangladeshi American.[6]

Intergenerational change among Asian Americans occurred in the midst of massive and rapid replenishment of the foreign born. The evolution of family lines and social structure took shape in communities with continuously refreshed and expanding transnational ties, a terrain for social development that differed profoundly from the truncated communities of the first wave of immigrants from Asian countries. Koreans, Asian Indians, and immigrants from the Philippines represented the most extreme historical cases of Asians who built communities in which family structures evolved through a century-long swing from extreme dearth of the foreign born enforced under policies of anti-Asian exclusion to plenitude of the foreign born in the post–World War II era of nondiscriminatory global admissions policies. A new generational cycle started by immigrant parents who were educated and had middle class horizons produced the millennial generation of Asian Americans possessing a transnational ethnic identity and expectations for a globalist life shaped by cultural internationalism.

Replenishment of the foreign-born in an era of globalization tended to strengthen transnational identities across the spectrum of immigrant communities. Replenishment affected immigrants who were imbedded in transborder social geography and cultural movements in particular ways. Among Mexican Americans, the "raw materials" of ethnic identity remained close at hand and vibrant across generations, in contrast to intergenerational identities among American ethnic groups formed from shorter and less continuous transoceanic mass immigration from European countries.[7] Canadian Americans whose homelands lay in former British and French colonies to the north also had originated as transregional peoples who developed enclaves around an international land border.[8] The ease of cross-border mobility allowed Canadian immigrants and their descendants in the United States, like Mexican Americans, to receive continuous waves of replenishing migration and influences from their nearby home districts. Mexican American communities, however, diverged in their social and political development from those of Canadian Americans, who blended into the melting pot like European immigrants. Mexican immigrants and their descendants developed new collective identities that expressed their ambivalent and ambiguous position relative to the mainstream of assimilation. Comparatively low levels of income and education, Hispanic culture and language, racial politics, and bureaucratic ethnic classification led to the categorization of Mexican Americans as an increasingly racialized group.

After World War II, immigration swelled into flows from all around the world, including such unexpected places as Asia and Africa. A new social fabric woven of global identities and cross-cultural exchanges took shape. Regional compartments that had evolved from previous centuries in the Atlantic basin, the Pacific basin, and the Indian Ocean extruded new transnational linkages through new mass migrations. Large-scale dynamic connections formed across the Pacific between the western hemisphere and eastern hemisphere. Asian immigrant entrepreneurs and professionals galvanized the development of Silicon Valley, the aero-space industry, international finance, education, and the health-care industry. Business and student migrants from the Asia Pacific flocked to the United States and Canada. Japanese-Brazilians immigrated to Japan to work in industrial plants. The population of immigrant Australians and New Zealanders increased by nearly 50 percent in the 1990s, and a sizable percentage settled in California. From New Zealand came Maoris, indigenous Polynesians, often chose to immigrate to Utah because they had converted to Mormonism. Texas and Florida became popular destinations for Australians. White immigrants from Australia and New Zealand usually had attended college, obtained corporate business, managerial, or professional jobs, and had annual household incomes higher than the majority of immigrants.[9]

Atlantic and Pacific regions were increasingly involved together in mutual development. The new trans-Atlantic and transcontinental mass migrations to the Pacific coast brought there the North Atlantic developmental forces of labor, human capital, cultural capital, and social capital. Concurrently, immigrants from across the Pacific and the Indian Ocean disseminated similar assets of labor and forms of capital, which by the late twentieth century had a transformative impact on the United States. Immigrants arrived from East Asia, South Asia, Southeast Asia, and places for the transit and resettlement of refugees. They were joined by a flow of Pacific Islanders from U.S. Samoa and former German Samoa, Tonga, Fiji, and French Polynesia, as well as newcomers from Australia and New Zealand.[1.] These trans-Pacific currents burnished the popular image of the United States as the global hub for multicultural diversity and economic integration.

The United States that emerged into the twenty-first century was the product of a transforming immigration from Asian and Pacific countries, along with larger currents of newcomers from Latin America, the Middle East, and Africa. The mass exodus from Europe of the nineteenth and early twentieth centuries could no longer be regarded as representing the culmination of nation-building through immigration. Instead, they appeared, in a new light, as a preliminary stage in a massive re-alignment of world population that accelerated in the twentieth century. The movement of people across the Pacific to western-hemisphere societies originally formed by Atlantic regional development rose to a new historical high point. Mass migration, which had been suppressed by decades of anti-Asian exclusion, was rejuvenated as a force for integration of the Pacific basin from East Asia to the Americas.

In the two decades after World War II, the law of immigration and nationality evolved steadily in the direction of ending discriminatory national-origins quotas. The quota system was finally abolished by congressional passage of the Hart–Celler Act of 1965, which revived the cosmopolitan ideals of membership in the American nation by establishing a global system of admissions. Congress replaced admissions based on discriminatory ethnic screening operating from 1924 to 1965 with an expanded selective system of skill and family screening. Admitting immigrants to match immigrants with occupational needs and to promote family reunion reinforced tendencies toward permanent settlement. In the twentieth century, these two entry "preferences" proved to be the telling signs of countries most strongly committed to receiving and assimilating immigrants. No other country built its immigration policy more aggressively on these admissions principles than the United States, creating its unparalleled receptivity to immigration from all over the world.[11]

By these innovations in policy, lawmakers ensured that occupational and family networks would form around nationality categories. Once the networking process started among particular nationalities it tended to "cascade" and increase their numbers. Lawrence H. Fuchs, a leading immigration expert, illustrated how this process worked, using an anecdote about a hypothetical medical professional who immigrated from India:

> Asians who made use of non-family [occupational] preferences often were able to use the family preferences later. For example, 2,208 immigrants arrived from India through one of two occupational preferences in 1982, bringing with them 1,786 spouses and children. An Indian anesthesiologist who had left his wife in India to care for their small children to come to the United States in 1982 would be entitled immediately as a lawful resident alien to petition under the second preference . . . to bring his family in as immigrants the following year. Their ability to immigrate was limited only by the ceilings set for the world and for India for second preference. . . .[12]

After 1965, the federal government operated a worldwide system of admissions regulated by an annual ceiling for total arrivals, "per-country" visa allotments, a permanent refugee program, and preferences and exemptions from visa-allotment limits for highly trained personnel and their family members. The reform of immigration policy continued to be shaped by congressional and presidential efforts to further American global power in the Cold War, but it also promoted immigrant-centered opportunities for admission. Such special efforts were made to serve the interests of immigrants that it can be said that the United States developed a kind of program to empower occupational and family networks. The United States continued its world leadership in refugee admissions with the passage of the Refugee Act of 1980, which established provisions for the regular admission of refugees. The Immigration Reform and Control Act of 1986 supplied legal alien status to undocumented immigrants and expanded certain categories of admission. In 1990 Congress passed another major immigration bill that renewed the worldwide system of regular and refugee admissions. The pace of immigration legislation grew in unison with the globalizing forces of the late twentieth century. In the 1980s, the absence of a popular ideology of restriction and the political effectiveness of pro-immigration advocates made expansion and diversity the central trends of admissions policies.[13]

American institutions promoted the integration of newcomers in the 1970s and 1980s, as policy experts and ordinary citizens debated whether American society's capacity for absorption was becoming overtaxed. The negotiating and skirmishing before the passage of the Immigration Reform and Control Act (IRCA) of 1986 that legalized undocumented immigrants was a harbinger of a long-term struggle to redesign the whole system of immigration. Policies selecting for occupational skills and family reunification admitted newcomers who contributed to a modern, technological economy and who had the family investments to reside permanently and to acquire citizenship. The increasing globalization of communications had made them more familiar with American life and even English before arrival than were many immigrants in the early twentieth century who hailed from the remote hinterlands of the Mediterranean and Eastern Europe.

The new worldwide immigration, like the wave in the early twentieth century, was noted for the great variety of groups it brought into the country. Indeed, the newest immigrants came from nations in the third world where cultural traditions were quite different from the popular customs brought by immigrants from Europe. The infusions from enormously diverse foreign communities increased internal cultural distances that had been shrinking as immigrant communities that formed in the early twentieth century gradually blended into the core of American society.

Transnational migration intensified in the era of globalization, leading some experts to visualize the unfolding present and the future in terms of the end of assimilationist patterns within the nation-state. Technology reached a higher level for furthering communications and movement between home and host societies. Immigrants were able to obtain status as transnationals in homelands from which they had departed. For example, new forms of transnational status were created by India, allowing immigrants from India to be officially recognized as "NRIs" (Non-Resident Indians), "OCIs" (Overseas Citizens of India), and "PIOs" (Persons of Indian Origin). Numerous countries in Latin America afforded dual citizenship that permitted their national citizenship and U.S. citizenship to co-exist concurrently. In a less formal recognition of transnationalism, Chinese Americans labeled themselves as "ABC": "American born Chinese." These examples of transnational identities were indeed innovative, but they had precursors rooted in earlier eras of immigration when, as in the late twentieth century, migrants were not fully assimilated in one country or maintained corridors with homelands through international mass transportation and communication. Chinese immigrants in the nineteenth century, Italian and Slavic immigrants at the turn of the century, and West Indian, Mexican, and Puerto Rican newcomers in the early twentieth century previously had developed features of transnational life in their communities.[14]

Flows of economic and social remittances created by immigrant communities have formed a vital conduit connecting the United States with homeland societies. Economic remittances—monetary payments sent by immigrants to relatives and organizations at home—helped boost economic activity in local communities. Social remittances—forms of social assistance provided to pay back received social favors or support—lubricated the workings of interpersonal networks of chain migration. In the decades at the end of the twentieth century, the provision of economic and social remittances by immigrants was enhanced by the rapid communication and cultural link-ups made possible by the global telecommunications revolution. Informal support networks based on family or neighborhood connections helped immigrants to cross international frontiers of opportunity shaped by economic differentials between the United States and other countries.

Mass immigration returned to the United States on a scale comparable to the early twentieth century. In the three decades after 1960, fifteen million immigrants entered the country legally, and probably three to five million entered illegally. The percentage of the foreign born in the population rose to 11.5 percent, the highest level since 1910 when it reached 14.8 percent. The United States had the greatest intake of immigrants of any country. In the size of its net international migrant stock in 2000, the United States rose above the rest of the world with an estimated 35 million newcomers. The next closest countries—the Russian Federation and Germany—lagged far behind with 13.3 and 7.3 million, respectively. New sources of immigration to the United States produced an influx increasingly representative of worldwide cultures, especially from homelands in Latin America, Asia, and Africa; a pattern which contrasted with immigration in the early twentieth century, when the vast majority of newcomers were from Europe (Figure 4-2).

From the onset of the Cold War, the expansion of corporate businesses, telecommunications, commercial exchanges, and military bases created new platforms for international and interregional connections that enlarged the global flow of immigration to the United States.[15] By hosting the greatest population of international migrants, the United States functioned as a reception center for the human networks and intercultural linkages that forged the worldwide integration of societies and economies.

The general trend toward political integration of the world intensified global patterns of migration. Inter-state frameworks for managing international labor migration in the Middle East, in Europe, and in Asian states were drafted through treaties and agreements. The United States and Mexico arranged a collaborative framework to bring Mexican guest workers, called the "bracero" program, which lasted from 1942 to 1964. The United States and Mexico signed the North American Fair Trade Agreement (NAFTA) in 1995, aiming to strengthen the regional economy but also to contain the flow of both legal and undocumented migration to the United States by creating more employment in Mexico. The creation of the European Union fostered migration between member states. The expansion of relationships between states that permitted immigrants to hold dual nationality also promoted immigration.

Forced migrations multiplied in the late twentieth century, generated by schemes of states for partition, repopulating new territories, ethnic cleansing, and engineering mega-projects for economic development. In the aftermath of wars and the post-colonial emergence of new independent states, "displaced persons" uprooted by civil conflict and governmental regime changes sought havens

Decade

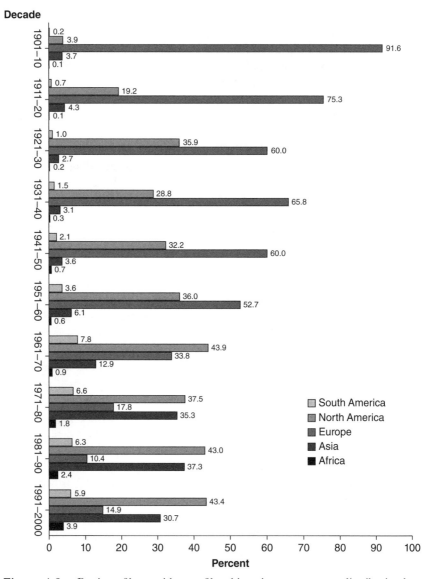

Figure 4-2. Region of last residence of legal immigrants, percent distribution by decade.

in foreign countries. The world's population of refugees and internally displaced persons (IDPs) grew to thirty million by the end of the twentieth century as more people were put at risk by war and domestic chaos of becoming forced migrants. After the Vietnam War, the United States became the leader in refugee resettlement of displaced people from Southeast Asia and throughout the world's crisis and conflict zones.

The increasing integration of the international political order in the course of the twentieth century moved U.S. immigration policy in closer tandem with diplomatic maneuvers. The United States orchestrated its refugee admissions policies to strengthen its alliances with friendly foreign nations and to counteract the interests of rival powers. This strategic use of refugee policies and programs became especially prominent during the Cold War.

The United States, like many countries in Europe, received a growing flow of undocumented aliens, whose numbers had mounted to several million illegal residents by 2000. The growth of undocumented alien populations reflected the worldwide rise of state activism in the control of admissions. Illegal immigration became severely problematic after states installed more stringent admissions and administrative requirements, which increased the numbers of excludable people who clamored for entry.

SOCIAL MOBILITY

Empirical indicators showed that America's newest immigrants from the Asia Pacific were moving up the socioeconomic ladder, ethnically integrating America's social-class structure and propelling growth and enterprise. Pursuing various routes and techniques for economic self-betterment, immigrants possessed a common set of positive attitudes toward work, savings, and collective effort. They were willing to invest the bulk of their daily time and energies in the tasks of earning incomes, often to maximal levels of productive output. The immigrant family disciplined, socialized, assigned roles, and distributed resources, stressing collective welfare and interdependence among its members. Immigrants from China, the Philippines, South Korea, Vietnam, and India developed strategies for cooperative resource sharing in the family and the community to capitalize on new opportunities.

Many new Asian immigrants recapitulated the saga of social ascent blazed by previous waves of newcomers from Asia, Europe, and elsewhere. Many were poised on the threshold of assimilation, as these were well-educated and mobile newcomers who had essentially been in the middle class or its periphery in their home countries. They and their children were edging their way across social and cultural boundaries, forming a vanguard in the front of multi-ethnic diversity advancing toward the mainstream. The Asian Indian community reflected these characteristics perhaps most impressively among all Asian immigrant populations (Table 4-5). Among Asian Indian immigrant adults in 1990, 25.0 percent had a bachelor's degree, and 84.7 percent had attended at least twelve years of school. These qualities can be seen in greater detail by exploring the Asian Indian community of Kalamazoo, Michigan, a microcosm of the religious and linguistic diversity of India, and American immigrant social mobility of the new millenium. In the 1990s, over half of those employed were in professional or white-collar occupations, nearly 70 percent had become naturalized U.S. citizens by the end of the decade, and parents concentrated their resources on support for their children's education.

Table 4-5.   Selected Characteristics of Asian Indian Population in the
United States, 1990 and 2000.

1990 U.S. Population of Asian Indian Descent, Education Level (Adults)

Percent with at least a bachelor's degree	25.0%
Percent with at least a high school degree	11.6
Percent with at least 12 years of school	84.7

Asian Indians (Adults) in Kalamazoo, Michigan 2000

Principal Native Indian Language

Gujarati	34.1%
Punjabi	9.5
Hindi	17.7
Tamil	8.2
Urdu	5.7

Religious Affiliation

Hinduism	77.5%
Jainism	6.5
Islam	5.6
Christianity	4.7
Sikhism	4.0

Country of Citizenship

United States	68.0%
India	30.0

Principal Occupations

Engineer	10.4%
Medical doctor	14.9
Business owner	13.1
Architect, pharmacist	19.6 (in 1990)
Dentist	14.1 (in 1990)
Teacher, professor	6.3 (in 1990)

Source: Arthur W. Helweg, Asian Indians in Michigan (East Lansing: Michigan State University Press, 2002).

For many other immigrants, the pathway to move up economically often involved taking unexpected and unattractive detours. An immigrant from Taiwan, Mai Lin, remembered how her highly educated professional parents had to take lesser jobs during the years after arrival in the United States:

"We settled in [a small town in Washington]. [My father became] a janitor. His pride was shot. He had been the head editor of a newspaper. He came and went whenever he wanted to in his jobs, and he had a lot of influence in the community and in Taiwan. . . . He became very withdrawn and he was depressed. . . . My mother was trying to get a job at a hospital. She worked as a nurse's aide then went to be waitress. They told her, 'Your schooling back in Taiwan and your experience there doesn't count as anything because you're a foreigner. You have to be certified in the States.'"[16]

Two areas of employment offered economic pathways to the large number of working-class "labor migrants" from Asia who flocked to the United States after World War II. Although heavy manufacturing industries declined during the Cold War era, low-wage and light manufacturing industries such as electronics assembly and garment-making grew in both rust-belt and sun-belt cities. Thousands of Asian immigrant women gained employment in these fields. Also the expansion of professional and upper middle class employment in the work force caused by the rise of a global information and knowledge economy raised demand for service workers in office maintenance, health and recreation, family care, food provisioning, and home services. Here, too, large numbers of Asian women found new job opportunities.[17]

The correlation of dynamic American economic opportunities and globalization produced a rapid growth in the immigrant population from Asian countries (Table 4-6). As Asian immigration increased after World War II, old and new Asian immigrant groups also achieved a rising income standard. From 1950 to 1980, the largest historic Asian American groups, the Japanese, Chinese, and Filipinos, converged upon the income norm for whites. Both Japanese men and women surpassed the median income of whites. Chinese men and Filipino men lagged behind the income median of white males, as many new arrivals earned low incomes. Despite the arrival of many wage earners and refugees in the communities of Chinese, Koreans, Vietnamese, Filipinos, Laotians, and Cambodians, the annual income for Asian and Pacific Americans as an aggregate forged ahead, and generally increased with the length of time they had been settled in the country. In 1989, a Current Population Survey of the U.S. Census Bureau disclosed that the average income for Asian and Pacific American men was $22,090, compared to $22,500 for white men. The mean income for Asian and Pacific American women was $13,550; for white women it was $11,518.[18] Chinese and Filipino women were particularly able to earn higher than the average incomes earned by women. Asian immigrant families operated on the principle of role collaboration and labor intensity. All family members were expected to work. In 1979, Asian American families more often than white families had two or even three income earners. The general tactic to increase household income was to multiply the number of earners and extend work periods beyond the norm of eight hours.

New immigration from Asian countries and transcontinental migration gradually expanded the regional cores of Asian immigrants started in the early twentieth century. By the 1980s, Asians who were heavily concentrated in the far west before World War II had become national minorities, settling in the east

Table 4-6. Race and Origin for the United States, 1980 and 1990.

Race and Origin	1980 Census		1990 Census		Percent Change 1980–1990
	Number	Percent	Number	Percent	
Asian or Pacific Islanders	3,500,439	1.5	7,273,662	2.9	107.8
Japanese	700,974	0.3	847,562	0.3	20.9
Chinese	806,040	0.4	1,645,472	0.7	104.1
Korean	354,593	0.2	798,849	0.3	125.3
Filipino	774,652	0.3	1,406,770	0.6	81.6
Asian Indian	361,531	0.2	815,447	0.3	125.6
Vietnamese	261,729	0.1	614,547	0.2	134.8
Hawaiian	166,814	0.1	211,014	0.1	26.5
Samoan	41,948	0.0	62,964	0.0	50.1
Guamanian	32,158	0.0	49,345	0.0	53.4
Other	*	*	821,692	0.3	*
Hispanic origin	14,608,673	6.4	22,354,059	9.0	53.0
Black	26,495,025	11.7	29,986,060	12.1	13.2
White	188,371,622	83.1	199,686,070	80.3	6.0
Totals	226,545,805	100.0	248,709,873	100.0	9.8

*N/A

Source: Herbert Barringer, Robert W. Gardner, and Michael J. Levin, Asians and Pacific Islanders in the United States (New York: Russell Sage, 1993) (Table 1-1), p. 4.

coast, the midwest, and the south.[19] Immigrants and their descendants invented a variety of ways of coping with the simultaneous needs of joining the mainstream and of maintaining a different ethnic life in these very different regions. Notwithstanding their initial cultural and social distance, immigrant parents negotiated a middle course as they raised their American-born children in the diverse locales of the United States.

Asians and Pacific Islanders perceived progress as the result of group solidarity and the loss of connections to the family and community as a liability. The family household of immigrants was a high functioning organized unit that instrumentalized the roles and relations of family members. It aimed at collective welfare and interdependence between family members. This focus promoted capital accumulation to provide for the continuation of the lineage. The extended family of Samoans and Tongans provided a safety net when individuals encountered difficulties in employment or education. Stressing labor intensity, saving, and economic teamwork, Koreans, Chinese, Vietnamese, and Asian Indians who immigrated after 1965 started small businesses at the highest per capita rate among the foreign born and exhibited high levels of self-employment compared to the general population.[20]

Immigrants from Asia organized to help kinsmen and countrymen through innovative forms of mutual assistance. The Japanese Benevolent Society of Honolulu's Japanese American community founded the Japanese Charity Hospital to provide free care for Japanese plantation laborers. Its services expanded to the point where the hospital had to move to a suburban area near Kuakini Street, where it was renamed in 1975 as the Kuakini Medical Center, and operated as the only general hospital in the United States established by Japanese immigrants. By 2000, Kuakini Medical Center had evolved into a non-profit corporation that served the entire community regardless of ethnicity or religious affiliation. Religious organizations often served immigrants as community centers for mutual assistance. When Taiwanese immigrants founded the largest Buddhist temple in the United States, the Hsi Lai Temple, just east of Los Angeles, they used it as a base for educational programs and other services. Each new enclave of Korean immigrants that established a Korean Christian church similarly made sure that it functioned as a social and civic center for their members.

A large number of professionals arrived in the waves of migration from India, Pakistan, the Philippines, and Taiwan and took up positions in medical, health, engineering, and other scientific fields. Economist Thomas Muller pointed out that legal immigrants arriving since the late 1960s had higher levels of education than earlier immigrants or native-born Americans. The career of Dr. A. L. Sarkar illustrated this pattern of highly educated "human capital" migration. He had received graduate training in science and technology at an Indian university and immigrated to Boston to work for a "high tech" company in the field of corporate scientific research. Dr. Sarkar was grateful that the government of India had subsidized his science training and felt that he was putting it to good use in the United States where he was contributing to the good of the wider world and gaining new opportunities for himself. "I work on compromises, as you can very well tell," he once said about his decision to immigrate to the United States. When he became a parent, Dr. Sarkar reflected on how his son will be growing up in the American mainstream, while still staying in touch with his heritage:

> "So, I don't think I would like to impose my decision on my child. At sixteen, having been brought up here, he's at the age where he thinks what he's doing, at least *he* thinks that. He becomes completely Americanized. . . . He still has some habits because we try to inject on him. We observe the festivals, we observe the values, we have fairly good, in fact very good, interaction with the community from back home. Being a large group here we get together almost every weekend or so. So he does get pretty good exposure to our culture, our values."[21]

Many immigrants from Asia arrived with high levels of education compared to immigrants from other regions of the world (Table 4-7). Data collected by the U.S. Census Bureau in 1960, 1970, and 1980 on Asian immigrants showed that a significant percentage of men had a college education, as did women at slightly lower rates. The wave of immigrants from India epitomized this trend, being notable for the

Table 4-7. Average Years of Schooling of Recent-Entrant Men and Women, Aged 25–34, by Area of Origin and Census Year.

Average Years of Schooling of Recent-Entrant Men Aged 25–34, by Area of Origin and Census Year

Characteristic	1960		1970		1980	
Asia	14.2	(14.1)[a]	14.2	(27.3)	14.2	(37.0)
Europe	10.9	(47.1)	11.1	(31.6)	13.4	(12.0)
Western Hemisphere	8.1	(36.8)	9.5	(34.7)	9.2	(37.2)
Other	11.4	(1.96)	12.5	(6.39)	13.5	(13.7)
Total Recent Entrants	10.3	(100.0)	11.5	(100.0)	12.2	(100.0)
Native-Born	10.8		11.7		13.3	

[a]Percentage of total recent-entrant men aged 25–34

Average Years of Schooling of Recent-Entrant Women Aged 25–34, by Area of Origin and Census Year

Characteristic	1960		1970		1980	
Asia	10.6	(17.2)[a]	12.5	(23.9)	13.2	(40.7)
Europe	9.8	(54.6)	10.3	(34.0)	12.7	(12.7)
Western Hemisphere	9.1	(25.8)	8.9	(36.2)	9.4	(34.7)
Other	9.5	(2.3)	10.2	(5.9)	12.3	(11.8)
Total Recent Entrants	9.8	(100.0)	10.3	(100.0)	11.7	(100.0)
Native-Born	10.6		11.2		13.0	

[a]Percentage of total recent-entrant women aged 25–34.
Source: Guillermina Jasso and Mark R. Rosenzweig, The New Chosen People: Immigrants in the United States (New York: Russell Sage Foundation, 1990), p. 65.

proportion of highly educated professionals in medical and health care.[22] When they became parents, Asian immigrants were determined that their children would obtain a college education in their new American home. Like previous immigrants such as the Jews, Greeks, Germans, and Armenians, Asian immigrants invested in education, particularly for their children, to qualify for professional and white-collar occupations.

The drive of parents to make education a resource for the future placed great pressure on children and their relations with their parents. Mai Lin, the Taiwanese immigrant whose father and mother had to undergo a decline in occupational status in their early years of settling into their new American lives, recalled that her parents "were very encouraging in terms of my making something of myself, but at the same time they were also worried about the cost of education." She entered MIT with a scholarship while her brother went to the University of Washington. However, when he majored in psychology instead of engineering her father began "telling him what an ungrateful son that he was; they had come over all this way and were trying to give him an education, and here he was going to go into psychology." The goal of achieving success through education was an intense force in high-achieving immigrant families and remained a staunch guidepost on the avenues to adulthood for the children of immigrants.

The road to education for the Asian second generation was also a path toward developing a sense of personhood and community that transcended the boundaries of the homelands in which their parents had been socialized. In public elementary and secondary institutions, the children of immigrants were taught according to new federal and state "K to 12" curricular frameworks and standards installed from the 1990s. The diversity orientation of schools provided knowledge and values that presented the United States as an ethnic and racial democracy in which all cultures were granted equal respect. Asian American students learned that the multicultural pluralism idealized in their schools required shouldering a future responsibility as American citizens to oppose prejudice and discrimination and to maintain an interest in ethnic heritage.

In colleges and universities, where Asian American students constituted a disproportionately high percentage of the student body, ethnic studies centers and their programs brought together students in shared experiences and common activities whose parents were from home countries that regarded each other as rivals or enemies. Asian American ethnic studies and programming involved Chinese Americans, Korean Americans, Japanese Americans, and Filipino/a Americans, as well as Indian, Pakistani, and Bangladeshi American students, and thus served to build bridges between these clusters of students. As the numbers of Asian and Asian American students increased rapidly at universities and colleges, academic centers for research on Asia and its countries multiplied to expand programs in Asian studies. Founded in 1990, the innovative Center for South Asian and Indian Ocean Studies at Tufts University pioneered in establishing broad geographic frameworks to encompass multiple Asian countries. Harvard's South Asia Initiative embarked from its beginnings in 2001 on a collaborative research project titled "South Asia: Bridging the Great Divides," that crossed the divisions among states; Hindu, Muslim, and other religious communities; castes; and genders. These path-breaking academic initiatives brought together students of diverse Asian ancestries into a unified academic environment for mutual intellectual exchanges. In the twenty-first century, at least eight centers on the study of South Asia, emphasizing regionalism or trans-regionalism rather than nationalism, had been founded in colleges and universities. Keeping pace with the rising interest in interregional and transnational coverage, the University of Illinois, Urbana, founded a Center for Middle Eastern and South Asian Studies. Harvard University's Asia Center housed the Fairbank Center for Chinese Studies, the Reischauer Institute for Japan studies, and the South Asia Institute, which had evolved from the innovative South Asian Initiative. These academic centers complemented and enhanced the ethos of intergroup interaction to which undergraduates were exposed through ethnic studies courses and extracurricular activities offered by college ethnic studies centers.

Concurrent with the multicultural education gained by American-born generations of Asians, and their engagement in other assimilating forms of lifestyle and behavior, rates of interethnic and interracial marriage began to rise. In most immigrant families that prioritized endogamy, intermarriage represented a new phenomenon but one that spread inescapably as a part of assimilation. National data on ancestry gathered in 1979 demonstrated that even the newest ethnic groups from Asia showed notable rates of mixed ancestry, reflecting the frequency of intermarriage. Multiple ancestry was reported by 31 percent of Filipinos, 23 percent of Chinese, and 22 percent of Japanese who responded to a population survey conducted by the U.S. Bureau of the Census in 1979. The 1990 U.S. population report showed that among native-born married persons between twenty-five and thirty-four years of age, 50 percent of Asians had married spouses from a different ethnic or racial group. The rates of intermarriage among Asians were quite high when taking into account their historic cultural sanctions toward endogamy and the existence of U.S. laws barring miscegenation that were not stricken from state statutes until the 1960s.[23]

Social scientists and historians found that rising intermarriage became a defining force of group interaction in the twentieth century. Historian David A. Hollinger described the "extraordinary increase in marriage and reproduction across" racial lines as "a fundamental challenge to the authority of descent-defined categories." He saw the dramatic spread of intermarriage as a ratification of the principle that "individuals decide how tightly or loosely they wish to affiliate with one or more communities of descent." The intermarried and their offspring provided a kind of renewed social support to the principle of assimilationist pluralism. According to Hollinger, "they are reanimating a traditional American emphasis on the freedom of individual affiliation."[24]

Hawai'i had an important historic role as a demographic "breakout" point of interracial relationships. Hawai'i's cross-cultural pluralism fostered a relatively tolerant atmosphere for racially mixed marriages, and it was not burdened by laws like those in the mainland states that barred intermarriage. People of European ancestry who came to Hawai'i from the mainland, the other Americas, and Europe intermarried with indigenous Hawaiians, newcomers from Asia, and immigrants from other distant parts of the world. Inter-racial marriage rates (proportion of marriages involving non-white spouses) in the 1920s for white males who married was 24 percent and 15 percent for white females who married, and by the 1980s climbed to 38 percent for white males and 28 percent for white females. Inter-racial marriages involving whites combined with inter-racial marriages among racial minorities to make Hawai'i the state with the highest proportion of multi-racial individuals (descended from two or more races) in the country. The U.S. Census of 2000 reported that one out of five persons in Hawai'i was multi-racial compared to the national average of one out of forty persons being multi-racial. President Barack Obama emerged as the leading example of a public figure who originated in the Hawaiian matrix of racial intermarriage formed out of the intermingling of migrations from the Atlantic and Pacific worlds.[25]

THE POLITICS OF GLOBAL IMMIGRATION

As in the Progressive era, immigration emerged in the 1990s as a pivotal issue galvanizing political conflict over the demographic destiny of American society. While the 1980s had been a decade of immigration "romanticism," as policy expert Lawrence H. Fuchs concluded, the 1990s became the decade of immigration pessimism. Immigration turned into a grave national issue as public discourse focused on the negative effects of immigration. Prominent elected officials in both the Democratic and the Republican Party urged public action to stem the alleged disorders caused by immigrants.

When California voters passed in 1994 Proposition 187, a ballot initiative aimed at cutting off social services, public education, and health care to illegal immigrants, it quickly became a lightning rod for popular anti-immigrant feelings. It provided a "wedge" issue for incipient restrictionists to escalate charges that immigrants, both illegal and legal, damaged the lot of the average native American by taking away jobs, abusing welfare, causing crime, failing to assimilate, and overloading schools, hospitals, prisons, and other public institutions. Defenders of the immigrants counterattacked by demonstrating that immigrants brought many economic and cultural benefits and were good citizens.

By the mid-1990s, support for public policies that empowered immigrants was challenged by mounting interest in policies that discriminated against aliens as a class or subjected foreign cultures to derogated status. The Presidential Platform Committee of the Republican Party in 1996 endorsed a proposed constitutional amendment that would deny U.S. citizenship to the children of illegal aliens. Furthermore, nativists called for protection and conservation of the historic cultural basis of American life. The U.S. House of Representatives acted on a bill in 1996 that would have established English as the official language of the United States.

In transitional neighborhoods occupied by whites and blacks, the rise of nativist reaction against new immigrant enclaves sprang in part from perceptions that they benefitted from special welfare and government assistance. The feeling that immigrants were entitled minorities appeared to have been connected with the rise of hostilities and violence toward Hispanics, Southeast Asians, and Koreans in various locales across the nation. From Oakland to Los Angeles, natives—both black and white—resented Asian and Hispanic newcomers who received or were thought to receive government assistance. Resentment over the mobility of Asian newcomers and fears of international Asian economic competition appeared to foster a potential for assaults against Asian Americans. Acts of anti-Asian violence increased from the 1980s to the early 1990s. Similar resentments against Hispanic business success appeared to have been an important factor underlying assaults by blacks on Cubans in the 1980 Miami riot in which two persons of Cuban ancestry were killed.

The United States mirrored some of the xenophobic patterns of reaction to immigrants found in European countries. In France, cultural conflicts with immigrants from North Africa and the Middle East produced national efforts to promote conformity and assimilation to official French culture. European leaders and their public supporters doubted whether Muslim immigrants could be assimilated and whether Christianity and Islam were compatible within the same state. Ireland, throughout its history one of the world's primary emigration or "sending" countries, experienced unprecedented tensions as its dynamic economy began to attract immigrants from Asia, Africa, and Eastern Europe. An immigrant to Ireland who was from Sri Lanka decided that the backlash against immigrants made it necessary to leave, even after she married an Irish engineer, had become a naturalized Irish citizen, attended Trinity College (Ireland's most prestigious university), and named her daughter "Aoife" after a mythical Irish princess. Mary Toomey lamented, "I thought I belonged here. I thought my family belonged. But we don't. We did everything expected of us, and still we don't belong." She left Dublin for a new home in Connecticut.

The ideology and long history of absorbing immigrants into a democratic country gave the United States a different perspective from European countries. This was likely a factor that kept the doors open in America, one that was subjective and intangible yet powerful. Many Americans still saw themselves as a diverse people and their country as an immigrant nation from its beginnings. Naturalizations of immigrants from Asia and the western hemisphere (chiefly Latin America) surged upward (Figure 4-3). While seriously concerned with the pressures and problems created by mass immigration, many Americans were able to grasp the benefits brought by the foreign born and the connection of their contributions to democratic values. It seemed that the public was willing to accept immigration as long as it was perceived to serve the national interest. To many Americans, their national interest

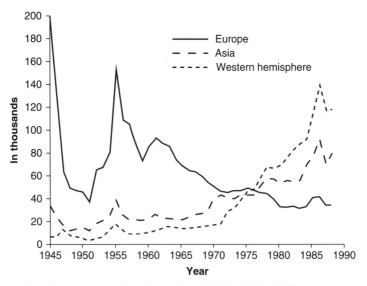

Figure 4-3. Persons naturalized by region of birth, 1945–1988.

required effective immigration controls, but, above all, the need to promote assimilation in a democratic spirit. Many newcomers and natives agreed with President Bill Clinton when in 1998 he advised immigrants, "Honor our laws. Embrace our culture. Learn our language. Know our history." Otherwise, the President warned, ethnic pride would lead to ethnocentrism and a withdrawal from the larger community. President Clinton's speechwriter, Eric Liu, described how he sought in his book, *The Accidental Asian* (1998), to express a deep concern over group identity. It can start from a political strategy, Liu cautioned, but could move into a more abstract realm of the reductive racial label that does not reflect the reality of choosing "what degree of in-between, which of the innumerable possible combinations, what sort of synthesis we will bring into being," while popular experience shows there is not a single way to be ethnic in America. Liu suggested it would be realistic in the best sense to embrace "the in-between," expressed socially by intermarriage, assimilation, or globalization, to be accepting of the flux of change and choice and to see the outcome of life in America as a "palimpsest" that represents "neither monoculturalism [nor] multiculturalism" but an "omniculturalism."[26]

Notwithstanding Liu's concerns, the will and effort of Asian immigrants to become part of the American nation has been demonstrated in their rapid achievement of naturalized citizenship. The new Asian immigrants had brought their ethnic identities and cultures, but they were committed to becoming integrated as U.S. citizens and to make American nationality the center of their core identity.

Notes

1. Nancy Foner, *From Ellis Island to JFK: New York's Two Great Waves of Immigration* (New Haven, Conn.: Yale University Press, 2000), pp. 10, 18.

2. Susan Schulten, *The Geographical Imagination in America, 1880–1950* (Chicago: University of Chicago Press, 2001), pp. 214–222, 229–238.

3. Marcus Lee Hansen, "The Problem of the Third Generation Immigrant" (Delivered to the Augustana Historical Society, Rock Island, Illinois, 1937), reprinted in Peter Kivisto and Dag Blanck, *American Immigrants and Their Generations: Studies and Commentaries on the Hansen Thesis after Fifty Years* (Urbana: University of Illinois Press, 1990), pp. 194–195.

4. Victor R. Greene, "Ethnic Confrontations with State Universities, 1860–1920" in Bernard J. Weiss, ed., *American Education and the European Immigrant, 1840–1940* (Urbana: University of Illinois Press, 1982), pp. 189–207.

5. Mary Patrice Erdmans, *Opposite Poles: Immigrants and Ethnics in Polish Chicago, 1976–1990* (University Park: Pennsylvania State University Press, 2007), pp. 210–215.

6. Bill Ong Hing, *Making and Remaking Asian America through Immigration Policy, 1850–1990* (Stanford, Calif.: Stanford University Press, 1993), ch. 1–3.

7. Tomas R. Jimenez, *Replenished Ethnicity: Mexican Americans, Immigration, and Identity* (Berkeley: University of California Press, 2010), pp. 126–127.

8. Marcus Lee Hansen, *The Mingling of the Canadian and American Peoples* (New Haven, Conn.: Yale University Press, 1940), ch. 6, 8, 9, 10, 11.

9. Nana Oishi, "Pacific: Japan, Australia, New Zealand," in Mary C. Waters, Reed Ueda, Helen Marrow, eds., *New Americans: A Guide to Immigration since 1965* (Cambridge, Mass.: Harvard University Press, 2007).

10. Tolu Muliaina, "Remittances, the Social System and Development in Samoa," in Robyn Iredale, Charles Hawksley, and Stephen Castles, eds., *Migration in the Asia Pacific: Population, Settlement and Citizenship Issues* (Cheltenham, UK: Edward Elgar, 2003), pp. 259–272; Craig R. Janes, *Migration, Social Change, and Health: A Samoan Community in Urban California* (Stanford, Calif.: Stanford University Press, 1990), pp. 38–43, 44–58; Cathy A. Small, *Voyages: From Tongan Villages to American Suburbs* (Ithaca, N.Y.: Cornell University Press, 1997), pp. 193–205, 217–229.

11. Stephen Castles and Mark J. Miller, *The Age of Migration: International Population Movements in the Modern World* (New York: Guilford Press, 1993), p. 223.

12. Lawrence H. Fuchs, *The American Kaleidoscope: Race, Ethnicity, and the Civic Culture* (Hanover, N. H.: Wesleyan University Press, 1990), p. 279.

13. Lawrence H. Fuchs, "Immigration Reform in 1911 and 1981: The Role of Select Commissions," *Journal of American Ethnic History* 3 (Fall 1983): 58–89; Peter H. Schuck, "The Transformation of Immigration Law," *Columbia Law Review* 84 (1984); Peter H. Schuck, "The Politics of Rapid Legal Change: Immigration Policy in the 1980s," *Studies in American Political Development* 6 (Spring 1992): 37–92; Gil Loescher and John Scanlan, *Calculated Kindness: Refugees and America's Half-Open Door* (New York: Free Press, 1986), pp. 153–155.

14. Michael Jones-Correa, "Under Two Flags: Dual Nationality in Latin America and Its Consequences for Naturalization in the United States," *International Migration Review* 35, no. 4 (Summer 2004): 997–1029; Jones-Correa, *Between Two Nations: The Political Predicament of Latinos in New York City* (Ithaca, N.Y.: Cornell University Press, 1998); Irene Bloemraad, "Who Claims Dual Citizenship? The Limits of Postnationalism, the Problems of Transnationalism, and the Persistence of Traditional Citizenship," *International Migration Review* 38, no. 2 (Summer 2004):389–426.

15. Robyn Iredale, Charles Hawksley, and Stephen Castles, eds., *Migration in the Asia Pacific: Population, Settlement and Citizenship Issues* (Cheltenham, UK: Edward Elgar, 2003), Parts One and Two.

16. June Namias, *First Generation: In the Words of Twentieth-Century American Immigrants*, rev. ed. (Urbana: University of Illinois Press, 1992), pp. 231ff.

17. Victor G. and Brett de Bary Nee, *Longtime Californ': A Documentary Study of an American Chinatown* (Stanford, Calif.: Stanford University Press, 1972), pp. 253–261.

18. Herbert Barringer, Robert W. Gardner, and Michael J. Levin, *Asians and Pacific Islanders in the United States* (New York: Russell Sage Foundation, 1993), pp. 237, 239, Tables 8.3 and 8.4.

19. Barringer, Gardner, and Levin, *Asians and Pacific Islanders*, pp. 110–111, Table 4.1; Peter Kwong, *The New Chinatown* (New York: The Noonday Press, Farrar, Straus and Giroux, 1987), pp. 39–42; and Kwong, *The New Chinatown*, rev. ed. (1996), ch. 10.

20. Barringer, Gardner, and Levin, *Asians and Pacific Islanders*, Table 7.6, pp. 210–211.

21. Namias, *First Generation*, rev. ed., pp. 183–187.

22. Arthur W. Helweg and Usha M. Helweg, *An Immigrant Success Story: East Indians in America* (Philadelphia: University of Pennsylvania Press, 1990); Arthur Helweg, *Asian Indians in Michigan* (East Lansing: Michigan State University, 2002).

23. U.S. Bureau of the Census, *Current Populations Reports, Series P-23, no. 116, Ancestry and Language in the United States: November 1979* (Washington, D.C.: U.S. Government Printing Office, 1982), p. 7.

24. David Hollinger, *Post-Ethnic America: Beyond Multiculturalism* (New York: Basic Books, 2006), pp. 42–46.

25. In the 2000 U.S. Census of Population, a new enumeration category for persons of multi-racial ancestry appeared. Hawai'i had largest proportion of "multi-racials" of any state.

26. Eric Liu, *The Accidental Asian: Notes of a Native Speaker* (New York: Random House, 1998), p. 201.

FIVE

The Pacific Coast as a National and Global Hub

"The Far West has hitherto been to Americans of the Atlantic States the land of freedom and adventure and mystery. . . ."[1]
Lord James Bryce, *The American Commonwealth*

"[It is the] 'third space' which enables other positions to emerge . . . displaces the histories that constitute it, and sets new structures of authority, new political initiatives, which are inadequately understood through received wisdom."[2]
Homi Bhabha, "Third Space"

"Pictures often convey values more powerfully than words, and Hollywood is the world's greatest promoter and exporter of visual symbols. Even the consumption of fast food can make an implicit statement about rejecting traditional ways."[3]
Joseph S. Nye, Jr., *Soft Power*

Transcontinental migrants to the Pacific coast brought quests for rebuilding lives, earlier generated by immigrants in the Atlantic region, into a far western realm open to innovation and experimentation. Historian Hasia R. Diner has noted that for American Jews who moved from east-coast urban centers to build new lives and communities in western states like California, "The West has functioned as the place from which they emphasize their embrace of America and its transformative power."[4] This historical insight can probably be applied to Swedes who moved from Wisconsin, Minnesota, and Iowa to Hilmar in California's central valley; the Danes who also came from the midwest to start Solvang in the Santa Ynez Valley; Irish Catholics who moved from Boston, New York City, and Philadelphia to San Francisco; and numerous other immigrants who first established themselves in the east coast and the midwest before re-settling in California where they could probe fuller possibilities for social mobility, pluralism, and assimilation.[5] Allensworth, in the central valley near Bakersfield, was one of the first enclaves in California started by African Americans who sought to build

164

communities away from racially segregated southern states. The move to California by these transcontinental migrants also involved a search for new and higher educational opportunities. The leaders of Solvang established Atterdag College, whose purpose was to promote Danish ethnic studies, and the town of Allensworth endeavored to build an industrial school for its youth.

Newcomers from other regions of the United States formed over half of the American-born population resident in California in 1970. Many were white easterners, midwesterners, and southerners seeking new avenues of social mobility (Table 5-1). From the south and southwest came African Americans, Hispanic Americans, and Native Americans departing from areas where they had endured a long history of white supremacy. By the late twentieth century, California had a larger black population than any state except for New York and Illinois, and a larger Hispanic population than Texas. Prominent African Americans in California who came out of the westward mass migrations of blacks included Ralph Bunche, Tom Bradley, and Jackie Robinson.[6] Los Angeles attracted one of the largest populations of Mexicans in the western hemisphere, and in the first decade of the twenty-first century elected a Mexican-American mayor, Antonio Villaraigosa.

The diverse newcomers to California, both whites and minorities, held in common the aspiration of moving to new communities to escape the limiting life conditions in their old hometowns (Map 3). Their displacement from the confines of the "rust belt" and provincial worlds released them into a "third space" where they could intermingle in innovative ways and styles and initiate the creation of a new political economy.[7] The Pacific coast region stood for solving the problems and limitations, and realizing the unfulfilled goals, of the older societies of the U.S. Atlantic coast and its hinterlands.

A NEW POLITICAL ECONOMY OF DIVERSITY

Opportunistic migrants moved across the continent to the Pacific coast and built social, economic, and institutional connections between the Atlantic and Pacific worlds. American society on the Pacific Rim acted as a catalyst of the global transformation that swept the country in the late twentieth century. In the long perspective of history, California cities became successors to nineteenth-century metropolitan Chicago. "Chicago dreaming" and "booster dreams" once defined the "self-making" spirit of the "Windy City."[8] The westward gaze fixed at the turn of the twentieth century on the midwest, where Chicago was seen as a city of newcomers and limitless innovation. Historian Timothy B. Spears described Chicago "as a city for restless dreamers and doers . . . populated chiefly by people who came from somewhere else . . . a city where anything seemed possible."[9] This evocation of creative destiny in Chicago would be applied almost word for word to behold the "California dream" in Los Angeles in the twentieth century. The *Los Angeles Times* newspaper dynasty formed by Harrison Gray Otis and Otis Chandler, both from families that originated in New England, started the process

Table 5-1. 1970: California Population by Native and Foreign Birth.

Born in California: As Percent of Total Native Born Residents, Calif.	Born in Other U.S. Region: As Percent of Total Native Born Residents, Calif.						
	North-east	North Central	South	West (not Calif. born)	State of Birth Not Reported	Native, Born Abroad	Foreign Born
47.4	7.4	17.3	13.4	7.7	5.2	1.5	8.8

1990: California Population by Native and Foreign Birth.

Born in California: As Percent of Total Native-Born Residents, Calif.	Born in Other U. S. Region: As Percent of Total Native-Born Residents, Calif.					
	North-East	North Central	South	West (not Calif. born)	Native Born, Abroad	Foreign Born
59.2	7.8	13.5	10.8	7.0		21.7

Source: Compiled and computed from Reports of the 1970 U.S. Census of Population, Characteristics of the Population Volume 1, Part 6: California, Section 2, p. 1148; Reports of the 1990 U.S. Census of Population, Social and Economic Characteristics, California, Section 1, Table 23, p. 197.

of making Los Angeles the nation's guiding star of urban development, "the city of the future."[10]

At the center of this transcontinental shift swirled newcomers who brought the human capital and labor for new corporate enterprises, which skillfully tapped financial assets from eastern and international corporate institutions. The parallel between the relocation of the Brooklyn Dodgers baseball team to Los Angeles and the postwar migration there of Jews from New York symbolized California's dream of the arrival of east-coast institutions and people that would find an important new role in its regional development. Historian Deborah Dash Moore noted, "The deep identification of Brooklyn with the Dodgers suggested that Los Angeles, too, could achieve the same renown, the same commonality of purpose and culture, if the baseball team moved to the city."[11] Jewish New Yorkers brought with them cultural life created by and for earlier generations in New York. For example, Camp Roosevelt, a summer camp for Jewish children located in the foothills of the San Jacinto Mountains outside of Los Angeles, was based on summer camps in the Catskills and Adirondacks of New York state. Historian Neal Gabler described the central role of the entertainment industry in allowing Jews from the east coast and midwest to produce an "empire of their own." Instead of the caste-like structure dominated by Protestant elites and Catholic masses, Los Angeles appeared as a social blank slate in which Jews could rise to new heights of social mobility and religious accommodation.[12]

Areas from which migrants had long been coming to the far west continued to send newcomers into the late twentieth century. The descendants of enslaved African Americans continued to leave southern states for Pacific shores. Asian Americans located across the country but their largest inter-regional migrations were from the northeast, upper Midwest, and Gulf states to the Pacific coast states (Map 5-1). Cross-border migrations from Canada and Mexico, and regional immigration from the Caribbean and Latin America, flowed into the far west with a greater diversity of subgroups. The federal government spurred rural-to-urban migration in Los Angeles through sponsored resettlement of Native Americans from southwestern reservations. As a result, Los Angeles became a city with one of the largest populations of residents with American Indian ancestry in the country.

Transcontinental movements of people from older established regional communities in the east, north, and south propelled the emergence of the modern Pacific coast. A panoply of groups, each with different skill sets and collective expertise but united by the common objective of rebuilding their lives through social mobility in new surroundings, composed the human material with the potential to power regional transformation.

California became the pacesetter for urban population growth through migration and expanding diversity. A volume by social scientists on aspects of Los Angeles diversity stated, "Since 1960, L. A. has been transformed from the Whitest large city in the country to its most diverse . . . [as] international migration, primarily of Latinos and Asians, replaced internal migration [of native-born whites

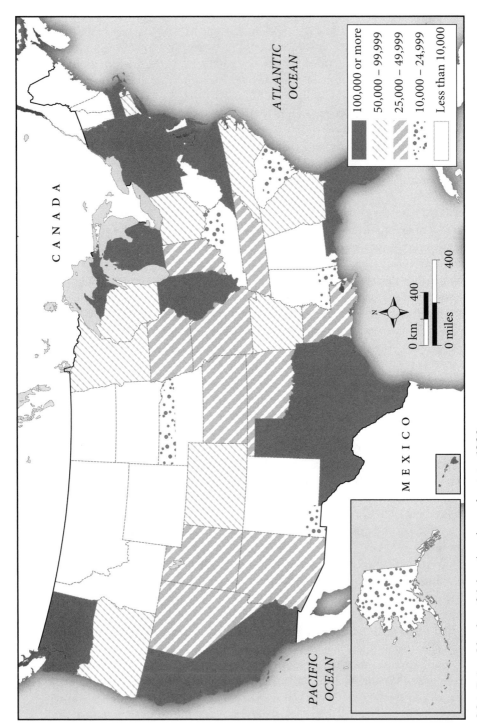

Map 5-1. Number of Asian Americans, by state, 1980.

and Africans] as the 'feeder' of Los Angeles."[13] At the start of the twenty-first century, California had become home to one out of eight Americans, nearly forty million people, which was greater than the population of four-fifths of the countries in the world. Several cities had developed into the largest and fastest growing urban centers in the nation. California had eight of the fifty most populous U.S. cities: Los Angeles (the nation's 2nd largest), San Diego (8th), San Jose (10th), San Francisco (13th), Fresno (34th), Sacramento (35th), Long Beach (36th), and Oakland (47th). Los Angeles County alone had a greater population than forty-two states and continuously ranked as the most populous county in the United States for many decades.

Once a raw and remote borderland between the Atlantic and Pacific regions, the U.S. west coast transformed itself after World War II into a new core sector, more open to innovations and their progressive development than other parts of the country. It grew into a control center for national and global development, with sophisticated new economies in high technology, mass consumer industries, and mega-projects for urban and suburban expansion.[14]

The role of the southern California region of the west coast as an interdisciplinary innovation leader in high technology was epitomized by the establishment in 1999 of the Institute for Creative Technologies (ICT) at the University of Southern California. Funded by a long-term contract from the U.S. Army, the mission of ICT was "to explore a powerful question: What would happen if leading technologists in artificial intelligence, graphics, and immersion joined forces with the creative talents of Hollywood and the game industry?" ICT announced, "Los Angeles, the entertainment capital of the world, was a logical base of these endeavors. Each and every day ICT is able to leverage our location near major movie and game studios to achieve our goals." Furthermore, ICT found a natural academic home at the University of Southern California, "one of the nation's top research universities, renowned the world over for its programs in cinema, interactive media, education and computer science." The outcome of this regional synergy was described as follows: "ICT brings film and game industry artists together with computer and social scientists to study and develop immersive media for military training, health therapies, education and more. Research projects explore and expand how people engage with computers, through virtual characters, video games and simulated scenarios. ICT is a recognized leader in the development of virtual humans who look, think and behave like real people. . . . Being based in Los Angeles facilitates collaboration with major movie and game makers."[15]

As much as the Pacific coast formed a magnet for entrepreneurial talents who built new technology empires, it also offered a stimulating atmosphere for pioneers of social innovation. Since the 1960s, social movements on the Pacific coast became innovation leaders in politics and protests on college campuses, minority empowerment, religious revivalism, or one of California's numerous referendum causes such as anti-tax crusades or Proposition 187 aimed against immigration. The Pacific-coast breeding ground of social movements gave birth to new waves of social innovation, often commercialized by enterprising businessmen, that would spill over the far west and flow back east to change the rest of the country. Contemplating the relationship between a particular social movement and innovation, sociologist Todd Gitlin observed, "The identity of the movement that sprang up was a brilliant exercise in social innovation. It deserves an entrepreneurship award."[16]

California functioned as the quintessential space for envisioning new opportunities and lifestyles. The newcomers in California from "back east" judged the novel conditions of their displacement in a bicoastal frame of reference. The "Golden State" represented in the popular consciousness surroundings unburdened by de-humanizing overcrowding, post-industrial stagnation, urban decay, cold winter weather, and summer heat and humidity that characterized debilitating life "back east." Furthermore, the open and novel conditions of the California coast contributed to the liberating feeling, also found in other communities of hustle-and-bustle development, expressed as "if you're new to the community, you can carve out your own niche."[17]

Governmental institutions in California, from the municipal and county level up to the state capital, pioneered in the manipulation of new incentives for regional enterprise and development. The agencies of the state liberally provided the permitting, licensing, incorporation, and legal clearances for innovations in public works and private enterprises. William Mulholland, a civil engineer who immigrated from Ireland, headed an unprecedented construction project which redirected Owens River water across hundreds of miles of deserts and mountains to arid Los Angeles, which turned it into a green metropolis capable of massive population growth. Just north of Los Angeles, Kern County developed into one of the world's greatest centers for energy production. Oil drilling was conducted on an enormous scale by corporations from 1899, making Kern County a global leader in petroleum and gas production. A century later, Kern County was the home of some of the nation's largest "farms" of wind turbines, generating more electrical power through wind than any other county in California.[18]

California's political economy integrated natural resource development, automobile transportation, and suburbanization into a scaffolding for innovation that pulled burgeoning masses of consumers into glittering theaters, shopping centers, hotels, restaurants, malls, amusement parks, and resorts.[19] The business and political leaders of postwar California appeared to be guided by a "new basis of civilization," foreseen a half-century earlier by an east coast professor, Simon Patten of the University of Pennsylvania's Wharton School, which he described as follows: "The new morality does not consist in saving, but in expanding consumption; not in draining men of their energy, but in storing up a surplus in the weak and young; not in the process of hardening, but in extending the period of recreation and leisure; not in the thought of the future, but in the utilization and expansion of the present."[20]

Around the City of Los Angeles, a commercial penumbra extended through the vast built environment collectively labeled the "Southland," which was to a large extent an empire built by the real estate industry. Los Angeles evolved into a city of suburbs linked through the nation's most extensive urban automobile road network that replaced its former electrical trolley system, once the western hemisphere's largest street rail system. This geo-economic force field propagated new suburban tracts, industrial parks, and shopping centers supported by an automobile-based lifestyle of drive-to, drive-in, and drive-through daily activity, enabled by new road systems and ample, free or low-cost parking facilities. Commercial advertising was creatively adapted to selling products by roadside signage to consumers who drove by in cars. Los Angeles, which fast became the automobile metropolis par excellence, became the leader of "in-your-face" drive-by advertising. A drive through its streets became a tour through an environment of billboards and neon signs over which the ultimate sign spelling "HOLLYWOOD" stood in 50-foot-tall and 450-foot-long lettering.[21]

The forces of urbanization that had dominated the northeast and the upper midwest during the industrial revolution gravitated to the new economic frontiers of the Pacific coast. The coastal strip from the Bay area, with its triple colossi of San Francisco, Oakland, and San Jose down through Los Angeles to San Diego turned into a leading sector for urbanization in the country. The wide-open spaces of the "Inland Empire," the interior hinterlands where Los Angeles County, San Bernardino County, and Riverside County converged, became an "interlogistics corridor" that cradled a new transportation economy. It arose from the progression of "containerizing" cargo, first employed in ships in the Port of Oakland after World War II, into massive transshipment facilities where 80 percent of the goods arriving in the Port of Los Angeles and Long Beach, and also air freight from Los Angeles International Airport ("LAX"), were transferred in containers to trucks and railroads for further distribution across the country. Growth rates of Inland Empire urban centers accelerated to levels matching the metropolitan Pacific coast. Urbanization widened around cities such as San Bernardino, Riverside, Ontario, and in enclaves of Moreno Valley. Palm Springs became an example of "sprawl" as the once sleepy desert oasis resort sprouted into a zone of multiple centers including Palm Desert, La Quinta, Twenty-Nine Palms, Indio, and Desert Hot Springs, attracting both upscale vacation homeowners and immigrant workers who maintained the golf courses, restaurants, hotels, and condominiums.

After World War II, Pan American World Airways (which originally serviced Latin American and Caribbean routes) expanded to the west coast and the Asia Pacific and transformed travel between the Atlantic and Pacific—between Asia, Europe, and the Americas. Pan Am became the trailblazer for conveying the new global passenger traffic consisting not only of tourists but increasingly of immigrants. A multinational business corporation with worldwide branch offices and facilities, Pan Am was in and of itself an organizational network for global migration as it hired employees from all over the world.[22]

The west coast, Las Vegas, and Hawai'i were joined together in a triangle of mass migration formed out of tourists, retirees, and students attending regional universities and colleges. During the Cold War, the United States and Japan became the leading exporters of tourists in the Pacific region. Hawai'i, Guam, and California became the favorite vacation spots of Japanese tourists. Hawai'i also became a magnet for mass tourism from the U.S. mainland and achieved worldwide status as a vacation destination. Las Vegas grew into a new national model of mass entertainment after World War II and a global tourist mecca by the late twentieth century. It became the vibrant paradigm for casino resort centers from the Gulf Coast to the east coast. Las Vegas became such a regular and preferred destination of tourists from Hawai'i that real estate entrepreneur Sam Boyd (an Oklahoma native) started casino hotels in Las Vegas—such as the well-known California Hotel—catering specially to tourists from Hawai'i by serving local Hawaiian food and making discounted rates available to Hawaiian residents and anyone who had been born in Hawai'i.[23] Indeed, Las Vegas became a favorite place to relocate for retirees from Hawai'i: men and women quit their jobs in Honolulu and bought their retirement homes in the sandy neighborhoods of "Sin City." The University of Nevada at Las Vegas offered a hotel and hospitality industry program that attracted many students from Hawai'i who prepared for a career in the Hawaiian tourism economy.

Vacationers and the elderly from all over the United States followed the sun to the resorts of the beaches, deserts, and mountains of the Pacific coast. Enterprising boosters of tourism and retirement communities built on the century-old reputation of southern California as superior to arch-rival Florida in the salubriousness of its climate. R. W. C. Farnsworth's *A Southern California Paradise*, published in Pasadena in 1883, declared, "The surplus of water, the lowness of the land, and the long, hot summer make Florida subject to malaria and fever." *Bentley's Handbook of the Pacific Coast*, a guide published in Oakland in 1884 by a physician, disparaged Florida's "humid atmosphere." Florida's proximity to northeastern urban centers gave it a head start catering to vacationers and retirees seeking warmer regions, but California's state and local governments aggressively promoted the efforts of entrepreneurs to build resorts and homes rapidly in Los Angeles, Santa Barbara, and San Diego to overtake Florida's market.[24]

Travel to the Pacific far west from across the United States accelerated with the expansion of air travel and the interstate highway system in the postwar decades. People from "back east" seeking better living and working conditions could move easily to a land of change and opportunity simply by driving an automobile or taking an airplane. Colleges up and down the west coast annually attracted thousands of students from across the United States who flocked to the campuses of the highly developed and affordable public universities of California, Oregon, Nevada, and Washington. The waves of tourists spurred the development of a vast network of resorts and attractions in Los Angeles, San Diego, Las Vegas, and Orange County.

To provide travel accommodations for the millions of temporary and transient newcomers to California, the motel industry that had originated in the automobile subculture underwent an enormous expansion (Figure 5-1). Immigrant

Figure 5-1.   Super 8 Motel in San Jose, California.

entrepreneurs from India propelled the motel industry. Starting in the San Francisco Bay area, Indian immigrant families became managers or owner-operators of fifty percent of the motels in California, particularly in budget chains such as "Super 8" motels, and branched out to other parts of the country.[25]

All these migrating groups connected with each other in the far west to create human networks that contributed to the integration of worldwide social, cultural, and human capital. Migrations linked the Atlantic and Pacific regions to create a new pluralism that was the foundation for intergroup collaboration, expertise, and leadership. The Pacific coast harbored a novel international and bicoastal culture of enterprise and innovation involving immigrants, natives, and highly transient subgroups such as consumers of tourism, college students, and technology workers.[26] This interaction formed "bridging cultural capital"—a parallel to the "bridging social capital" described by political scientist Robert Putnam—that facilitated the inclusionary and outreaching activities of intercultural collaboration.

CULTURAL PRODUCTION AND INNOVATION

Since Sam Patch, America's first daredevil, and P. T. Barnum provided spectacle for the paying masses in the nineteenth century, popular consumer demand created rising expectations for entertainment. This trend turned California and nearby areas into new experimental spaces for cultural production and new markets for the consumption of entertainment.[27] The result was the production of commercialized popular culture on an industrial scale. The entrepreneurs of the motion picture industry, the iconic innovation of Los Angeles mass culture, sprang from the transcontinental migration of American entertainers and their producers and a wave of foreign talents to southern California. What had begun as their dreamlike visions for a new medium in the enclaves of eastern industrial cities or foreign countries were transformed into a commercial product in the sunny spaces for film-making of Los Angeles neighborhoods in Hollywood and the San Fernando Valley. Movie-making in and around Los Angeles gave the entire region an ethos of imaginative taste conducive to popular creativity. A bi-ographer of Amy Semple McPherson, a Canadian immigrant turned evangelist who electrified preaching with Hollywood spectacular effects at her famous An-gelus Temple of the Foursquare Gospel Church in 1920s Los Angeles, stated, "The whole sprawling city was a potential movie set, since one never knew when life might be absorbed by art; and once the Angelenos saw themselves on the silver screen [in location shots] they would in some degree regard life as a cinematic spectacle."[28]

The migrating members of the Hughes family of Texas, the Cochrane family of Chicago, the Laemmle family of Oshkosh, Wisconsin, and the Rubin family of Brooklyn typified the networking of talented newcomers from dispersed origins who came to southern California to pioneer motion pictures by leveraging their accumulated economic and human capital. They were representative examples of the crisscrossing intergenerational networks of talents from all over the country whose transcontinental convergence energized the making of the movie indus-try. Howard Hughes was an iconic figure who personified the transition from the industrial revolution to the new political economy of innovation and enterprise fostered in California. He converted his vast inherited wealth from the Texas oil industry into pioneering enterprises in aerospace by founding Hughes Aircraft and in mass entertainment where he ran Hollywood motion picture studios such as RKO. Robert Cochrane, whose father had been a famous judge and head of the Wheeling and Lake Erie Railway of Toledo, Ohio, and whose brother, Negley, was one of the great "muck-raking" journalists of the Progressive era, worked at the first modern advertising agency in the downtown Loop section of Chicago, where he became a business partner of one of the ad firm's clients, Carl Laemmle. A German Jewish immigrant who operated the Oshkosh, Wisconsin, branch of a men's clothing store, Laemmle, with Cochrane's mentorship and financial back-ing, started distributing and showing movies in the Chicago area. Together Laemmle and Cochrane decided to seize the entrepreneurial "bull by the horns" and move to California to make their own movies. Laemmle became the founder of Universal Studios and Pictures in the San Fernando Valley area near Holly-wood. Robert Cochrane used his expertise to run the advertising department at Universal, where he created the "movie poster": a new form of advertisement in which every movie would receive a unique, sizable, and artistic poster depicting scenes and actors. His brother, Phil, also left the Chicago advertising agency to join him at Universal. Their creative older brother Witt K. Cochrane, the agency's founder, followed. The three Cochrane ad men had exchanged the "windy city" for sunny Los Angeles. Witt's daughter, Nan Cochrane, who attended the Dana Hall School for Girls in Wellesley, Massachusetts and the University of Chicago, moved to Pasadena and became one of the first woman executives at Universal, as head of script development, and then at RKO movie studios, run by the oil and aviation magnate Howard Hughes. At RKO, Nan Cochrane's daughter, Nancy, who worked as a secretary, met and married the studio attorney Edward Rubin, the son of Russian Jewish immigrants from Brooklyn. Rubin became Hughes' attorney, and later headed the preeminent entertainment law firm in Los Angeles, Mitchell, Silberberg, and Knupp, and served as president of the California Bar Association and Beverly Hills Bar.[29]

The motion picture industry of Hollywood and nearby neighborhoods was formed out of the interplay of transcontinental migrant networks of entrepreneurial talents such as these members of the Hughes, Cochrane, Laemmle, and Rubin families. The heads of Metro-Goldwyn-Mayer (MGM), Warner Brothers, Twentieth Century Fox, and other studios were from Jewish families newly arrived in the United States. Countless talents—aspiring moguls, actors, screenwriters, artists, musicians, and craftsmen—moved across the country to southern California to start careers in the movie-making enterprise.[30]

The Los Angeles entertainment industry known as "Hollywood" became a mecca that brought together theatrical talents from immigrant and minority communities of the Atlantic region with those of the west coast and the Asia Pacific. Hollywood was a hearth of cosmopolitan culture and social networks. International cinema talents migrated from Europe and Asia and declared their U.S. citizenship in federal courts near the Hollywood studios where they made movies. Many, like Marlene Dietrich, left Europe during the rise of fascism; others, like actress Joan Fontaine (previously Joan de Beauvoir de Havilland) and Oscar-winning cinematographer James Wong Howe, came from Asia (Figure 5-2a, b, c).

After World War II, motion picture, television, and music productions popularized romantic images of trans-Pacific encounters. The Pacific-region image in the national media was formed in entertainment vehicles such as the musical "South Pacific," Elvis Presley movies shot in Hawai'i ("Blue Hawaii" and "Paradise Hawaiian Style"), "surfin' songs" (by the Beach Boys and Jan and Dean), surfin' music by Dick Dale (a California transplant from Massachusetts), and the hit television shows *Hawaiian Eye, Hawaii Five-O,* and *Magnum, P.I.* Other imagined figures cast from the Pacific who became important mass media icons were Charlie Chan, once the most famous and recognizable consulting detective in U.S. movies next to Sherlock Holmes, who hailed from Honolulu according to the script; David Carradine, the star of the legendary television series *Kung Fu,* who played Kwai Chang Caine, a half-Chinese vagabond martial artist who dispensed Asian-style justice and wisdom to the "wild west"; and Pat Morita, who became the "sensei," karate master "Mister Miyagi" in a series of popular movies that began with *The Karate Kid.*

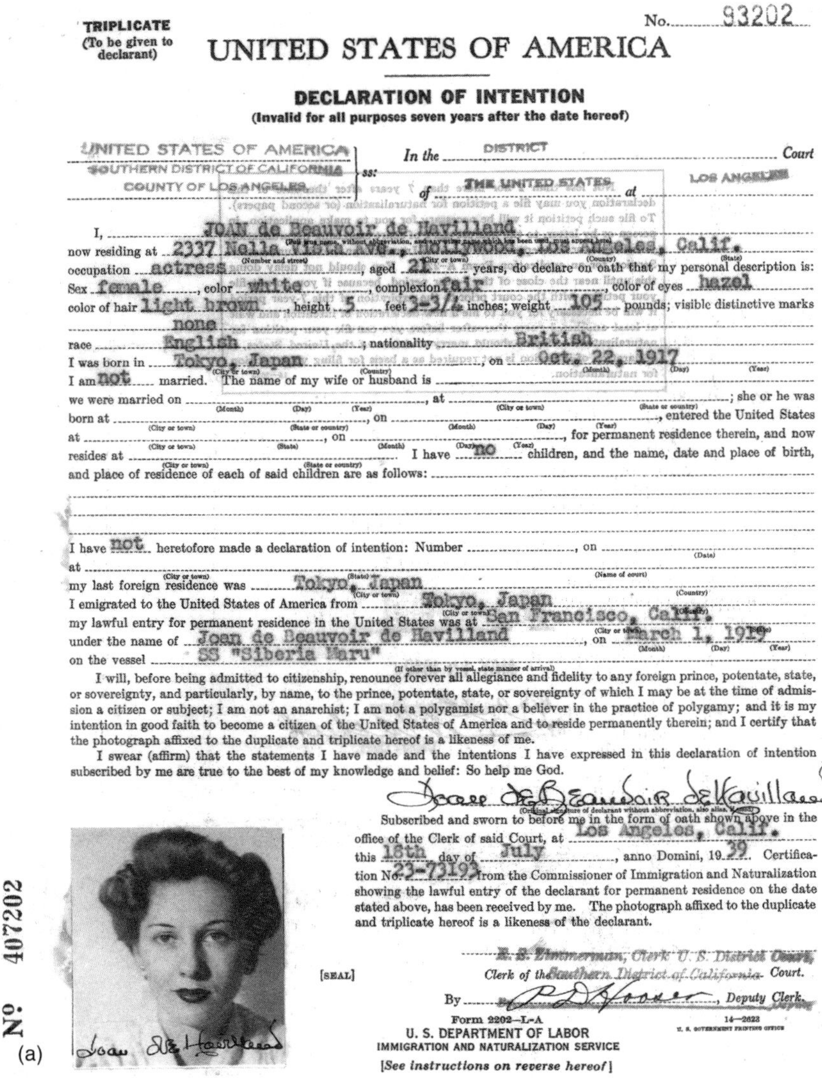

TRIPLICATE
(To be given to declarant)

No. 93202

UNITED STATES OF AMERICA

DECLARATION OF INTENTION
(Invalid for all purposes seven years after the date hereof)

UNITED STATES OF AMERICA
SOUTHERN DISTRICT OF CALIFORNIA } ss:
COUNTY OF LOS ANGELES

In the DISTRICT Court

of THE UNITED STATES at LOS ANGELES

I, Joan de Beauvoir de Havilland
now residing at 2337 Nella Vista Ave., Hollywood, Los Angeles, Calif.
occupation actress, aged 21 years, do declare on oath that my personal description is:
Sex female, color white, complexion fair, color of eyes hazel
color of hair light brown, height 5 feet 3-3/4 inches; weight 105 pounds; visible distinctive marks none
race English; nationality British
I was born in Tokyo, Japan, on Oct. 22, 1917
I am not married. The name of my wife or husband is

we were married on , at ; she or he was
born at , on , entered the United States
at , on , for permanent residence therein, and now
resides at . I have no children, and the name, date and place of birth,
and place of residence of each of said children are as follows:

I have not heretofore made a declaration of intention: Number , on
at ; my last foreign residence was Tokyo, Japan
I emigrated to the United States of America from Tokyo, Japan
my lawful entry for permanent residence in the United States was at San Francisco, Calif.
under the name of Joan de Beauvoir de Havilland, on March 1, 1919
on the vessel SS "Siberia Maru"

I will, before being admitted to citizenship, renounce forever all allegiance and fidelity to any foreign prince, potentate, state, or sovereignty, and particularly, by name, to the prince, potentate, state, or sovereignty of which I may be at the time of admission a citizen or subject; I am not an anarchist; I am not a polygamist nor a believer in the practice of polygamy; and it is my intention in good faith to become a citizen of the United States of America and to reside permanently therein; and I certify that the photograph affixed to the duplicate and triplicate hereof is a likeness of me.

I swear (affirm) that the statements I have made and the intentions I have expressed in this declaration of intention subscribed by me are true to the best of my knowledge and belief: So help me God.

Joan de Beauvoir de Havilland

Subscribed and sworn to before me in the form of oath shown above in the office of the Clerk of said Court, at Los Angeles, Calif.
this 18th day of July, anno Domini, 19 39. Certification No. 2-7219 from the Commissioner of Immigration and Naturalization showing the lawful entry of the declarant for permanent residence on the date stated above, has been received by me. The photograph affixed to the duplicate and triplicate hereof is a likeness of the declarant.

[SEAL]

R. S. Zimmerman, Clerk U. S. District Court.
Clerk of the Southern District of California Court.
By , Deputy Clerk.

Form 2202-L-A
U. S. DEPARTMENT OF LABOR
IMMIGRATION AND NATURALIZATION SERVICE
[See instructions on reverse hereof]

Nº 407202

(a)

Figure 5-2. Naturalized immigrants in the transnational American motion picture industry: (a) Joan Fontaine (previously Joan de Beauvoir de Havilland). (b) Marlene Dietrich, and (c) James Wong Howe.

The movie studios found new neighbors in the television studios of Warner Brothers, Walt Disney, Quinn Martin, Ziv, and Desilu, and the recording studios of Capitol Records, Dunhill Records, and A&M Records. Innumerable talents in the Los Angeles-based media productions of the 1950s and 1960s were transcontinental "transplants." Actor Leonard Nimoy came from Boston, Patty Duke from New York City, and Kim Novak from Chicago to achieve fame and fortune and demonstrate the great opportunities in motion pictures and television that lured masses of aspiring talents to Los Angeles. Phil Spector, a record producer,

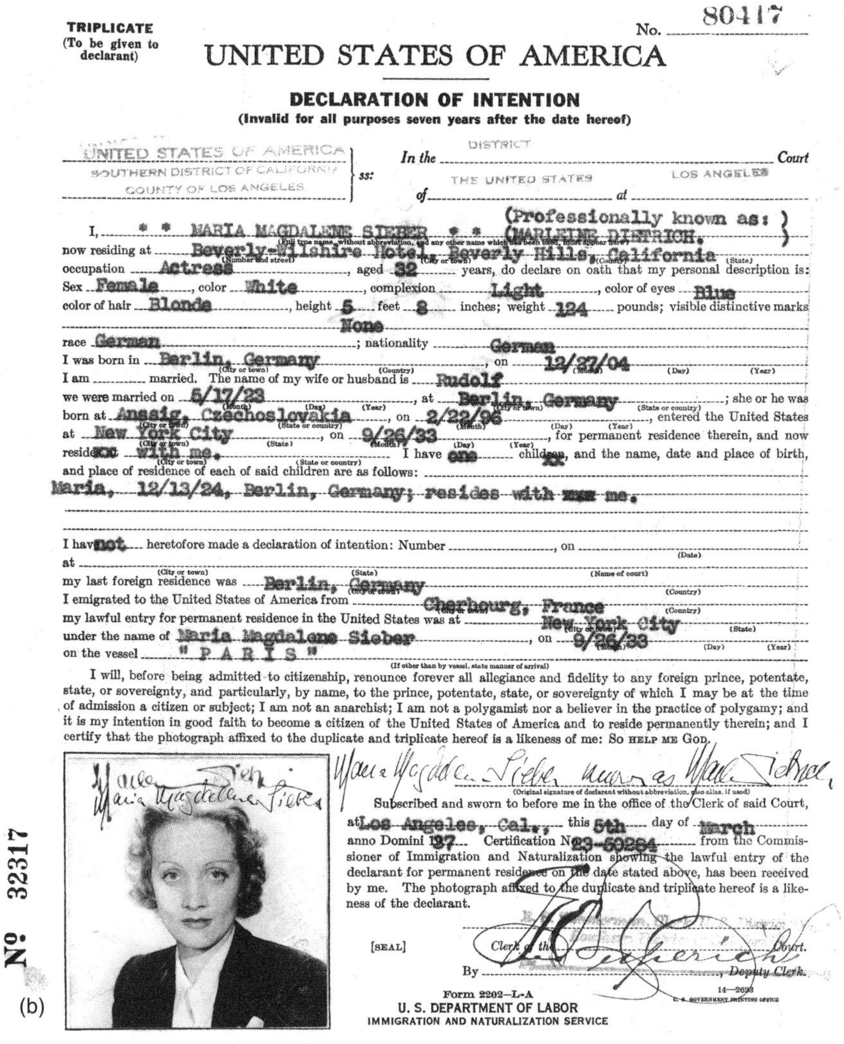

TRIPLICATE
(To be given to declarant)

No. 80417

UNITED STATES OF AMERICA

DECLARATION OF INTENTION
(Invalid for all purposes seven years after the date hereof)

UNITED STATES OF AMERICA
SOUTHERN DISTRICT OF CALIFORNIA　} ss:
COUNTY OF LOS ANGELES

In the DISTRICT _____ *Court*
THE UNITED STATES　　LOS ANGELES
of _____ *at* _____

I, * * MARIA MAGDALENE SIEBER * * (Professionally known as: MARLENE DIETRICH.)
now residing at Beverly-Wilshire Hotel, Beverly Hills, California
occupation Actress, aged 32 years, do declare on oath that my personal description is:
Sex Female, color White, complexion Light, color of eyes Blue
color of hair Blonde, height 5 feet 8 inches; weight 124 pounds; visible distinctive marks None
race German; nationality German
I was born in Berlin, Germany on 12/27/04
I am married. The name of my wife or husband is Rudolf
we were married on 5/17/23 at Berlin, Germany; she or he was
born at Anssig, Czechoslovakia, on 2/22/96, entered the United States
at New York City, on 9/26/33, for permanent residence therein, and now
resides with me. I have one children, and the name, date and place of birth,
and place of residence of each of said children are as follows:
Maria, 12/13/24, Berlin, Germany; resides with me.

I have not heretofore made a declaration of intention: Number _____, on _____
at _____
my last foreign residence was Berlin, Germany
I emigrated to the United States of America from Cherbourg, France
my lawful entry for permanent residence in the United States was at New York City
under the name of Maria Magdalene Sieber, on 9/26/33
on the vessel "P A R I S"

I will, before being admitted to citizenship, renounce forever all allegiance and fidelity to any foreign prince, potentate, state, or sovereignty, and particularly, by name, to the prince, potentate, state, or sovereignty of which I may be at the time of admission a citizen or subject; I am not an anarchist; I am not a polygamist nor a believer in the practice of polygamy; and it is my intention in good faith to become a citizen of the United States of America and to reside permanently therein; and I certify that the photograph affixed to the duplicate and triplicate hereof is a likeness of me: So HELP ME GOD.

Subscribed and sworn to before me in the office of the Clerk of said Court,
at Los Angeles, Cal., this 5th day of March
anno Domini 19__. Certification No 23-59294 from the Commissioner of Immigration and Naturalization showing the lawful entry of the declarant for permanent residence on the date stated above, has been received by me. The photograph affixed to the duplicate and triplicate hereof is a likeness of the declarant.

[SEAL]

Clerk of the Court.
By _____ Deputy Clerk.

Form 2202–L–A
U. S. DEPARTMENT OF LABOR
IMMIGRATION AND NATURALIZATION SERVICE

N°: 32317

(b)

Figure 5-2. *Continued.*

moved from New York City to Los Angeles and created "the wall of sound" of rock-and-roll African American "girl groups" whose families came from the south and "back east." Lou Adler, founder of Dunhill Records, hailed from Chicago. California-style teenager music that glorified the beach and car subcultures was originally popularized in Los Angeles-area secondary schools such as University High School, Torrance High School, and Palisades High School. It made a spectacular rise from a regional genre to a national music sensation through the ballads of the Beach Boys and Jan and Dean, produced by Capitol Records.

The growth of Asian immigrant enclaves and their movie theaters on the Pacific coast and Hawai'i provided entry points for Asian cinema, which exerted a profound influence on American movie making. The Toho La Brea and Kokusai

100

Form N-405
UNITED STATES DEPARTMENT OF JUSTICE
IMMIGRATION AND NATURALIZATION SERVICE
(Rev. 2-10-55)

Form approved.
Budget Bureau No. 43-R083.8.

ORIGINAL
(To be retained
by Clerk of Court)   316

UNITED STATES OF AMERICA

No. 205700

PETITION FOR NATURALIZATION

U.S. DISTRICT COURT, LOS ANGELES, CALIFORNIA

To the Honorable the _____ Court of _____ at _____

This petition for naturalization, hereby made and filed, respectfully shows:

(1) My full, true, and correct name is TUNG JIM WONG   aka   JAMES WONG HOWE

(2) My present place of residence is 1562 Queens Road Los Angeles LA California

(3) My occupation is Cameraman

(4) I am 58 years old. (5) I was born on 8/28/99 in Sai Choon Village, China

(6) My personal description is as follows: Sex M , complexion med , color of eyes brn , color of hair grey , height 5 feet 3 inches, weight 150 pounds, visible distinctive marks none ; country of which I am a citizen subject, or national China

(7) I am married; the name of my wife or husband is Sanora Louise Howe nee Babb we were married on 9/16/49 at Hawthorne, California he or she was born at Leavenworth, Kansas on 4/21/07 and entered the United States at _____ on _____ for permanent residence in the United States and now resides at with me

and was naturalized on _____ at _____ certificate No. _____ ; or became a citizen by _____

(7a) (If petition is filed under section 319 (a), Immigration and Nationality Act.) I have resided in the United States in marital union with my United States citizen spouse for at least 3 years immediately preceding the date of filing this petition for naturalization, and have been physically present in the United States at least half of that time.

(7b) (If petition is filed under section 319 (b), Immigration and Nationality Act.) My husband or wife is a citizen of the United States, is in the employment of the Government of the United States, or of an American institution of research recognized as such by the Attorney General of the United States, or an American firm or corporation engaged in whole or in part in the development of foreign trade and commerce of the United States, or subsidiary thereof or of a public international organization in which the United States participates; and such husband or wife is regularly stationed abroad in such employment. I intend in good faith upon naturalization to live abroad with my spouse and to resume my residence within the United States immediately upon termination of such employment abroad.

(8) I have no children; and the name, sex, date and place of birth, and present place of residence of each of said children who is living, are as follows:

_____

_____

_____

WONG CHIN CHIN

(9) My lawful admission for permanent residence in the United States was at Port Townsend, Washington under the name of James Wong Howe on 5/12/04 on the SS Empress SS Tremont

(10) Since my lawful admission for permanent residence I have not been absent from the United States, for a period or periods of 6 months or longer, except as follows:

DEPARTED FROM THE UNITED STATES			RETURNED TO THE UNITED STATES		
PORT	DATE (Month, day, year)	VESSEL OR OTHER MEANS OF CONVEYANCE	PORT	DATE (Month, day, year)	VESSEL OR OTHER MEANS OF CONVEYANCE
New York City	4/15/36	Europa or Bremen	NYC	2/4/37	Europa or Bremen

(11) It is my intention in good faith to become a citizen of the United States and to renounce absolutely and entirely all allegiance and fidelity to any foreign prince, potentate, state, or sovereignty of whom or which at this time I am a subject or citizen. (12) It is my intention to reside permanently in the United States. (13) I am not and have not been for a period of at least 10 years immediately preceding the date of this petition a member of or affiliated with any organization proscribed by the Immigration and Nationality Act or any section, subsidiary, branch affiliate or subdivision thereof nor have I during such period engaged in or performed any of the acts or activities prohibited by that Act. (14) I am able to read, write and speak the English language (unless exempted therefrom). (15) I am, and have been during all the periods required by law, a person of good moral character, attached to the principles of the Constitution of the United States and well disposed to the good order and happiness of the United States. I am willing, if required by law, to bear arms on behalf of the United States, or to perform noncombatant service in the Armed Forces of the United States, or to perform work of national importance under civilian direction (unless exempted therefrom). (16) I have resided continuously in the United States since 5/12/04 and continuously in the State in which this petition is made for the term of 6 months at least immediately preceding the date of this petition and I have been physically present in the United States for at least one-half of the 5 year period immediately preceding the date of this petition. (17) I have heretofore made petition for naturalization: No. 145656 on Nov. 24, 1950 at Los Angeles, California in the United States District Court, and such petition was denied by the Court for the following reasons and causes, to wit: withdrawn at my request

(18) Attached hereto and made a part of this, my petition for naturalization, are the affidavits of at least two verifying witnesses required by law.

(19) Wherefore I, your petitioner for naturalization, pray that I may be admitted a citizen of the United States of America, and that my name be changed to James Wong Howe I, aforesaid petitioner, do swear (affirm) that I know the contents of this petition for naturalization subscribed by me, and that the same are true to the best of my knowledge and belief, and that this petition is signed by me with my full, true name: SO HELP ME GOD.

ALIEN REGISTRATION NO. A2 954 265 1b

X Tung Jim Wong
(Full, true, and correct signature of petitioner, without abbreviation)

(c) 16—41078-7

Figure 5-2. *Continued.*

theaters of Los Angeles and the Toyo in Honolulu showed Japanese movies weekly. The Linda Lea in downtown Los Angeles showed Japanese and Filipino movies, while in nearby Chinatown, movie theaters showed films from Hong Kong made by the Shaw Brothers movie studios. The audience base for Chinese and Japanese movies grew in conjunction with the introduction and popularization of martial arts among Americans. Clint Eastwood and James Coburn viewed samurai movies and derived stylistic pointers in how to film combat and dueling scenes in their cowboy western movies.

Movies about samurai swordsmen and kung fu karate masters attracted moviegoers from outside Asian communities. Hollywood studios and mainstream theater chains decided to capitalize on the rising interest in Asian martial arts and began to showcase films with the Hong Kong kung-fu master Bruce Lee, Pat Morita (a Nisei) who played the karate master of the *Karate Kid* movies, Sho Kosugi (who played the Japanese Ninja on the American screen), Chuck Norris, David Carradine, and Uma Thurman.

Clint Eastwood, George Lucas, and Steven Spielberg viewed the films of Japanese director Akira Kurosawa at the Toho La Brea Theatre and other Los Angeles foreign film theaters that featured classic Japanese movies. The films of Kurosawa had the greatest influence on American cinema: John Sturges' *Magnificent Seven* cowboy epic replicated Kurosawa's *Seven Samurai*. Spielberg's *Star Wars* was based partly on Kurosawa's *Hidden Fortress,* the Jedi knights and their light sabres on the swords and swordsmanship of the samurai in Kurosawa's films. Clint Eastwood's "spaghetti westerns" were based on Kurosawa's *Yojimbo* and *Sanjuro.* The character of the ronin (masterless samurai), played by the legendary Toshiro Mifune, was played by Eastwood as a cowboy gunslinger and also was played comically by John Belushi in the first seasons of the television show *Saturday Night Live.* Directors Francis Ford Coppola and George Lucas produced Kurosawa's *Kagemusha,* an epic film about a famous warlord in sixteenth-century Japan. When Kurosawa was given an Oscar (his second) for lifetime achievement, it was presented at the Academy Awards ceremony to him in person by Lucas and Spielberg.

The convergence of Atlantic and Pacific diasporas in the far west produced a transcultural table of food styles (Figure 5-3a, b, c, d, e). European immigrants became purveyors of exotic new tastes in the food industries of California. Domenico Ghirardelli produced and popularized a new style of chocolate candies and beverages that would sweep California and then the rest of the country. Other Italian immigrants, like the Gallo Brothers and Robert Mondavi, developed European-style wine-making in the fertile valleys of Napa, Sonoma, and Mendocino Counties in the areas to the north and east of San Francisco Bay. They made this California region into the national center of wine production that would revolutionize the American public's taste for Italian and other European wines. The diaspora from the Asia Pacific brought into the west coast and Hawai'i Americanized Asian foods like San Francisco-style chop suey and chow mein. In Los Angeles, Man Fook Low, a favorite Cantonese restaurant with Hollywood stars such as Mae West, served

(a)

(b)

(c)

Figure 5-3. Faces of interregional and globalized food styles: (a) Zarlito's, National City, California; (b) Ketchie's Stand, Sawtelle, West Los Angeles; (c) "The King's Hawaiian Story"; (d) The roots of McDonald's, the pioneer of global American fast food, were in southern California and its automobile subculture. The chain's oldest operating restaurant is in Downey, California (shown in the photograph), a Los Angeles suburb near the freeways; (e) Yaadgar Pakistani and Indian Restaurant, Redding, California.

Figure 5-3. *Continued.*

dumplings known as "dim sum", long popular in the Hawaiian Islands, where it was called "manapua."

Food styles were created in California and Hawai'i out of an eclectic blend of ingredients found in a diversity of food traditions and ethnic markets. In National City, a major San Diego enclave of immigrants from the Philippines, Zarlito's Restaurant offered its customers Filipino American-style Chinese food. In Hawai'i, a slice of spam on a ball of rice with a seaweed wrapper became the ubiquitous "spam musubi," which was good for a fast-food breakfast, snack, or lunch meal.[31] Indeed, Hawai'i's commercial fast food with its mixture of Chinese, Japanese, Korean, Filipino, Portuguese, Puerto Rican, and American dishes in "plate lunches" and "bento boxes" pioneered the innovation of "fusion" Asian food style that would become popular on the mainland. Traditional Japanese sushi evolved into many new types including the popular "California maki" (a roll of sweetened sticky rice with avocado and crab wrapped in seaweed). Los Angeles vendors selling Mexican food added Korean kim-chee (pickled cabbage) to their tacos and burritos. Lonnie Ketchie, who hailed from Little Ax, Oklahoma, created a legendary taco with a California twist that became a food icon at his stand serving Japanese and Mexican American customers in the Sawtelle neighborhood of West Los Angeles.[32]

California-style fast food diffused into areas where it had been virtually nonexistent. The food scene in New England was typical of this national transformation. In the early 1970s, only one restaurant in Boston, the El Phoenix Room, offered Mexican food, and no sushi restaurants existed. In New Haven, Connecticut, customers at Chinese restaurants ate only Polynesian Cantonese style food and were frequently served by white waiters. By 2000, Mexican fast food had become commonplace in Boston; stands serving burritos and tacos, like Chipotle and Boloco, multiplied near mass transit stations and commercial districts. Chinese restaurants in Boston specialized in Sichuan, Beijing, and Taiwanese-style Chinese food and Cantonese dim sum. Sushi was on the menu of numerous "high end" eateries and could also be purchased at the major supermarket chains such as Shaw's, Star Market, and Stop and Shop. King's Bakery, established in Honolulu by the Tairas, a Japanese immigrant family from Hilo, Hawai'i, told "The King's Hawaiian Story" to customers in Boston's supermarkets on the wrappers of their popular "Hawaiian sweet bread":

> "The Taira family story began over 50 years ago in Hilo, Hawai'i. Our father, Robert Taira, borrowed $382 from a family friend and opened a small but successful bakery. While he baked many delicious treats, it was the popularity of his 'King's Hawaiian Sweet Bread' that took us far beyond our island home . . . [inspired] by Portuguese 'keeper bread,' a sweet, hearty recipe favored by sailors on long ocean voyages. . . . Mahalo (thanks) from our ohana (family) to yours."

King's sweetbread went "virally" national when Arby's Roast Beef adopted it as a bun for its sandwiches. The southern California-style hamburger of the drive-through stand became a worldwide standard through McDonald's Hamburgers, which had its commercial start in the Los Angeles and San Diego areas.

South Asian food styles purveyed in the diaspora of immigrants from India and Pakistan evolved in a "third space" providing the room and distance from homelands to re-position the rivalry between these two nations into new paths of constructive interaction. On the west coast, combined "Pakistani and Indian Restaurants," which were virtually non-existent when Ronald Reagan was governor of California, rapidly gained a popular following at the turn of the twenty-first century, even locating in small towns such as Redding, in far northern California.

In 2012, a British journalist described how rival powers India and Pakistan could have a cooperative and fruitful relation in the transnational "third spaces" of food diaspora styles as follows:

> "India and Pakistan are two nations who share a common passion for good food," said Smeeta Chakrabarti, the CEO of NDTV Lifestyle, which is broadcasting the show in India. "And this love for food is something that binds the two nations, despite the numerous differences." The producers of the show, filmed over three weeks in Delhi, are tapping into a growing appetite among the region's upper-middle class for food, fashion and "lifestyle" products. In India especially, television programmes about food and travel are increasingly popular.
>
> India recently completed the second series of its franchise of MasterChef, and Australian MasterChef, shown on Star World, is said to have been one of the most successful imports. In Pakistan, the show will be broadcast on Geo TV.
>
> One of the Pakistani chefs taking part in the series, Poppy Agha, has her own culinary institute in Karachi and a show on Pakistani television, A Taste of Fusion. She said of her time in India: "I made some fantastic friends. There is a rivalry, but in this programme we all came together. I learned so much."[33]

The sports transcultural diaspora revolved around Asian martial arts and celebrity athletes. Martial arts such as judo, karate, aikido, tae kwon do, and kung fu became popularized through commercialized training schools. They combined with martial sports from the Atlantic world to create the popular form of "mixed martial arts" that originated in Brazilian Japanese and Portuguese communities. The fighters of the Gracie family of Brazil established a mixed martial arts training academy in the Los Angeles suburb of Torrance. Asian athletes entered the arena of American sports competition. From the 1990s, baseball players from Japan, South Korea, and Taiwan joined Major League Baseball teams. The most successful, like Hideo Nomo, Ichiro Suzuki, Hideki Matsui, Daisuke Matsuzaka, and Chan-Ho Park, become international trans-Pacific celebrities, even known in the Latin American and Caribbean countries, whose teams played against teams from Asia in the World Baseball Classic. The University of Hawai'i football team became the first from the Pacific Islands to play in the Orange Bowl (2008) and displayed a Hawaiian cultural style of football teamwork based on a concept of the Hawaiian extended family to a national American television audience.

As the diverse groups from Asian countries coalesced into communities, they created new expressions for collective ethnic identities rooted in intergroup differences and reflecting casualness or disrespect. Chinese in Hawai'i were colloquially called "pa-ke," which meant "uncle," and Koreans were "yobo," meaning spouse. In the U.S. mainland, Japanese immigrants described caucasians as "hakujin": white people. In Los Angeles, Japanese Americans referred to American Jews as "ku-ichi" (ku meant the number nine and ichi the number one, which added together yielded the number ten: in Japanese, ten was the word "ju," a homonym for Jew). Japanese Americans in Hawai'i referred to Japanese Americans in the mainland U.S. as "kotonks," a slang for empty-headed. In Hawai'i, all white Europeans were labeled "haoles" except the Portuguese, who were called "Portugee." Haole came to signify northern European ethnicity while Portugee described "not Haole," in a local Hawaiian version of the early-twentieth-century identification of southern Europeans as a different subcategory of the white race to be differentiated from "nordics."

The acculturation tactics of migrants from the Atlantic and Pacific regions—formed as they encountered, adjusted, and adapted to each other in creole borderlands of the United States—created new fields of cultural interchange with a deep influence on American culture. Historian Warren I. Cohen contemplated, "It is clear that the interaction between East Asia and the United States has had an enormous impact on American culture. Indeed, American culture has been affected *more* profoundly than has Asian culture. The effects are intensifying, and—more so than the Americanization of East Asia—they are certain to be permanent."[34] American migrants and European immigrants who encountered Asian Americans learned new cross-cultural communications and exchanges to function within an Asian-Pacific cultural fabric. In Hawai'i, they adopted customs such as removing shoes when indoors and participated in the creation of a Hawaiian pidgin English and creole culture. Even Asian popular music became notable among American audiences in the Pacific region. "Kan-kan Musume," became a hit song of postwar Japan and communities in Hawai'i. Its opening line in the original Japanese lyrics "Ana ko kawai ya" ("That pretty girl") was changed into "Anna go Hawai'i" by audiences who sang along in Honolulu. "Sukiyaki," a popular ballad by the Japanese singer Kyu Sakamoto, became a number one hit record on the primary mainstream rock-and-roll charts and music stations on the west coast in 1963.

Pacific coast America also produced a new sports diversity as it became a corridor for the growing flow of black migration from the east, south, and midwest. From World War II to the Cold War, California colleges became magnets for black athletes. Jackie Robinson (from Georgia) and Lew Alcindor (from New York City) became stars at UCLA; Bill Russell (from Louisiana) and K. C. Jones (from Texas) led the basketball team at the University of San Francisco to two NCAA championships. The Brooklyn Dodgers, who moved west to become the Los Angeles Dodgers, bridged between east coast and west coast in more ways than one. In a bi-coastal twist, Jackie Robinson, a UCLA student from Pasadena who broke the color barrier as a Brooklyn Dodger player, received a worthy biography, *Baseball's Great Experiment: The Jackie Robinson Story*, from historian Jules Tygiel who had moved from New York City to Los Angeles to attend UCLA for his graduate studies in history. The Los Angeles Dodgers continued the Brooklyn Dodgers tradition of ethnic "trailblazing" by hiring pitchers Fernando Valenzuela from Mexico and Hideo Nomo, who became the first star baseball player from Japan.[35]

The post–World War II boom in the tourism industry grew out of attractions that were unique to the far west and Pacific region. The Ramona Pageant, a summertime festival in the Southern California town of Hemet that revolved around the play *Ramona*, based on Helen Hunt Jackson's best-selling 1884 novel by the same title about California's Indians, was one of the first great tourist attractions in California.[36] The Rose Parade coupled with the Rose Bowl college football game in Pasadena to produce another of California's oldest seasonal tourist attractions. San Francisco's Chinatown became a year-around tourist destination with its exotic stores and restaurants and was the home of the famous and popular nightclub "The Forbidden City," which featured Asian and Pacific American star singers and dancers.

The rising demand for recreational nightlife and entertainment that had started in the downtowns of big eastern cities found new outlets for scale and innovation in the far west. New, neon-lit urban centers mushroomed that were dedicated entirely to the provision of mass culture entertainment. The cities of Las Vegas and Reno, Nevada, just across the California state line, grew rapidly into resorts for casino hotels, setting a new standard that would be replicated cross country in places like Foxwoods in Connecticut and Atlantic City in New Jersey.

California, with its unique mix of sunny weather, mountains, and beaches was a natural experimental space for developing a new market for participatory and recreational sports activity. Austrian immigrants imported the sport of skiing and created the prototype for ski resorts in the Sierra Nevada and other Pacific mountain regions. In 1936, Austrian skiers Bill and Fred Klein opened the Klein school of skiing at the "flagship" lodge of the Sierra Club near the top of the 7,000-foot-high Donner Pass. Austrian skiing champion Hannès Schroll founded the Sugar Bowl resort in 1938 in northern Placer County near Norden, California. Within just several hours drive by car from the mountains, California provided the sandy shores and the waves for swimming and surfing. Patrons of the California beach resort were socialized into a "sun and surf" subculture that served as a stepping stone to the trans-Pacific development of the premier Hawaiian areas for beach resorts: Waikiki in Oahu, Kaanapali in Maui, Poipu in Kaua'i, and Kona-Kailua on the "Big Island" of Hawai'i.

Southern California became a cradle of new amusement centers known as theme parks. These new institutions represented the next evolutionary stage of amusement parks that had started in eastern urban areas such as Coney Island in New York and Whalom Park in Massachusetts. The first of the California-style theme parks was Olvera Street in downtown Los Angeles, which was a low-keyed tourist attraction featuring colonial buildings, shops, restaurants, and entertainments that were found in California when it was part of Mexico. Then came Knotts Berry Farm in Orange County with an Old West theme, followed by Disneyland; Marineland of the Pacific, which featured marine life; and the "thrill" center known as Magic Mountain. Even motion picture studios became mini-theme parks. When Carl Laemmle and Robert Cochrane founded Universal Pictures and Studios in 1915, they realized that movie making was an exciting tourist attraction and a natural stage for advertisement. With Cochrane's leadership and expertise in advertising, Universal Studio Tours was born and became one of the earliest and most important tourist spectacles in Los Angeles.[37] The tours expanded in the 1970s into a parkland of movie sets that set the pace for similar movie-making theme parks at Warner Brothers and Paramount Studios. Solvang, a small town in central California that had been originally settled by Danish immigrants, converted itself into a major tourist center based on the ethnography and history of Danish American life. The central Hawaiian island of Oahu established one of the most ambitious theme parks, the Polynesian Cultural Center, founded by the Church of the Latter Day Saints, that exhibited the traditions and performing arts of indigenous Pacific Islanders. This ethnographic theme park was visited by tourists and officials from China who supported similar parks in Yunan Province in China designed to showcase the traditions of the diverse ethnic groups in that region.[38]

HUMAN CAPITAL AND EDUCATION

Innovative spaces for the role of migrating human capital flowing into California was exemplified in the growth of Pasadena, a suburb just east of downtown Los Angeles. Pasadena developed into an elite enclave of innovation, an area for the facilitation and culmination of creative forces from Boston and Chicago, as it grew into a magnet for intellectual elites of the eastern establishment. Henry L. Huntington, a railroad magnate from a leading Boston family, established the Huntington Library, which, like its Boston ancestor the Massachusetts Historical Society, became a national institution dedicated to historical research and archival collections. The Huntington Library lured Frederick Jackson Turner, Professor of History at Harvard, away from Cambridge, Massachusetts, to take a new position as the Library's first director. Astronomer Charles Yerkes of the University of Chicago found new opportunities in Pasadena and nearby mountains, which surpassed any eastern observatory site for the development of modern astronomical research that had been pioneered at Harvard. Yerkes' projects to build ever greater telescopes from the Mount Wilson observatory to the Palomar Observatory radiated from his base in Pasadena, the fledgling California Institute of Technology.

Pasadena was only the forerunner for initiatives that enabled California to leap-frog over other states in developing multiple fields of world-class high-technology research enterprises. From World War II to the early years of the Cold War, Los Angeles and nearby areas became the headquarters of new corporate industries generated by aerospace engineering and Department of Defense contracts (Map 5-2). These gigantic new enterprises were conveniently located next to dozens of military bases for advanced aircraft and naval vessels that also served as training and testing sites. Military personnel who manned installations such as Edwards Air Force Base, Vandenberg Air Force Base, Pearl Harbor, Schofield Barracks, and Camp Pendleton constituted some of the largest migrant populations in the Pacific coast region.

California received by far the most funding of any western state from federal contracts for manufacturing and infrastructure construction. During World War II, contracts to California for equipment and material and the building of harbor, manufacturing, and air transport facilities amounted to $35 billion, while Texas, ranking next among western states, received only $8 billion. Manufacturing tripled in value-added amounts from just before the war to just after the war. Los Angeles County, which had been an industrial backwater a few decades earlier, began to surpass the powerhouse region of Detroit in production. The number of defense manufacturers rose to four thousand, and Los Angeles textile producers grew nearly five times. In the early 1950s, companies that had built war planes, like Douglas and Lockheed, shifted design and output to meet the new demand for civilian aircraft, and made southern California into a global producer of civilian aircraft like the DC-6 and the Constellation.[39]

Applied and basic research firms drew thousands of scientists and engineers to California from across the country and from foreign nations seeking new careers. These new companies built upon the tradition of a scientific research community that had gathered earlier in the Pasadena area to form the nucleus of Cal Tech and the Jet Propulsion Laboratory, and turned southern California into a vast breeding ground of aerospace industries. German scientists in rocketry were recruited to jumpstart the development of the missile industry. Simon Ramo, a creative genius in engineering, moved from Utah to Los Angeles, became a founding partner of the aerospace corporate giant TRW (Thompson, Ramo, Wooldridge) and was hailed as a "father" of the intercontinental ballistic missile,

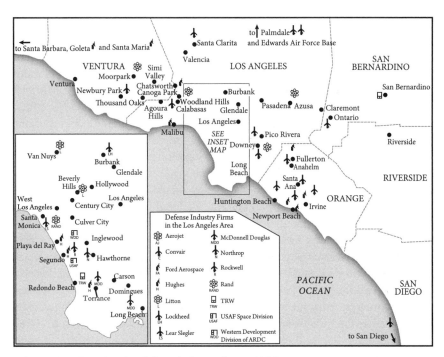

Map 5-2.   Los Angeles defense industry firms, 1991.

the ICBM, a weapon that became modified for use in space exploration by the National Aeronautics and Space Administration (NASA). Led by visionary entrepreneurs such as Howard Hughes and Donald Douglas, Hughes Aircraft and Douglas Aircraft formed the vanguard of new companies such as Northrup, McDonnell, Grumman, Lear-Siegler, and other manufacturers of jet aircraft for military and civilian purposes. The urban sprawl south of San Francisco between San Jose and Palo Alto became the home of an engineering complex that became the pace-setter for innovation in the computer industry and was renowned worldwide as "Silicon Valley." It became a core sector for young entrepreneurs, many from South Asia and East Asia, who launched a wave of "start-up" companies that went on to great success.

After World War II, the state of California launched an unprecedented program of expansion in its public system of higher education. The earliest major public institution of higher education was the University of California in Berkeley, founded in 1868. In the twentieth century, the University of California grew into the largest public university system in the nation through the founding of branch campuses. The University of California, Los Angeles (UCLA) became the southern branch of the University of California in the 1920s and 1930s, and then, during the post-war decades, a rapid construction program added in swift succession additional University of California campuses at Davis, Santa Barbara,

San Diego, Santa Cruz, Irvine, and Riverside, which grew into giant institutions. California also created a secondary tier of state colleges, such as California State College at San Diego (Cal State San Diego), Cal State Los Angeles, Cal State Northridge, Cal State Long Beach, and Cal State San Jose, which were re-branded as California State Universities and whose enrollments eventually rivaled those of the University of California campuses. Such supreme investment in public higher education in California was seen as crucial to the region's character and social structure. "California's public colleges—so central to the state's identity that their independence is enshrined in its Constitution—have long been seen as gateways to the middle class," commented a journalist.[40]

The swift expansion of public higher education in California responded to the surge of postwar transcontinental and international migration that was rapidly multiplying the state's population. Massive enrollments meant that new faculty with advanced training had to be found immediately. Without the major doctoral programs of eastern and midwestern states, the University of California had to look eastward to recruit its new faculty members. It became a place of skyrocketing demand for young Ph.Ds from the top Ivy League schools and the great research universities of the midwest, such as Michigan, Chicago, and Wisconsin. Students from doctoral programs back east obtained jobs in west coast universities and brought the leading edge of academic research. Graduates of Columbia and Harvard doctoral programs provided new intellectual leadership in the burgeoning UCLA History Department which grew into one of the largest academic history departments in the country.

Specialized academic centers brought scholars into the field of Pacific Ocean regional studies. In Hawai'i, the East-West Center was founded in the early 1960s by the State Department and Congress to be a research institute, located in Honolulu and affiliated with the University of Hawai'i, that would support studies of the Asia Pacific. It was a flagship for subsequent centers on the Pacific coast that hosted scholars from all over the country and the world to create new intellectual communities of researchers and policy makers. The East-West Center provided an institutional home for re-visioning the Pacific Rim and Oceania as an area that could be properly understood only through an interregional developmental perspective.

Much more numerous than the ranks of doctoral graduates from leading universities from the east were the new teachers in elementary and secondary schools. Many had originally aspired to work in the public schools of metropolitan New York City, Boston, Philadelphia, Chicago, and numerous smaller urban centers in the northeast or the midwest. This pool of teaching talent made possible the rapid expansion of California's vaunted K-to-12 public school systems and enabled them to reach a standard of nationally recognized excellence.[41]

The elites of the Pacific far west nurtured new initiatives for culture and public art (Figure 5-4a, b, c). A UCLA literature professor dubbed Los Angeles "Weimar on the Pacific" because Los Angeles, particularly the suburb of Pacific Palisades, became famed as a retreat for German writers and artists, such as Thomas Mann

Figure 5-4.   Public statues in Honolulu memorializing leaders of anti-colonial movements: (a) Mohandas K. Gandhi, Indian nationalist and independence leader in British India (*top left*); (b) Jose P. Rizal, Filipino nationalist, writer, and reformer (*top right*); (c) Sun Yat-Sen, first president of the Republic of China (*bottom*).

and Arnold Schoenberg, during the interwar years. Later in the twentieth century and twenty-first century, young talents in music such as Zubin Mehta from India and Gustavo Dudamel from Venezuela found a home and an appreciative celebrity audience as directors of the Los Angeles Philharmonic Orchestra. The trust of J. Paul Getty, a billionaire once reputed to be the world's wealthiest person, endowed the Getty Center of Los Angeles with part of his fortune, which made "the Getty" the richest art museum in the country and a center of new museological research when it opened in 1997.[42] To honor his wife, Bernice P. Bishop, a member of the Hawaiian royal family, philanthropist and businessman Charles Reed Bishop established the Bishop Museum for Pacific ethnology in Honolulu in 1889. UCLA founded the Fowler Museum for cultural and ethnographic history. The discipline and administration of museum studies of the Pacific region responded to popular expressions of America's interest in world cultures that previously had been publicly exhibited in world's fairs.[43] The wide cultural horizon of the Pacific coast region functioned according to the theoretical expectation of a commentator on the future of the humanities: "What I see in this experimental space is the opportunity for reconnecting forms of high-level research and knowledge in arts and humanistic fields to that very big and frankly expanding audience for culture and knowledge."[44]

Institutions that preserved public historical memory expanded from the activist base of local communities. Immigrant ethnic groups became sponsors and audiences for cultural museums such as the Waipahu Plantation Museum of Oahu, the Japanese American National Museum of Los Angeles, and the Wing Luke Museum of Seattle.[45] Community groups in ethnic neighborhoods established public landmarks and memorials that commemorated heroic homeland leaders like Sun Yat-sen, Jose Rizal, and Mohandas K. Gandhi, who had led independence movements against colonial domination.

POLITICS AND POPULATION

Population shifts to the west coast propelled the rise of Pacific regional political power. California, the home of one out of eight Americans at the turn of the twenty-first century, had by far the largest congressional delegation of any state, fifty-three members of the House of Representatives. Lifted by the enormous political gravity of the state, many California politicians vaulted into national prominence, such as U.S. Presidents Richard Nixon and Ronald Reagan, Speaker of the House Nancy Pelosi, Governors Arnold Schwarzenegger and Jerry Brown.

The cultural spaces of diversity and innovation in California had a new potential for defining peoplehood and minoritization, the process of developing an identity as a minority group. California produced a new paradigm for group relations built out of new multiracial empowerment categories, Afro-American, Hispanic, Asian-Pacific Islander, and Native American Indians. This new categorical set supplanted the hegemonic racialized categories of white supremacist domination created under the conditions of white–black biracialism, Asian exclusion, Mexican-American borderlands, and Native American reservation life. The new empowerment categories designed for a political goal coexisted with a scalar field of ethnic relations in which ethnic groups adjusted and interacted fluidly with each other, moving up and down, through the ordinary channels of social mobility and acculturation.

The mobilization of empowerment movements in minority communities developed slowly in the years after World War II. Blacks, Asians, Latinos, and Native Americans occupied separate and divided niches in California's social structure, and their community leaders found it difficult to organize a multiracial coalition in a situation where minority groups operated at a distance from each other. Edward Roybal, a Mexican American activist and City Councilman from east Los Angeles, stood out as a lone pioneer and exception who succeeded in garnering political support from black and Japanese American leaders. However, an acid test came when the Brooklyn Dodgers moved to Los Angeles and evicted low-income Latinos from Chavez Ravine to build Dodger Stadium. The nascent multi-racial coalition could not stop the bulldozers and evictions. Historian Scott Kurashige noted that ". . . few of the city's residents backed the Mexican American holdouts against the Dodger Stadium landgrab, Blacks, Asians, and organized labor were no exception."[46]

A new front of social innovation in race relations emerged on college campuses, and particularly in public institutions like the University of California, Berkeley, and Cal State–Dominguez Hills. Students organized the Afro-American movement, the Chicano movement, the Asian American movement, and the Native American movement to build a Third World Liberation Front that coalesced around antiracism and overlapped with the antiwar movement. Mexican American students and community organizers adopted a new collective identity as "Chicanos" and labeled themselves in a new discourse of peoplehood as "La Raza" with a historic homeland, "Aztlan."[47] Chinese, Japanese, Korean, and Filipino/a students and community leaders replaced the collective labels of "orientals" with "Asians" and "Asian Americans." Campus ethnic studies and ethnic student centers multiplied and created a national model that was reproduced in campuses throughout the country. Among Japanese Americans, the traditional festivals of Hana Matsuri, Obon, and Nisei Week, which were once chiefly neighborhood events, became part of a wider public culture of California multiculturalism.[48] Ron Karenga (born Ronald Everett) moved as a youngster from Maryland and attended Los Angeles Community College and UCLA. In the 1960s, Karenga created Kwanzaa, a holiday during the Christmas season with elements of African tradition. Later, he became a professor of philosophy and politics at California State University at Long Beach.[49]

Black power came to the forefront of the racial empowerment movement of the late 1960s. The Black Panthers of Oakland and Berkeley, California, became its militant vanguard. It emerged as a local institution for neighborhood self-defense and organization, but it developed an ideology that adapted the anticolonial Marxism of Algierian thinker Franz Fanon to conditions in the United States. Its leaders came from African American families who had migrated from the south to the west coast. Founding leaders Bobby Seale and Huey P. Newton were born in Texas and Louisiana, respectively. A historian of their impact on Berkeley and Oakland found that the Panthers "came from families without influence who had only recently migrated from the South . . . where black distrust of whites was far more endemic than it had been in the North" and were alienated from traditional black leaders of the Bay area whose families had long been in the north. The Black Panthers' innovative style of leadership was produced by recently arrived outsiders. It caught on in other cities in the midwest and east with African American neighborhoods that had received the large black exodus from the south in the mid-twentieth century.[50]

Ultimately, in the last quarter of the twentieth century, a new multiracial politics that was accommodationist as well as minority-empowering crystallized from earlier drives for community progress and integration in Los Angeles under mayors Tom Bradley and Antonio Villaraigosa, who respectively became the city's first black and Latino mayors. Bradley, whose family roots were in Texas and who had risen through the ranks of the Los Angeles Police Department, provided an agenda that coupled multiracialism with the realignment of Los Angeles as a "world city" of emergent globalization and economic internationalism. Bradley empaneled the "Los Angeles 2000 Committee," which declared in its *LA 2000: A City for the Future* report that their metropolis was a "crossroads" city, "a leading hub of world trade, especially as the United States gateway to the Pacific Rim nations."[51]

The dominant role of the entertainment and mass media industry in California produced a profound transformation of political leadership. Partly involving the stylistics of campaigning and self-presentation, but also a forerunner of the growth of television in politics, California led the way in connecting acting careers to political careers. Actor Peter Lawford, a British immigrant who married Patricia Kennedy, a sister of President John F. Kennedy, became a key link in Democratic Party politics to Hollywood. Political leaders who first were prominent as actors included President Ronald Reagan, U.S. Senator George Murphy, Governor Arnold Schwarzenegger, and George Takei of the Southern California Rapid Transit Board.

If California's political leaders operated from the nation's greatest demographic base of power, Hawai'i's political leaders rose from the nation's dominant base of Asian and Pacific multiracial diversity. As Barack Obama grew up in the Hawaiian environment, he witnessed a political establishment, from local officeholders in city and state government, to members of its congressional delegation, that included Asians, Pacific Islanders, and other races. U.S. Senator Daniel Inouye of Hawai'i was part of a vanguard political generation of Asian American politicians that included U.S. Senators Hiram Fong and Spark Matsunaga of Hawai'i, Congresswoman Patsy T. Mink of Hawai'i (Figure 5-5a, b), and California's U.S. Senator S. I. Hayakawa. They were forerunners of political leaders who

Figure 5-5.   Patsy T. Mink, first congresswoman from Hawai'i.

emerged from the newer waves of Asian immigration, like Ed Lee, a son of Chinese immigrants who became Mayor of San Francisco, and Governor Bobby Jindal of Louisiana and Governor Nikki Haley of South Carolina, whose families came from India. Frank Fasi, an Italian American from Connecticut, served as mayor of Honolulu for twenty-two years and married into a local Japanese American family. Jack Burns, an Irish Catholic from Montana, became the mentor to Nisei political leaders such as U.S. Senator Daniel Inouye, who regarded Burns as a "political father," as did other local politicians spearheading the successful drive for Hawaiian statehood in 1959. Linda Lingle, a Jewish woman from Los Angeles, became governor of Hawai'i in 2002. By becoming President, Hawai'i's Barack Obama epitomized the internationalism of the political leadership that sprang from the globalizing Pacific region. Historian Douglas Brinkley described Barack Obama as "our first global president" who "came of age, really, after the Cold War, with the Internet being the transformative engine of society, and he now takes his multicultural heritage and the geographical diversity of his upbringing [to the world]."[52]

PERSONHOOD, PEOPLEHOOD, AND NATIONHOOD

The borderland between the Atlantic and Pacific worlds on the west coast provided the diversity and innovative spaces for new explorations in individual and collective identity. In the twentieth century, the world of amateur and professional sports constituted a major source for the production of new ethnic identities. The first celebrity from the Pacific was Hawai'i's Duke Kahanamoku, an Olympic swimming champion. The Duke, a Polynesian Hawaiian, grew up in the shadow of Diamond Head (Hawai'i's iconic tourism symbol) on the waters of Waikiki Beach where he became a "beach boy" and "king of the surfers." His personality, celebrity and entrepreneurialism launched the popularization of the sport of surfing, which he came to personify.

Asian American athletes in competitive sports provided new models of personal excellence for their communities, particularly significant for Asian Americans whose talents were often overlooked by comparison with white and black athletes. After World War II, Wally Yonomine of Honolulu's Farrington High School, a Japanese American who was an outstanding football and baseball player, became a trans-Pacific and international professional sports star. As a halfback, Yonomine played with the San Francisco 49ers and scored four touchdowns in one season. His achievements playing in the professional baseball leagues of Japan, where he was known as the Jackie Robinson of Japan because he integrated Japanese baseball as an American, earned him induction into the Japanese baseball Hall of Fame.[53] Wat Misaka, another Japanese American, led the University of Utah men's basketball team to championships in the NCAA (1944) and NIT (1947) tournaments and became the first non-white player in the professional Basketball Association when he played for the New York Knickerbockers in 1947. Tommy Kono, a Nisei from the bay area of California, became an Olympic medalist and world champion in weightlifting.

With the expansion of jet air links between the coasts, "bicoastalism" came to define the lifestyles and personality styles of elite leaders in the public eye. The interchanges of elites between Massachusetts and California exemplified a new transregionalism in which notable individuals defined themselves by their back-and-forth movement or their professional linkages bridging the east and west coast. The mobile elite of intercoastal networkers much earlier included Henry L. Huntington, Harrison Gray Otis, and Josiah Royce, and more recently notable figures in the popular media such as Julia Childs, Bonnie Raitt, Matt Damon, Ben Affleck, Mark Wahlberg, Jay Leno, and Conan O'Brien, and public academics James Q. Wilson, Derek Bok, and Albert Carnesale.

The west-coast borderland of the Atlantic and Pacific transoceanic world offered spaces for cultural production centered on the reinvention of selfhood and peoplehood (Figure 5-6a, b). It was an area that nurtured the public interplay and display of multiple diversities in the backgrounds of prominent individuals and celebrities which became integral to their cultural impact. Dwayne "The Rock" Johnson, whose ancestry was African Canadian and Samoan, spent part of his youth in Honolulu and achieved stardom as a heavyweight wrestling champion and movie actor. Tiger Woods of California, predominantly Thai and African by ancestry, became the world's leading golfer. Brian Clay, a track athlete at Honolulu's Castle High School who was half Japanese and half African American, won a gold medal in the decathlon in the 2008 Olympics. Bruno Mars, a part African American singer of popular crossover hit songs, attended Honolulu's Roosevelt High School. New bicoastal celebrity thematics emerged in this crosscultural borderland. Dick Dale (a part-Lebanese musician from Quincy, Massachusetts) brought Middle-Eastern rhythms to "surfin'" music to become "King of the Surf Guitar." Elvis Presley made several movies on location in Honolulu, Los Angeles, and Las Vegas to make a transition from early rock-and-roll to the west coast sound. Jack Lord,

THE

BLACK SURFING ASSOCIATION's

STATEMENT OF
PURPOSE AND INTENT

THIS association of surfers, black surfers, is the first of its kind. Our intent and purpose is the continuous search for our unique character and individuality so fluidly expressed in dancing, wave dancing. We are the literal main ingredient of a developing organization of young and old, male and female, Black persons who seek to share the pleasures of our Creator's oceanic rhythms.

Our distinctive group, which is increasing in number, is greatly diversified in our individual perspectives and pursuits. Our politics, philosophies, vocations and social relations are as varied as our personalities and spiritual realizations. Yet with our varied lifestyles, we are bonded together by two cosmic forces, blood and water. The blood, being our ancestral African roots, and the water, being the oceans and seas of the world.

The focal point of this bond is the sharing of the sport and art-form of surfing. This water sport, believed to have been created by our own oceanic ancients, is enjoyed today throughout the coastal regions of the world. Though comparitively small in numbers, surfing, like tennis, golf, and skiing, is enjoying an increasing number of Black participants. From this growth of interest, participation, and the need for sharing arose the conception of the developing BLACK SURFING ASSOCIATION.

UMOJA, together as one, in God's name, let us surf, share, and save our Oceans and Seas.

Founder
Anthony L. Corley
California, 1981
revised: Jan, 2004

Black Surfing Association
Tony Corley
2222 Olive Street
Paso Robles, CA 93446

tonycblacksurf@hotmail.com

(a)

Figure 5-6. Cultural innovation and peoplehood. (a) Black Surfing Association's Statement of Purpose and Intent. (b) Mission Statement of the Black Surfing Association.

BSA MISSION STATEMENT

To expose and encourage people of African ancestry to witness, experience, participate and enjoy the ancient oceanic activity of surfing throughout the oceans and seas of the world. And, with this exposure and participation, the BSA will demonstrate, educate, and help to implement aquatic skills, ecological awareness and activism, and overall athleticism. Ultimately, it is the BSA's goal to expose and advance the sport and activities of wave-riding in the Black communities while generating well-being, harmony, and heightened awareness amongst surfing individuals, clubs, organizations, businesses, and related media interest groups. We also encourage and support our members to compete and represent Black people and the Black Surfing Association with good sportsmanlike conduct and ethnic ambassadorism.

(b)

Figure 5-6. *Continued.*

a Brooklyn native and Fordham University alumnus, starred as police chief "McGarrett" of the on-location hit television show *Hawaii Five-O*, and became an iconic and honorary Asian-Pacific "haole" to locals.

Board riding and board making took root in the youth subculture of African Americans and came to define inner-city recreation. For young black skateboarders and skateboard makers in neighborhoods of South Central L.A., Watts, and Compton, skateboarding not only represented an urban version of ocean surfing but also a link with the popularity of roller skating among blacks in the south. Tony Curley, one of the first black surfers on the beaches of San Luis Obispo County on California's central coast, started the Black Surfing Association in 1975.

This organization, whose motto was "Umoja" (unity: together as one), described its growth arc as follows: "From the need for companionship, camaraderie, and socialization on a path shared by so few of our own, the inception and development of the Black Surfing Association has evolved and continues to grow."

CONCLUSION

In the far western U.S. periphery, a social fabric emerged out of trans-oceanic and transcontinental migration that contrasted with communities "back east" shaped by historic settler migrations of the Atlantic basin. The mass movements from Asia and the Pacific, consisting of Chinese, Japanese, Koreans, Filipinos, and Pacific Islanders, infused unique cultural influences into the Pacific coast region that interacted creatively with the multiple waves of U.S. internal migrants; immigrants from Europe; foreign-born migrants from the border regions of Canada and Mexico; and the further hemispheric regions of the Caribbean and Latin America. Even in the aftermath of 9/11, international migration continued to abound on a global scale, and the momentum toward creating diversity remained strong.[54] The interaction of these currents of international and domestic migrants who were located in long-distance social networks made the Pacific coast into a region with far-reaching and even global connections. As a consequence, these newcomers enlarged the eclectic component of American national identity and diversified the national culture to reflect global heterogeneity. The people flocking to the west coast gave rise to a new model of democracy in which transoceanic interregional diversity from the Atlantic and Pacific worlds had a central place in the civic sphere and in politics.

The Pacific coast was no longer secondary and provincial after World War II. It emerged as a new and powerful core or metropole, a primary source for creative expertise and leadership that would transform the wider world. It was a transoceanic control point for a "feedback loop" from the Pacific coast to the Atlantic coast in which the dynamism of the former propagated innovation and growth eastward to the rest of the country. California itself was a global powerhouse, with a population larger than found in 80 percent of other countries. The industrial labor force of Los Angeles, Orange, and Santa Clara counties alone surpassed the number of workers in manufacturing in many states (Figure 5-7). If California were ranked as a country in the scale of annual domestic output, the Golden State would be one of the top ten most productive nations in the world.

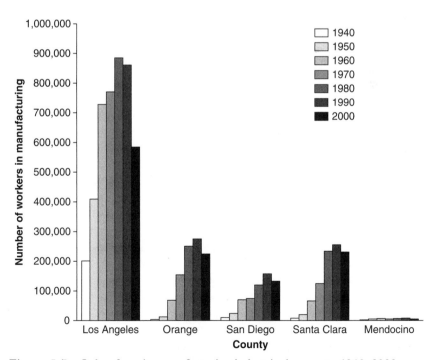

Figure 5-7.   Labor force in manufacturing industries by county, 1940–2000.

California's economic leadership arose with the globalization of trade and entrepreneurialism that provided new opportunities for economic interaction joining Pacific and Atlantic regions. Asian immigrant entrepreneurs, students, and professionals galvanized the development of Silicon Valley, the aerospace industry, international finance, education, and the healthcare industry. Rising high in the entertainment industry were Asian Americans like Kevin Tsujihara who became CEO of Warner Brothers. Newcomers from the northeast, midwest, and south were drawn by technology, service industries, consumerism, entertainment and the innovative outlook of the Pacific coast, the latest stage in the westward transcontinental shift of the American population that propelled the rise of west-coast regional power to new lofty heights. It was, in fact, a new global and transformative force, a form of what political scientist and policy maker Joseph S. Nye, Jr., has identified as American "soft power," "the means to success in world politics," the ability to achieve strategic objectives without "coercion or payments," that " arises from the attractiveness of a country's culture," as well as politics.[55] The California edge of the Pacific coast was the epicenter of a wave of innovative culture that had the capacity to shift collective consciousness and mass behavior over the entire world toward patterns at work in the United States. It was the ultimate outcome of the historical arc from transoceanic emergence, to innovation, to convergence of multiple peoples and their cultures.

The political economy of California directed regional development into profitable innovative enterprises that spurred mass entertainment, consumerism, and technology industries in aerospace and computing for a globalist age. The infrastructure of metropolitan suburbanization that was coupled with mass automobile transportation functioned as the basis for new mass-consumption patterns, energizing the shopping and entertainment centers that integrated consumer behavior with the worship of celebrity, youth culture, and materialistic lifestyles. Urban planners across the country aspired to build the post-industrial city by borrowing from the California experience, especially Los Angeles, the paradigmatic city of suburbs and automobile traffic. Robert Moses, the development czar of New York City, was impressed by the transportation revolution in California and was bent on reconfiguring metropolitan New York City to accommodate the automobile with expressways that led to suburban Long Island or counties just across the Hudson River in New Jersey.

A Pacific coast region of long-distance migrants nourished a dual capacity for innovation and repeated self-transformation in individuals as well as collective groups. Late-twentieth-century California epitomized the image of the United States described by immigration expert Lawrence H. Fuchs as a kaleidoscope of old fragments continually resetting themselves into new and unexpected patterns. Repeated composition of new patterns coexisted with their repeated decomposition in the hectic, less regulated political economy and experimental spaces in which people from across the country and the oceans sought to reach their horizons of aspiration on the western oceanic edge of America. The establishment of Disney Hall in downtown Los Angeles symbolized the unique combination of

Figure 5-8. Walt Disney Concert Hall.

innovation and talent produced by migrants nurtured by coastal California (Figure 5-8). The new home of the Los Angeles Philharmonic Orchestra, conducted by the brilliant Venezuelan maestro, Gustavo Dudamel, Disney Hall was funded by the entertainment megacorporation founded by a transplanted Chicagoan, Walt Disney, and designed by a Canadian immigrant to Los Angeles, Frank Gehry, perhaps the preeminent architect of his time. According to the *Los Angeles Times*, "He wanted his design to protect the idea of the concert hall as refuge—but also to embody the essential informality of Los Angeles. He wanted to demystify and democratize classical music. . . ."[56]

During the late twentieth century, the pressures of mass migration and rapid economic and environmental change had produced a host of new problems. Underlying the achievements in the field of motion pictures, television, and high technology were the mountainous deficit sheets of business failure. The judicial and legal documents for bankruptcy proceedings filed away in the course of many decades overflowed the filing cabinets of the federal record center in Southern California. Anxious residents were drawn toward nativism and xenophobia: reviving the Pacific coast traditions of anti-immigrant politics. Urban riots, such as those in Watts in 1965 and central Los Angeles in 1992, the proliferation of new urban gangs, and the growth of an underclass exacerbated historic racial divisions and furthered backlashes that escalated the racialization of majority and minority relations. Environmental degradation and sprawl became faces of a new dysfunctionalism brought on by mass transportation based on polluting automobiles and a barely manageable density of suburbs and consumer marketplaces.[57] The interregional migrations of opportunistic newcomers, human capital, entrepreneurs, labor, and consumer groups between the Atlantic and Pacific worlds had produced new manifestations of a core historical pattern in the history of the Americas: creative forces being renewed, reshaping national life, transforming the wider world, and producing a new horizon of problems and promises under the glow of evanescence.

Notes

1. James Bryce, *The American Commonwealth*, 3rd ed. (New York: Macmillan, 1893), Vol. 2, p. 930.

2. Homi Bhabha, "Third Space: Interview with Homi Bhabha," in Jonathan Rutherford, ed., *Identity: Community, Culture, Difference* (London: Lawrence and Wishart, 1990), p. 211; Homi Bhabha, *The Location of Culture* (New York: Routledge, 1994), pp. 37–39.

3. Joseph S. Nye, Jr., *Soft Power: The Means to Success in World Politics* (New York: PublicAffairs, 2004), p. 47.

4. Hasia R. Diner, "American West, New York Jewish," in Ava F. Kahn, *Jewish Life in the American West: Perspectives on Migration, Settlement, and Community* (Los Angeles: Autry Museum of Western Heritage, 2002), p. 50.

5. Carolyn Larson and Geraldine Johnson, "Turlock: A Center of Swedish Settlement," in Helen Alma Hohenthal et al., John Edwards Caswell, ed., *Streams in a Thirsty Land: A History of the Turlock Region* (Turlock, Calif.: City of Turlock, 1972), p. 74; Patrick J. Blessing, *West among Strangers: Irish Migration to California, 1850–1880* (doctoral dissertation, University of California, Los Angeles, 1977).

6. Josh Sides, *L. A. City Limits: African American Los Angeles from the Great Depression to the Present* (Berkeley: University of California Press, 2003), pp, 37–54.

7. See Bhabha, "Third Space," p. 211, and *The Location of Culture*, pp. 37–39.

8. William Cronon, *Nature's Metropolis: Chicago and the Great West* (New York: W. W. Norton, 1991), ch. 1; Timothy B. Spears, *Chicago Dreaming: Midwesterners and the City, 1871–1919* (Chicago: University of Chicago Press, 2005), pp. xiii, 4.

9. Spears, *Chicago Dreaming*, p. 3.

10. William Andrew Spalding, *Autobiography of a Los Angeles Newspaperman, 1874–1900*, ed.by Robert V. Hine (San Marino, Calif.: Huntington Library, 1961), ch. 9–10.

11. Deborah Dash Moore, *To the Golden Cities: Pursuing the American Jewish Dream in Miami and L.A.* (Cambridge, Mass.: Harvard University Press, 1994), pp. 41–52, 224.

12. Neal Gabler, *An Empire of Their Own: How the Jews Invented Hollywood* (New York: Crown Publishers, 1998).

13. Robert Gottlieb, Mark Vallianatos, Regina M. Freer, and Peter Dreier, *The Next Los Angeles: The Struggle for a Livable City* (Berkeley: University of California Press, 2006), pp. 74–75.

14. W. Bernard Carlson, *Innovation as a Social Process: Elihu Thomson and the Rise of General Electric, 1870–1900* (Cambridge, Eng.: Cambridge University Press, 1991), pp. 350–351.

15. http://ict.usc.edu (retrieved January 19 and August 2, 2014).

16. Chris Faraone, "Volcanic: Todd Gitlin Looks at Occupy," *The Boston Phoenix* (September 14, 2012), p. 46.

17. Michael S. Schmidt and Sheryl Gay Stolberg, "Tampa as Scandal's Social Link," *New York Times*, November 14, 2012.

18. Jules Tygiel, *The Great Los Angeles Swindle: Oil, Stocks, and Scandal during the Roaring Twenties* (New York: Oxford University Press, 1994), pp. 20–21.

19. Gottlieb et al., *The Next Los Angeles*, p. 76.

20. Simon N. Patten, *The New Basis of Civilization* (New York: Macmillan, 1907), p. 215.

21. Gottlieb et al., *The Next Los Angeles*, p. 76.

22. George E. Burns, in "The Jet Age Arrives," Pan American World Airways, 1927–1991, documents the commercial passenger jet plane revolution that launched a global network of mass air travel and mass migration. Retrieved from Pan Am Historical

Foundation http://www.panam.org/online-archives/chronicles/216-jet-age-arrives
.html (retrieved August 2, 2014).

23. Dennis Ogawa and John Blink with Mike Gordon, *California Hotel and Casino: Hawai'i's Home Away* (Honolulu: Japanese Cultural Center of Hawai'i, 2008), pp. 3–40.

24. The quotations from R. W. C. Farnsworth, ed. *A Southern California Paradise* (Pasadena: R. W. C. Farnsworth Publisher, 1883), p. 94, and William R. Bentley, *Bentley's Handbook of the Pacific Coast* (Oakland, Calif.: Pacific Press, 1884), p. 26 are cited in John E. Baur, *The Health Seekers of Southern California, 1870–1900*, 2nd ed. (San Marino: The Huntington Library, 1959), pp. 15–16.

25. Pawan Dhingra, *Life Behind the Lobby: Indian American Motel Owners and the American Dream* (Stanford, Calif.: Stanford University Press, 2012), pp. 1–8.

26. Rob Wilson and Arif Dirlik, eds., *Asia/Pacific as Space of Cultural Production* (Durham, N.C.: Duke University Press, 1995).

27. See accounts of public entertainments in Paul E. Johnson, *Sam Patch: The Famous Jumper* (New York: Hill and Wang, 2003), and Neil Harris, *Humbug: The Art of P. T. Barnum* (Boston: Little, Brown, 1973).

28. Daniel Mark Epstein, *Sister Aimee: The Life of Aimee Semple McPherson* (New York: Harcourt Brace, 1993), p. 251.

29. I. G. Edmonds, *Big U: Universal in the Silent Days* (Cranbury, N.J.: A. S. Barnes and Co.), pp. 18–21; Frederica Sagor Maas, *The Shocking Miss Pilgram: A Writer in Early Hollywood* (Lexington: University Press of Kentucky, 1999), p. 235.

30. Lary May, *Screening Out the Past: The Birth of Mass Culture and the Motion Picture Industry* (New York: Oxford University Press, 1983), ch. 1; Scott Berg, *Goldwyn: A Biography* (New York: Riverhead Books, 1989), Part 1.

31. Debra Samuels, "Spam Goes Glam in This Japanese-American Snack," *Boston Globe*, February 20, 2013.

32. Jack Fujimoto, *Sawtelle: West Los Angeles's Japantown* (Charleston, S.C.: Arcadia Publishing, 2007), ch. 4, 5.

33. Andrew Buncombe, "Will Battle of TV Chefs Be a Recipe for Peace—Or Are the Two Enemies Sharpening Knives?" *The Independent,* January 18, 2012. Retrieved from http://www.independent.co.uk/news/world/asia/now-india-and-pakistan-have-started-a-food-fight-6291030.html.

34. Warren I. Cohen, *The Asian American Century* (Cambridge, Mass.: Harvard University Press, 2002), p. 81.

35. Jules Tygiel, *Baseball's Great Experiment: Jackie Robinson and His Legacy* (New York: Oxford University Press, 1983).

36. Helen Hunt Jackson, *Ramona* (New York: Robert Brothers, 1884).

37. Edmonds, *Big U*, pp. 53–54.

38. Dru C. Gladney, *Dislocating China: Reflections on Muslims, Minorities, and Other Subaltern Subjects* (Chicago: University of Chicago Press, 2004), pp. 31–46, and Parts 2–5.

39. Bruce Cumings, *Dominion from Sea to Sea: Pacific Ascendancy and American Power* (New Haven: Yale University Press, 2009), p. 330.

40. Jennifer Medina, "In California, Son Gets Chance to Restore Luster to a Legacy," *New York Times,* January 28, 2013).

41. "Today's Teen Agers"; "Students: On the Fringe of a Golden Era," *Time*, January 29, 1965.

42. Steven Conn, *Museums and Intellectual Life, 1876–1926* (Chicago: University of Chicago Press, 1998), pp. 244–260.

43. Neil Harris, "All the World a Melting Pot?: Japan at American Fairs, 1876–1904," in Akira Iriye, ed., *Mutual Images: Essays in American-Japanese Relations* (Cambridge, Mass.: Harvard University Press, 1975), pp. 24–30; Akira Iriye, *Cultural Internationalism and World Order* (Baltimore: Johns Hopkins University Press, 1997), pp. 78–79.

44. Bari Walsh, "An Expansive, Plugged-in Vision for the Humanities," *Colloquy Alumni Quarterly, The Graduate School of Arts and Sciences, Harvard University*, Fall/Winter 2011, pp. 2–5.

45. Dominic A. Pacyga, "Chicago: City of the Big 'Little' Museums"; Eileen H. Tamura, "Ethnic Museums in Hawai'i: Exhibits, Interpreters, and Reenactments"; Anju Reejhsinghani, "Museums in Austin and San Antonio, Texas, of Interest to Ethnic Historians" all in "Special Feature: Ethnic Museum Reviews," *Journal of American Ethnic History* 28, No. 3 (Spring 2009): 55–88.

46. Scott Kurashige, *The Shifting Grounds of Race: Black and Japanese Americans in the Making of Multiethnic Los Angeles* (Princeton, N.J.: Princeton University Press, 2008), pp. 229–230.

47. Mario T. Garcia, *Mexican Americans: Leadership, Ideology, and Identity, 1930–1960* (New Haven, Conn.: Yale University Press, 1989), pp. 299–302; Juanita Tamayo Lott, *From Racial Category to Multiple Identities* (Walnut Creek, Calif.: Altamira Press, 1998), ch. 4, 5; Juan Gomez-Quinones, "Outside Inside—The Immigrant Workers: Creating Popular Myths, Cultural Expressions, and Personal Politics in Borderlands Southern California," in David R. Maciel, Isidro D. Ortiz, and Maria Herrera-Sobek, eds., *Chicano Renaissance: Contemporary Cultural Trends* (Tucson: University of Arizona Press, 2000).

48. Lon Kurashige, *Japanese American Celebration and Conflict: A History of Ethnic Identity and Festival, 1934–1990* (Berkeley: University of California Press, 2002), Introduction.

49. Laura Pulido, *Black, Brown, Yellow, and Left: Radical Activism in Los Angeles* (Berkeley: University of California Press, 2006), ch. 3–6.

50. W. J. Rorabaugh, *Berkeley at War: The 1960s* (New York: Oxford University Press, 1989), pp. 76, 77, 79.

51. Kurashige, *The Shifting Grounds of Race*, pp. 280, 289.

52. Dan Boylan and T. Michael Holmes, in *John A. Burns: The Man and His Times* (Honolulu: University of Hawai'i Press, 2000), a biographical study of the state of Hawai'i's first elected governor, provide insight on the cultural and political adaptation of Americans who moved to the Hawaiian Islands in the postwar years; Douglas Brinkley, "Obama Is America's First Global President, Douglas Brinkley Says." *USA Today*, April 9, 2009.

53. Robert K. Fitts, *Wally Yonamine: The Man Who Changed Japanese Baseball* (Lincoln, Nebr.: University of Nebraska Press, 2008).

54. Reed Ueda, "Immigration in Global Historical Perspective, in Mary C. Waters, Reed Ueda, Helen Marrow, *New Americans: A Guide to Immigration since 1965* (Cambridge, Mass.: Harvard University Press, 2007).

55. Nye, Jr., *Soft Power*, p. x.

56. Christopher Hawthorne, "Gehry's Disney Concert Hall Is Inextricably of L.A.," *Los Angeles Times*, September 21, 2013.

57. Mike Davis, *City of Quartz: Excavating the Future in Los Angeles* (New York: Vintage Books, 1992), pp. 173–177, and *Ecology of Fear: Los Angeles and the Imagination of Disaster* (New York: Vintage Books, 1999), ch. 7.

CREDITS

Chapter 1

© John Elk III/Alamy, 4; © GlowImages/Alamy, 8; Courtesy of Karen Welsh, Woman's Board of Missions for the Pacific Islands, 9; Millicent Library, Fairhaven Massachusetts and Spinner Publications, Inc., New Bedford, Massachusetts, 9; Michael J. McAfee, courtesy of Irving Moy, 9; Source: Herbert R. Barringer, Robert W. Gardner, Michael J. Levin, Asians and Pacific Islanders in the United States (New York: Russell Sage Foundation, 1993), Figure 2-1, p. 23, 26.

Chapter 2

Courtesy of Lyman Museum, 37; San Francisco History Center, San Francisco Public Library, 46; National Archives and Records Administration of the United States, 52; National Archives and Records Administration of the United States, 52; Life Histories of Students, 1926–27. William Carlson Smith Collection, AX311. Special Collections & University Archives, University of Oregon Libraries, Eugene, Oregon, 53; Courtesy Special Collections & University Archives, California state University, Stanislaus, 63; National Archives and Records Administration of the United States, 64; National Archives and Records Administration of the United States, 67; The Granger Collection, New York, 73.

Chapter 3

Archives of Kuniichi Yoshimoto family, 99; Courtesy of The Bancroft Library, University of California, Berkeley, 100; From Theatres of Hawai'I by Lowell Angell. Used with permission, 101; Public Domain, 105; Dr. Sun Yat-Sen Hawaii Foundation. Collection of Lum Chee (Courtesy of Raymond and Yansheng Ma Lum), 110; Public Domain, 111; Sikh Temple, Stockton, c. 1920. Resource #: P80–138. Holt-Atherton Special Collections, University of the Pacific Library, 112; Korean American Digital Archive. Kada-m13923. East Asian Library, University of Southern California, 112; Courtesy of Deep Focus Productions, Inc., 126; Courtesy of Deep Focus Productions, Inc., 126; Courtesy McKinley High School, Honolulu, HI, 131; Seabrook Educational and Cultural Center, 133; Library of Congress Prints and Photographs Division, Washington, D.C. LC-USZ62-43767, 133.

Chapter 4

Collection of Elverhøj Museum of History and Art. Solvang, CA, 143; George Rose/Getty Images, 144; Collection of Elverhøj Museum of History and Art. Solvang, CA, 144; Source: U. S. Department of Justice, Immigration and Naturalization Service, 2000 Statistical Yearbook of the Immigration and Naturalization Service (Washington, D. C.: U. S. Government Printing Office, 2002), p. 16, 150; Source: Guillermina Jasso and Mark R. Rosenzweig, The New Chosen People: Immigrants in the United States (New York: Russell Sage Foundation, 1990), p. 104, 160.

Chapter 5

age fotostock/SuperStock, 173; Petitions for Naturalization, File Unit 97765. Joan de Beauvoir de Havilland Aherne (Joan Fontaine). The National Archives at Riverside, Perris, California, 176; Petitions for Naturalization, File Unit 63218. Marlene Dietrich. The National Archives at Riverside, Perris, California, 177; Petitions for Naturalization, File Unit 205700. James Wong Howe. The National Archives at Riverside, Perris, California, 178; Jeremy Artates of jartates.com, 180; Jerold Kress, 180; Courtesy of King's Hawaiian Bakery, 180; © Robert Landau/CORBIS, 181; Muhammad Mazhar, 181; "Mohandas K Gandhi" by Stephen C. Lowe, Gift of the Gandhi Memorial International Foundation and the Jhamandas Watumull Fund. Courtesy of the Honolulu Mayor's Office of Culture and the Arts, 189; "Jose Rizal" by Carl Ruiz, Gift of the Filipina Society of Hawaii with the Oahu Filipino Community Council. Courtesy of the Honolulu Mayor's Office of Culture and the Arts, 189; picturescolourlibrary.com/StockConnection USA/Newscom, 189; Collection of the U.S. House of Representatives, 193; Collection of the U.S. House of Representatives, 193; Black Surfing Association/http://www.blacksurfingassociation.com, 195; Black Surfing Association/http://www.blacksurfingassociation.com, 196; Source: Bruce Cumings, Dominion from Sea to Sea: Pacific Ascendancy and American Power (New Haven: Yale University Press, 2009), p. 331, 197; © John O'Neill, 199.

Color Inserts

Courtesy of the Harvard Map Collection, Inserts 4–8.

INDEX

Note: page numbers followed by *f* and *t* refer to figures and tables respectively.